The Land of Mist
with
The 'Baby Book' of
Denis Stewart Percy Conan Doyle

The Land of Mist

with

The 'Baby Book' of Denis Stewart Percy Conan Doyle

Sir Arthur Conan Doyle

IMPALA

Published by
Impala
(International Media Publication and Literary
Associates) Ltd
Registered Office:
c/o Davenport Lyons
30 Old Burlington Street
London W1S 3NL

The Land of Mist First published in 1912
The Baby Book of Denis Stewart Percy Conan Doyle
first published 2006
This edition first published 2006

The 'Baby book' Diary © Impala 2006
Introduction to the Diary © Irving Finkel 2006
IMPALA logo design © Impala 2006

FRONT COVER ILLUSTRATION by Barry Martin, courtesy of the
Ray and Annette Keene Collection, © Impala 2006

ISBN 0 9549943 8 8

Contents

Introduction to the Diary

Diaries are a wonderful - and often not appreciated – human phenomenon. They are usually intensely personal documents, compiled under myriad circumstances, and for very diverse reasons. Perhaps a majority of diarists never stop to ask themselves why they make such a painstaking record, but for many it becomes as necessary a prelude to going to bed as cleaning one's teeth.

Diaries vary, of course, in their content, and therefore their interest to other readers, but the genre as a whole should be valued as a unique form of human testament. Small scribbled pages will outlive their author in a way that few ever visualise, and with the passage of time they come to encapsulate, in some small measure, both an individual's lifetime, and the times in which he or she lived. Diarists write for themselves, and usually tell the truth as they see it. Private diaries must rank, therefore, among the most valuable of historical records.

This status does nothing to ensure their survival. While the diaries of famous or celebrated individuals – such as the unusual Conan Doyle child-development journal given in this book - are usually cherished, the diaries of private individuals do not survive so readily. Many individuals stipulate that their diaries are to be destroyed on their death. Countless unwanted diaries are unthinkingly burned or thrown away when inherited, since people think they must be private, or too hard to decipher, or simply too bulky to look after. In this way a great historical resource slips from our grasp. But what might be private now will not be, so urgently, in one hundred years time.

For this reason the present writer has started a rescue campaign to ensure the survival of unwanted private diaries, of any type, so that they can be stored and protected, to form a major resource for future historians. In this way the quiet voices of many faded generations will find a later echo, and convey their unlooked-for message to an ever more remote and unimaginable readership.

Dr Irving Finkel
British Museum

THE DIARY

Baby's Book

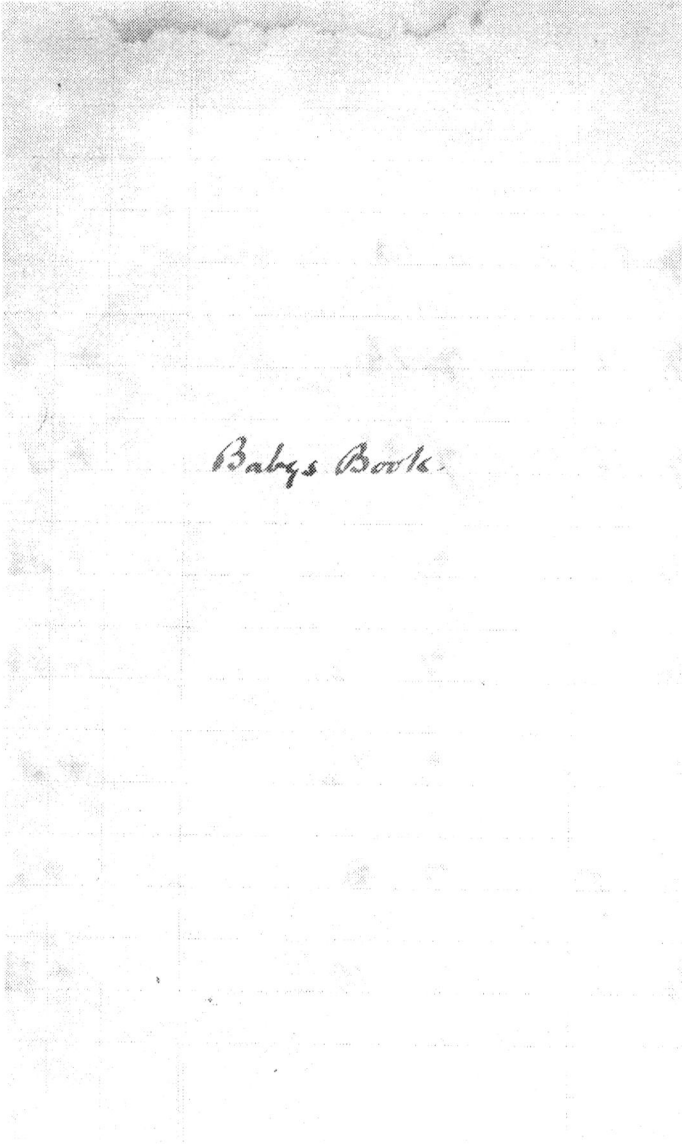

Babys Book

[Page 2]

Ap. 5.	*6.10*	
Ap. 12	*7.1½*	*+ 7½*
Ap. 15	*7 5½*	*+ 4*
Ap. 18	*7. 9.*	*+ 3½*
Ap. 21	*7 4½*	*-4½*
Ap. 24	*7 7½*	*+ 3*
Ap. 27	*7 8.*	*+½*
Ap. 29	*7 10½*	*+2½*

Ap. 5.	6. 10	
Ap. 12	7. 1½	+ 7½
Ap. 15	7 5½	+ 4
Ap. 18	7. 9.	+ 3½
Ap. 21	7 4½	− 4½
Ap. 24	7 7½	+ 3
Ap. 27	7 8.	+ ½
Ap. 29	7 10½	+ 2½

[Page 3]

Baby was born
*   March 17th about 6. PM.*
*   St Patrick's Day. 1909.*

He was Christened
*   Denis Stewart Percy Conan Doyle*
*   April 17th*

He was below the average size
and weight when born, but was
very well formed and intelligent.

He had much trouble with his
digestion, continual flatulence,
and pain. This caused his
weight to fluctuate as shown
opposite.

Long for his age and weight. A very

Baby was born
    March 17th about 6. PM.
    St Patricks Day. 1909.

He was Christened
· Denis Stewart Percy Conan Doyle.
    April 17th

He was below the average size
and weight when born, but was
very well formed and intelligent.

He had much trouble with his
digestion, continual flatulence,
and pain. This caused his
weight to fluctuate as shown
opposite.

    Long for his age & weight. A very

[Page 4]

May 7th	*8 lbs*
May 12th	*8.5.0.*
May 16th	*8.7.0*
May 20th	*8.6.0*
May 24th	*8.7.0*
May 29th	*9.2.½*
June 4th	*9.9.0*
June 7.	*9.13.8*
June 17	*10.9.0*
June 20	*10.7.0*

over

May 7th		8 lbs.
May 12th		8 . 5 . 0
May 16th		8 . 7 . 0
May 20th		8 . 6 . 0
May 24th		8 . 7 . 0
May 29th		9 . 2 . ½
June 4th		9 . 9 . 0
June 7		9 . 13 . 8
June 17		10 . 9 . 0
June 20		10 . 7 . 0

[Page 5]

finely formed brow and head. Eyes deep blue. hair darkish. No eye brows. Longish legs. Very long & well formed fingers and nails

Began to crow a little - googa noises - when about one month old.

About seven weeks his eye brows began to form. He went to London & had benefit.

Made a sudden rapid advance with Mellins Food. Put on 12 ounces in 3½ days.
Took to putting out his tongue & then laughing (10 weeks old).

finely ptched... brow & head. Eyes
deep blue. Hair darkish. No eye
brows. Longish legs. Very long &
well formed fingers & nails. .....

Began to crow a little — googa
noises — when about one month
old.

About seven weeks his eye brows
began to form. He went to London &
had benefit.

Made a sudden rapid advance
with Mellins Food. Put on 12 ounces
in 3½ days.
Took to putting out his tongue & then
laughing (10 weeks old).

[Page 6]

June 27.	*10.11½*
July 6	*11.3*
July 10	*11.3*
July. 21.	*11.12½*
July 25	*12.2¾*
July 29	*12.11.*
Aug. 3.	*13.3*

Aug. 9.	*14 lbs!*

June 27.	10 . 11½ .
July 6	11 . 3 .
July 10.	11 . 3 .
July 21.	11 . 12½ .
July 25	12 2¾
July 29.	12 . 11 .
Aug 3.	13 . 3 .
Aug 9.	14 lbs !

[Page 7]

June 20.   Some sign of teeth. Begins
*   to hold his hand to his mouth.*

June 26.   had a cold and went back
*   a little*

July 6.   Coming on again. Uses his
*   hands more.*

July 21.   Change to Deal. Seems
*   better than ever.*

Aug 3.   In splendid form. Developed
*   a very roguish laugh. More*
*   alert*

June 20. Some Signs of Teeth. Begins
to hold his hand to his mouth.

June 26. Had a cold & went back
a little.

July 6. Coming on again. Uses his
hands more.

July 21. Change to Deal. Seems
better than ever.

Aug 3. In splendid form. Developed
a very roguish laugh. more
alert.

[Page 8]

   *In March 1910 Baby was
one year old.*
   *He then weighed 24 pounds
and was a bonny boy, straight
lightish hair, blue eyes, lower
part of face promises to be
massive, well turned chin like
my mothers. Mouth firm.
Gaze steady. Strong character.*

*He says Dad! Dad! & Mam!
Mam! but I do not think they
mean anything. His favourite
noise is a kind of interrogative
ah? . Then he has a very shrill
cry for disapproval.*
   *He cannot walk or stand,
save with help. He moves his
legs rapidly when held up but*

In March 1910 Baby was one year old.

He then weighed 24 pounds and was a bonny boy. straight lightish hair, blue eyes, lower part of face promises to be massive, well turned chin like my mothers. mouth firm. Gaze steady. Strong character.

He says Dad! Dad & Mam! Mam! but I do not think they mean anything. His favourite noise is a kind of interrogative ah?. Then he has a very shrill cry for disapproval.

He cannot walk or stand, save with help. He moves his legs rapidly when held up but

[Page 9]

remains stationary.

He has an excellent memory. Having heard a bird in a certain tree he always afterwards looked at that tree as he passed.

In Feb 1911, being nearly two years old Denis showed some curious characteristics.

He spoke fairly well but had wordsof his own for many objects, for example sugar was Gillyum, water was Dappa, his comforter was Bungay and so on.

He showed considerable temper, squaling with rage when he thought he was crossed.

When he wanted to get rid or had enough of anyone or

remains stationary.

He has an excellent memory. Having heard a bird in a certain tree he always afterwards looked at that tree as he passed.

In Feb 1911, being nearly two years old Denis showed some curious characteristics.

He spoke fairly well but had words of his own for many objects, for example sugar was Gillyum, water was Dappa, his comforter was Bingay and so on.

He showed considerable temper, squealing with rage when he thought he was crossed.

When he wanted to get rid or had enough of anyone or

[Page 10]

anything he always said
Ta Ta. Ta Ta, man! to the
doctor. Ta Ta Noah to the Arc.
and so on.
          He is very strong and sturdy &
generous with his possessions.
Cries "Come here, Bicky" when he
wants a biscuit.

          Little Adrian, (3 months
old) weighs 10 lbs 6 ounces
which is just the same as Denis
at the same age.

Denis at two years old talks
glibly in his own language. Some
new words are Bungay for a
comforter, Nama for wind mill -

anything he always said
Ta Ta. Ta Ta, man! to the
doctor Ta Ta Noah to the Arc,
and so on.

He is very strong & sturdy, & is
generous with his possessions.
Cries "Come here, Bicky" when he
wants a biscuit.

Little Adrian (3 months
old) weighs 10 lbs 6 ounces
which is just the same as Denis
at the same age.

Denis at two years old talks
glibly in his own language. Some
new words are Bungay for a
Computer, Nama for wind mill —

[Page 11]

toot - toot for toast.
     He connects ideas very rapidly.
Thus on seeing a smoking rubbish
heap in the field he [said] made at once
a long imitation of a railway
whistle -
     He is a remarkable mimic,
taking off the exact note & tome. He
should have a very clear ear for
music.

Ap 15/11
Denis is now 2 years old. He
gets out such sentences as
'Have-a-drop-of-Mummy's-tea'
'Perfly impossble'
'Open-the-door'
He occasionally says 'greedy
Denis. Dirty boy.'

toot-toot for toast.

He connects ideas very rapidly. Thus on seeing a smoking rubbish heap in the field he ~~said~~ made at once a long imitation of a railway whistle —

He is a remarkable mimic, taking off the exact note & tone. He should have a very clear ear for music.

Ap 15/11

Denis is now 2 years old. He gets out such sentences as

'Have-a-drop-of-Mummy's-Tea'

'Perfectly impossible'

'Open-the-door'.

He occasionally says 'Greedy Denis. Dirty boy!'

[Page 12]

June 1912 He is now over three and
            can talk very well. His main
            interest is in motor cars and trains.
            He has an exceedingly loving
            sympathetic disposition.

May 1913 The above still holds
            good. He should surely be
            an engineer. He is a most
            loving and gentle boy.

June 1912. He is now over three and
can talk very well. His main
interests in motor cars & trains.
He has an exceedingly loving
sympathetic disposition

May 1913. The above still holds
good. He should surely be
an engineer. He is a most
loving & gentle boy.

[Page 13]

June 1912
Adrian is now 18 months. He is a
little backward in speech as he was in
walking. He walks now well. His
main words are Ada - which we
think is brother - Dadda, Mamma,
Bird - Away. [Th] Bang. He
says away whenever he sees a
picture of a railway train.

1913 Shows every sign of being a
        great comedian. Very subtle in
        his humour. Self conscious.
        Fond of dress and of looking at
        himself in a glass.

June 1912.

Adrian is now 18 months. He is a little backward in speech as he was in walking. He walks now well. His main words are Ada — which we think is brother — Dadda. Mamma. Bird — Away. ✕ Bang. He says Away whenever he sees a picture of a railway train.

1913 Shows every sign of being a great Comedian. Very subtle in his humour. Self conscious. Fond of dress & of looking at himself in a glass.

    "If if was Alfred the Greats time
I would have shot John because he is
a Dane."   *Babetty*
                                   Ap. 1915.

Story of Dennis
    He pretended all day to be the
German Emperor. On being told that
I would be angry he said "Who is
he? A common Doyle!"

March 3 / 16 Adrian nearly died
       of pneumonia.
       Recovering all right.
       Very good patient.

His mother having reproached Denis
by saying that Adrian & Baby took
their medicine well, he said
"Brave souls!"

" If it was ofred the greats time
I would have shot John because he is
a Dane."   Babillly.
                              Ap. 1915.

Story of Dennis
    He pretended all day to be the
German Emperor. On being told that
I would be angry he said " Who is
he ?. a common Doyle ! "

March 3. / 16. Adrian nearly died
        of Pneumonia.
        Recovering all right.
        Very good patient

. His mother having reproached Dennis
by saying that Adrian & Baby took
their medicine well, he said
" Brave souls ! "

37

[Page 15]

Denis (aged 8) said "I expect
the fairies are a training school
for angels."

Adrian asked in the middle of the
night "Do the roses know us?"

Adrian pretended all day to be a 30
foot rock python. On being asked how he
would fit into the bed he said "Oh, I'll
just coil up."

Adrian asked if God was listening
to his conversation. On being told that
he was he said "Well, its very rude of him."

Baby who had quarrelled with
Adrian but who had to include him in
his prayers said " God bless
horrid Adrian."

Denis (aged 8) said "I expect
the fairies are a training school
for angels"

Adrian asked in the middle of the
night "Do the roses know us?"

Adrian pretended all day to be a 30
foot rock python. On being asked how he
would fit into the bed he said "Oh, I'll
just coil up".

Adrian asked if God was listening
to this conversation. On being told that
he was he said "Well, it's very rude
of him"

Baby who had quarrelled with
Adrian but who had to include him in
his prayers said "God bless
horrid Adrian".

[Page 16]

On Adrian saying that he was
Dog Crusoe, Denis at once said
"down, pup, down!"

"How big is an acre". "About
the size of Daddy"

"I do hope God will give Jesus
a happy birthday."
"Fairies are the O.T.C. of
church."
"Would Christ play cricket?"
"Yes, if he could give pleasure."
"I wonder if he could bowl
Goglies?"

On Adrian saying that he was Dog Crusoe, Denis at once said "Down, pup, down!"

"How big is an acre." "About the size of Daddy"

"I do hope God will give Jesus a happy birthday"

"Fairies are the O.T.C. of angels"

"Would Christ play cricket?"
"Yes, if he could give pleasure"
"I wonder if he could bowl Googlies"

[Page 17]

THE LAND OF MIST

1. *In Which Our Special Commissioners Make a Start*

THE great Professor Challenger has been—very improperly and imperfectly—used in fiction. A daring author placed him in impossible and romantic situations in order to see how he would react to them. He reacted to the extent of a libel action, an abortive appeal for suppression, a riot in Sloane Street, two personal assaults, and the loss of his position as lecturer upon Physiology at the London School of Sub-Tropical Hygiene. Otherwise, the matter passed more peaceably than might have been expected.

But he was losing something of his fire. Those huge shoulders were a little bowed. The spade-shaped Assyrian beard showed tangles of grey amid the black, his eyes were a trifle less aggressive, his smile less self-complacent, his voice as monstrous as ever but less ready to roar down all opposition. Yet he was dangerous, as all around him were painfully aware. The volcano was not extinct, and constant rumblings threatened some new explosion. Life had much yet to teach him, but he was a little less intolerant in learning.

There was a definite date for the change which had been wrought in him. It was the death of his wife. That little bird of a woman had made her nest in the big man's heart. He had all the tenderness and chivalry which the strong can have for the weak. By yielding everything she had won everything, as a sweet-natured, tactful woman can. And when she died suddenly from virulent pneumonia following influenza, the man staggered and went down. He came up again, smiling ruefully like the stricken boxer, and ready to carry on for many a round with Fate. But he was not the same man, and if it had not been for the help and comradeship of his daughter Enid, he might have never

47

rallied from the blow. She it was who, with clever craft, lured him into every subject which would excite his combative nature and infuriate his mind, until he lived once more in the present and not the past. It was only when she saw him turbulent in controversy, violent to pressmen, and generally offensive to those around him, that she felt he was really in a fair way to recovery.

Enid Challenger was a remarkable girl and should have a paragraph to herself. With the raven-black hair of her father, and the blue eyes and fresh colour of her mother, she was striking, if not beautiful, in appearance. She was quiet, but she was very strong. From her infancy she had either to take her own part against her father, or else to consent to be crushed and to become a mere automaton worked by his strong fingers. She was strong enough to hold her own in a gentle, elastic fashion, which bent to his moods and reasserted itself when they were past. Lately she had felt the constant pressure too oppressive and she had relieved it by feeling out for a career of her own. She did occasional odd jobs for the London press, and did them in such fashion that her name was beginning to be known in Fleet Street. In finding this opening she had been greatly helped by an old friend of her father—and possibly of the reader—Mr. Edward Malone of the *Daily Gazette*.

Malone was still the same athletic Irishman who had once won his international cap at Rugby, but life had toned him down also, and made him a more subdued and thoughtful man. He had put away a good deal when last his football-boots had been packed away for good. His muscles may have wilted and his joints stiffened, but his mind was deeper and more active. The boy was dead and the man was born. In person he had altered little, but his moustache was heavier, his back a little rounded, and some lines of thought were tracing themselves upon his brow. Post-war conditions and new world problems had left their mark. For the rest he had made his name in journalism and even to a small degree in literature. He was still a bachelor, though there were some who thought that his hold on that condition was precarious, and that Miss Enid Challenger's little white fingers could disengage it. Certainly they were very good chums.

It was a Sunday evening in October, and the lights were just beginning to twinkle out through the fog which had shrouded London from early morning. Professor Challenger's flat at Victoria West Gardens was upon the third floor, and the mist lay thick upon the windows, while the low hum of the attenuated Sunday traffic rose up from an invisible highway beneath, which was outlined only by scattered patches of dull radiance. Professor Challenger sat with his thick, bandy legs outstretched to the fire, and his hands thrust deeply into his trouser pockets. His dress had a little of the eccentricity of genius, for he wore a loose-collared shirt, a large knotted maroon-coloured silk tie, and a black velvet smoking-jacket, which, with his flowing beard, gave him the appearance of an elderly and Bohemian artist. On one side of him ready for an excursion, with bowl hat, short-skirted dress of black, and all the other fashionable devices with which women contrive to deform the beauties of nature, there sat his daughter, while Malone, hat in hand, waited by the window.

" I think we should get off, Enid. It is nearly seven," said he.

They were writing joint articles upon the religious denominations of London, and on each Sunday evening they sallied out together to sample some new one and get copy for the next week's issue of the *Gazette*.

" It's not till eight, Ted. We have lots of time."

" Sit down, sir ! Sit down !" boomed Challenger, tugging at his beard as was his habit if his temper was rising. " There is nothing annoys me more than having anyone standing behind me. A relic of atavism and the fear of a dagger, but still persistent. That's right. For heaven's sake put your hat down ! You have a perpetual air of catching a train."

" That's the journalistic life," said Malone. " If we don't catch the perpetual train we get left. Even Enid is beginning to understand that. But still, as you say, there is time enough."

" How far have you got ?" asked Challenger.

Enid consulted a business-like little reporter's notebook. " We have done seven. There was Westminster Abbey for the Church in its most picturesque form, and Saint Agatha for the High Church, and Tudor Place for the Low. Then there was the Westminster Cathedral for Catholics, Endell Street for Presbyterians, and Gloucester Square for Unitarians. But to-night we are trying to introduce some variety. We are doing the Spiritualists."

Challenger snorted like an angry buffalo.

" Next week the lunatic asylums, I presume," said he. " You don't mean to tell me, Malone, that these ghost people have got churches of their own."

" I've been looking into that," said Malone. " I always look up cold facts and figures before I tackle a job. They have over four hundred registered churches in Great Britain."

Challenger's snorts now sounded like a whole herd of buffaloes.

" There seems to me to be absolutely no limit to the inanity and credulity of the human race. *Homo Sapiens !* *Homo idioticus !* Who do they pray to—the ghosts ?"

" Well, that's what we want to find out. We should get some copy out of them. I need not say that I share your view entirely, but I've seen something of Atkinson of St. Mary's Hospital lately. He is a rising surgeon, you know."

" I've heard of him—cerebro-spinal."

" That's the man. He is level-headed and is looked on as an authority on psychic research, as they call the new science which deals with these matters."

" Science, indeed !"

" Well, that is what they call it. He seems to take these people seriously. I consult him when I want a reference, for he has the literature at his fingers' end. ' Pioneers of the Human Race '—that was his description."

" Pioneering them to Bedlam," growled Challenger.

" And literature ! What literature have they ?"

"'Well, that was another surprise. Atkinson has five hundred volumes, but complains that his psychic library is very imperfect. You see, there is French, German, Italian, as well as our own."

" Well, thank God all the folly is not confined to poor old England. Pestilential nonsense !"

" Have you read it up at all, Father ? " asked Enid.

" Read it up ! I, with all my interests and no time for one-half of them ! Enid, you are too absurd."

" Sorry, Father. You spoke with such assurance, I thought you knew something about it."

Challenger's huge head swung round and his lion's glare rested upon his daughter.

" Do you conceive that a logical brain, a brain of the first order, needs to read and to study before it can detect a manifest absurdity ? Am I to study mathematics in order to confute the man who tells me that two and two are five ? Must I study physics once more and take down my *Principia* because some rogue or fool insists that a table can rise in the air against the law of gravity ? Does it take five hundred volumes to inform us of a thing which is proved in every police-court when an impostor is exposed ? Enid, I am ashamed of you !"

His daughter laughed merrily.

" Well, Dad, you need not roar at me any more. I give in. In fact, I have the same feeling that you have."

" None the less," said Malone, " some good men support them. I don't see that you can laugh at Lodge and Crookes and the others."

" Don't be absurd, Malone. Every great mind has its weaker side. It is a sort of reaction against all the good sense. You come suddenly upon a vein of positive nonsense. That is what is the matter with these fellows. No, Enid, I haven't read their reasons, and I don't mean to, either; some things are beyond the pale. If we re-open all the old questions, how can we ever get ahead with the new ones ? This matter is settled by common sense, the law of England, and by the universal assent of every sane European."

" So that's that !" said Enid.

" However," he continued, " I can admit that there are occasional excuses for misunderstandings upon the point." He sank his voice, and his great grey eyes looked sadly up into vacancy. " I have known cases where the coldest intellect—even my own intellect—might, for a moment have been shaken."

Malone scented copy.

" Yes, sir ?"

Challenger hesitated. He seemed to be struggling with himself. He wished to speak, and yet speech was painful. Then, with an abrupt, impatient gesture, he plunged into his story :

" I never told you, Enid. It was too ... too intimate. Perhaps too absurd. I was ashamed to have been so shaken. But it shows how even the best balanced may be caught unawares."

" Yes, sir ?"

" It was after my wife's death. You knew her, Malone. You can guess what it meant to me. It was the night after the cremation ... horrible, Malone, horrible ! I saw the dear little body slide down, down ... and then the glare of flame and the door clanged to." His great body shook and he passed his big, hairy hand over his eyes.

" I don't know why I tell you this; the talk seemed to lead up to it. It may be a warning to you. That night— the night after the cremation—I sat up in the hall. She was there," he nodded at Enid. " She had fallen asleep in a chair, poor girl. You know the house at Rotherfield, Malone. It was in the big hall. I sat by the fireplace, the room all draped in shadow, and my mind draped in shadow also. I should have sent her to bed, but she was lying back in her chair and I did not wish to wake her. It may have been one in the morning—I remember the moon shining through the stained-glass window. I sat and I brooded. Then suddenly there came a noise."

" Yes, sir ?"

" It was low at first —just a ticking. Then it grew louder and more distinct—it was a clear rat-tat-tat. Now comes the queer coincidence, the sort of thing out of which legends grow when credulous folk have the shaping of them. You must know that my wife had a peculiar way of knocking at a door. It was really a little tune which she played with her fingers. I got into the same way so that we could each know when the other knocked. Well, it seemed to me—of course my mind was strained and abnormal—that the taps shaped themselves into the well-known rhythm of her knock. I couldn't localize it. You can think how eagerly I tried. It was above me, somewhere on the woodwork. I lost sense of time. I daresay it was repeated a dozen times at least."

" Oh, Dad, you never told me !"

" No, but I woke you up. I asked you to sit quiet with me for a little."

" Yes, I remember that."

" Well, we sat, but nothing happened. Not a sound more. Of course it was a delusion. Some insect in the wood; the ivy on the outer wall. My own brain furnished the rhythm. Thus do we make fools and children of ourselves. But it gave me an insight. I saw how even a clever man could be deceived by his own emotions."

" But how do you know, sir, that it was *not* your wife ?"

" Absurd, Malone ! Absurd, I say ! I tell you I saw her in the flames. What was there left ?"

" Her soul, her spirit."

Challenger shook his head sadly.

" When that dear body dissolved into its elements—when its gases went into the air and its residue of solids sank into a grey dust—it was the end. There was no more. She had played her part, played it beautifully, nobly. It was done. Death ends all, Malone. This soul talk is the Animism of savages. It is a superstition, a myth. As a physiologist I will undertake to produce crime or virtue by vascular control or cerebral stimulation. I will turn a

Jekyll into a Hyde by a surgical operation. Another can do it by a psychological suggestion. Alcohol will do it. Drugs will do it. Absurd, Malone, absurd! As the tree falls, so does it lie. There is no next morning ... night—eternal night ... and long rest for the weary worker."

" Well, it's a sad philosophy."

" Better a sad than a false one."

" Perhaps so. There is something virile and manly in facing the worst. I would not contradict. My reason is with you."

" But my instincts are against!" cried Enid. " No, no, never can I believe it." She threw her arms round the great bull neck. " Don't tell me, Daddy, that you with all your complex brain and wonderful self are a thing with no more life hereafter than a broken clock !"

" Four buckets of water and a bagful of salts," said Challenger as he smilingly detached his daughter's grip. " That's your daddy, my lass, and you may as well reconcile your mind to it. Well, it's twenty to eight. Come back, if you can, Malone, and let me hear your adventures among the insane."

2. Which Describes an Evening in Strange Company

THE love-affair of Enid Challenger and Edward Malone is not of the slightest interest to the reader, for the simple reason that it is not of the slightest interest to the writer. The unseen, unnoticed lure of the unborn babe is common to all youthful humanity. We deal in this chronicle with matters which are less common and of higher interest. It is only mentioned in order to explain those terms of frank and intimate comradeship which the narrative discloses. If the human race has obviously improved in anything—in Anglo-Celtic countries, at least—it is that the prim affectations and sly deceits of the past are lessened, and that young men and women can meet in an equality of clean and honest comradeship.

A taxi took the adventurers down Edgware Road and into the side-street called "Helbeck Terrace." Halfway down, the dull line of brick houses was broken by one glowing gap, where an open arch threw a flood of light into the street. The cab pulled up and the man opened the door.

"This is the Spiritualist Church, sir," said he. Then, as he saluted to acknowledge his tip, he added in the wheezy voice of the man of all weathers: "Tommy-rot, I call it, sir." Having eased his conscience thus, he climbed into his seat and a moment later his red rear-lamp was a waning circle in the gloom. Malone laughed.

"*Vox populi*, Enid. That is as far as the public has got at present."

"Well, it is as far as we have got, for that matter."

"Yes, but we are prepared to give them a show. I don't suppose Cabby is. By Jove, it will be hard luck if we can't get in !"

There was a crowd at the door and a man was facing them from the top of the step, waving his arms to keep them back.

"It's no good, friends. I am very sorry, but we can't help it. We've been threatened twice with prosecution for over-crowding." He turned facetious. "Never heard of an Orthodox Church getting into trouble for that. No, sir, no."

"I've come all the way from 'Ammersmith," wailed a voice. The light beat upon the eager, anxious face of the speaker, a little woman in black with a baby in her arms.

"You've come for clairvoyance, Mam," said the usher, with intelligence. "See here, give me the name and address and I will write you, and Mrs. Debbs will give you a sitting gratis. That's better than taking your chance in the crowd when, with all the will in the world, you can't all get a turn. You'll have her to yourself. No, sir, there's no use shovin' . . . What's that ? . . . Press ?"

He had caught Malone by the elbow.

"Did you say Press ? The Press boycott us, sir. Look at the weekly list of services in a Saturday's *Times* if you doubt it. You wouldn't know there was such a thing as Spiritualism. . . . What paper, sir? . . . 'The *Daily Gazette.*' Well, well, we are getting on. And the lady, too? . . . Special article—my word! Stick to me, sir, and I'll see what I can do. Shut the doors, Joe. No use, friends. When the building fund gets on a bit we'll have more room for you. Now, Miss, this way, if you please."

This way proved to be down the street and round a side-alley which brought them to a small door with a red lamp shining above it.

" I'll have to put you on the platform—there's no standing room in the body of the hall."

" Good gracious !" cried Enid.

" You'll have a fine view, Miss, and maybe get a readin' for yourself if your lucky. It often happens that those nearest the medium get the best chance. Now, sir, in here !"

Here was a frowsy little room with some hats and top-coats draping the dirty, white-washed walls. A thin, austere woman, with eyes which gleamed from behind her glasses, was warming her gaunt hands over a small fire. With his back to the fire in the traditional British attitude was a large, fat man with a bloodless face, a ginger moustache and curious, light-blue eyes—the eyes of a deep-sea mariner. A little bald-headed man with huge horn-rimmed spectacles, and a very handsome and athletic youth in a blue lounge-suit completed the group.

" The others have gone on the platform, Mr. Peeble. There's only five seats left for ourselves." It was the fat man talking.

" I know, I know," said the man who had been addressed as Peeble, a nervous, stringy, dried-up person as he now appeared in the light. " But this is the Press, Mr. Bolsover. *Daily Gazette*—special article. . . . Malone, the name and Challenger. This is Mr. Bolsover, our President. This is Mrs. Debbs of Liverpool, the famous clairvoyante. Here is Mr. James, and this tall young gentleman is Mr. Hardy Williams, our energetic secretary. Mr. Williams is a nailer for the buildin' fund. Keep your eye on your pockets if Mr. Williams is around."

They all laughed.

" Collection comes later," said Mr. Williams, smiling.

" A good, rousing article is our best collection," said the stout president. " Ever been to a meeting before, sir ?"

" No," said Malone.

" Don't know much about it, I expect."

" No, I don't."

" Well, well, we must expect a slating. They get it from the humorous angle at first. We'll have you writing a very comic account. I never could see anything very funny in the spirit of one's dead wife, but it's a matter of taste and of knowledge also. If they don't know, how can they take it seriously ? I don't blame them. We were mostly like that ourselves once. I was one of Bradlaugh's men, and sat under Joseph MacCabe until my old Dad came and pulled me out."

" Good for him !" said the Liverpool medium.

" It was the first time I found I had powers of my own. I saw him like I see you now."

" Was he one of us in the body ?"

" Knew no more than I did. But they come on amazin' at the other side if the right folk get hold of them."

" Time's up !" said Mr. Peeble, snapping his watch. " You are on the right of the chair, Mrs. Debbs. Will you go first ? Then you, Mr. Chairman. Then you two and myself. Get on the left, Mr. Hardy Williams, and lead the singin'. They want warmin' up and you can do it. Now then, if _you_ please !"

The platform was already crowded, but the newcomers threaded their way to the front amid a decorous murmur of welcome. Mr. Peeble shoved and exhorted and two end seats emerged upon which Enid and Malone perched themselves. The arrangement suited them well, for they could use their notebooks freely behind the shelter of the folk in front.

" What is your reaction ?" whispered Enid.

" Not impressed as yet."

" No, nor I," said Enid, " but it's very interesting all the same."

People who are in earnest are always interesting, whether you agree with them or not, and it was impossible to doubt that these people were extremely earnest. The hall was crammed, and as one looked down one saw line after line of upturned faces, curiously alike in type, women predominating, but men running them close. That type was not distinguished nor intellectual, but it was undeniably healthy, honest and sane. Small trades-folk, male and female shopwalkers, better class artisans, lower middle-class women worn with household cares, occasional young folk in search of a sensation—these were the impressions which the audience conveyed to the trained observation of Malone.

The fat president rose and raised his hand.

" My friends," said he, " we have had once more to exclude a great number of people who desired to be with us to-night. It's all a question of the building fund, and Mr. Williams on my left will be glad to hear from any of you. I was in a hotel last week and they had a notice hung up in the reception bureau: ' No cheques accepted '. That's not the way Brother Williams talks. You just try him."

The audience laughed. The atmosphere was clearly that of the lecture-hall rather than of the Church.

" There's just one more thing I want to say before I sit down. I'm not here to talk. I'm here to hold this chair down and I mean to do it. It's a hard thing I ask. I want Spiritualists to keep away on Sunday nights. They take up the room that inquirers should have. You can have the morning service. But its better for the cause that there should be room for the stranger. You've had it. Thank God for it. Give the other man a chance." The president plumped back into his chair.

Mr. Peeblé sprang to his feet. He was clearly the general utility man who emerges in every society and probably becomes its autocrat. With his thin, eager face and darting hands he was more than a live wire—he was a whole bundle of live wires. Electricity seemed to crackle from his finger-tips.

" Hymn One !" he shrieked.

A harmonium droned and the audience rose. It was a fine hymn and lustily sung:

> " The world hath felt a quickening breath
> From Heaven's eternal shore,
> And souls triumphant over death
> Return to earth once more."

There was a ring of exultation in the voices as the refrain rolled out:

> " For this we hold our Jubilee
> For this with joy we sing,
> Oh Grave, where is thy victory,
> Oh Death, where is thy sting ?"

Yes, they were in earnest, these people. And they did not appear to be mentally weaker than their fellows. And yet both Enid and Malone felt a sensation of great pity as they looked at them. How sad to be deceived upon so intimate a matter as this, to be duped by impostors who used their most sacred feelings and their beloved dead as counters with which to cheat them. What did they know of the laws of evidence, of the cold, immutable decrees of scientific law ? Poor earnest, honest, deluded people !

" Now !" screamed Mr. Peeble. "" We shall ask Mr. Munro from Australia to give us the invocation."

A wild-looking old man with a shaggy beard and slumbering fire in his eyes rose up and stood for a few seconds with his gaze cast down. Then he began a prayer, very simple, very unpremeditated. Malone jotted down the first sentence: " Oh, Father, we are very ignorant folk and do not well know how to approach you, but we will pray to you the best we know how." It was all cast in that humble key. Enid and Malone exchanged a swift glance of appreciation.

There was another hymn, less successful than the first, and the chairman then announced that Mr. James Jones of North Wales would now deliver a trance address which would embody the views of his well-known control, Alasha the Atlantean.

Mr. James Jones, a brisk and decided little man in a faded check suit, came to the front and, after standing a minute or so as if in deep thought, gave a violent shudder and began to talk. It must be admitted that save for a certain fixed stare and vacuous glazing of the eye there was nothing to show that anything save Mr. James Jones of North Wales was the orator. It has also to be stated that if Mr. Jones shuddered at the beginning it was the turn of his audience to shudder afterwards. Granting his own claim, he had proved clearly that an Atlantean spirit might be a portentous bore. He droned on with platitudes and ineptitudes while Malone whispered to Enid that if Alasha was a fair specimen of the population it was just as well that his native land was safely engulfed in the Atlantic Ocean. When, with another rather melodramatic shudder, he emerged from his trance, the chairman sprang to his feet with an alacrity which showed that he was taking no risks lest the Atlantean should return.

"We have present with us to-night," he cried, "Mrs. Debbs, the well-known clairvoyante of Liverpool. Mrs. Debbs is, as many of you know, richly endowed with several of those gifts of the spirit of which Saint Paul speaks, and the discerning of spirits is among them. These things depend upon laws which are beyond our control, but a sympathetic atmosphere is essential, and Mrs. Debbs will ask for your good wishes and your prayers while she endeavours to get into touch with some of those shining ones on the other side who may honour us with their presence to-night."

The president sat down and Mrs. Debbs rose amid discreet applause. Very tall, very pale, very thin, with an aquiline face and eyes shining brightly from behind her gold-rimmed glasses, she stood facing her expectant audience. Her head was bent. She seemed to be listening.

"Vibrations!" she cried at last. "I want helpful vibrations. Give me a verse on the harmonium, please."

The instrument droned out "Jesu, Lover of my soul." The audience sat in silence, expectant and a little awed.

The hall was not too well lit and dark shadows lurked in the corners. The medium still bent her head as if her ears were straining. Then she raised her hand and the music stopped.

"Presently! Presently! All in good time," said the woman, addressing some invisible companion. Then to the audience, "I don't feel that the conditions are very good to-night. I will do my best and so will they. But I must talk to you first."

And she talked. What she said seemed to the two strangers to be absolute gabble. There was no consecutive sense in it, though now and again a phrase or sentence caught the attention. Malone put his stylo in his pocket. There was no use reporting a lunatic. A Spiritualist next him saw his bewildered disgust and leaned towards him.

"She's tuning in. She's getting her wave length," he whispered. "It's all a matter of vibration. Ah, there you are!"

She had stopped in the very middle of a sentence. Her long arm and quivering forefinger shot out. She was pointing at an elderly woman in the second row.

"You! Yes, you, with the red feather. No, not you. The stout lady in front. Yes, you! There is a spirit building up behind you. It is a man. He is a tall man—six foot maybe. High forehead, eyes grey or blue, a long chin, brown moustache, lines on his face. Do you recognize him, friend?"

The stout woman looked alarmed, but shook her head.

"Well, see if I can help you. He is holding up a book—brown book with a clasp. It's a ledger same as they have in offices. I get the words 'Caledonian Insurance'. Is that any help?"

The stout woman pursed her lips and shook her head.

"Well, I can give you a little more. He died after a long illness. I get chest trouble—asthma."

The stout woman was still obdurate, but a small, angry, red-faced person, two places away from her, sprang to her feet.

" It's my 'usband, ma'm. Tell 'im I don't want to 'ave any more dealin's with him." She sat down with decision.

" Yes, that's right. He moves to you now. He was nearer the other. He wants to say he's sorry. It doesn't do, you know, to have hard feelings to the dead. Forgive and forget. It's all over. I get a message for you. It is: ' Do it and my blessing go with you '! Does that mean anything to you ?"

The angry woman looked pleased and nodded.

" Very good." The clairvoyante suddenly darted out her finger towards the crowd at the door. " It's for the soldier."

A soldier in khaki, looking very much amazed, was in the front of the knot of people.

" Wot's for me ?" he asked.

" It's a soldier. He has a corporal's stripes. He is a big man with grizzled hair. He has a yellow tab on his shoulders. I get the initials J. H. Do you know him ?"

" Yes—but he's dead," said the soldier.

He had not understood that it was a Spiritualistic Church, and the whole proceedings had been a mystery to him. They were rapidly explained by his neighbours. " My Gawd !" cried the soldier, and vanished amid a general titter. In the pause Malone could hear the constant mutter of the medium as she spoke to someone unseen.

" Yes, yes, wait your turn ! Speak up, woman ! Well, take your place near him. How should I know ? Well, I will if I can." She was like a janitor at the theatre marshalling a queue.

Her next attempt was a total failure. A solid man with bushy side-whiskers absolutely refused to have anything to do with an elderly gentleman who claimed kinship. The medium worked with admirable patience, coming back again and again with some fresh detail, but no progress could be made.

" Are you a Spiritualist, friend ?"

" Yes, for ten years."

" Well, you know there are difficulties."

" Yes, I know that."

" Think it over. It may come to you later. We must just leave it at that. I am only sorry for your friend."

There was a pause during which Enid and Malone exchanged whispered confidences.

" What do you make of it, Enid ?"

" I don't know. It confuses me."

" I believe it is half guess-work and the other half a case of confederates. These people are all of the same church, and naturally they know each other's affairs. If they don't know they can inquire."

" Someone said it was Mrs. Debbs' first visit."

" Yes but they could easily coach her up. It is all clever quackery and bluff. It *must* be, for just think what is implied if it is not."

" Telepathy, perhaps."

" Yes, some element of that also. Listen ! She is off again."

Her next attempt was more fortunate. A lugubrious man at the back of the hall readily recognized the description and claims of his deceased wife.

" I get the name Walter."

" Yes, that's me."

" She called you Wat ?"

" No."

" Well, she calls you Wat now. ' Tell Wat to give my love to the children '. That's how I get it. She is worrying about the children."

" She always did."

" Well, they don't change. Furniture. Something about furniture. She says you gave it away. Is that right ?"

" Well, I might as well."

The audience tittered. It was strange how the most solemn and comic were eternally blended—strange and yet very natural and human.

" She has a message: ' The man will pay up and all will be well. Be a good man, Wat, and we will be happier here then ever we were on earth '."

The man put his hand over his eyes. As the seeress stood irresolute the tall young secretary half rose and whispered something in her ear. The woman shot a swift glance over her left shoulder in the direction of the visitors.

" I'll come back to it," said she.

She gave two more descriptions to the audience, both of them rather vague, and both recognized with some reservations. It was a curious fact that her details were such as she could not possibly see at the distance. Thus, dealing with a form which she claimed had built up at the far end of the hall, she could none the less give the colour of the eyes and small points of the face. Malone noted the point as one which he could use for destructive criticism. He was just jotting it down when the woman's voice sounded louder and, looking up, he found that she had turned her head and her spectacles were flashing in his direction.

" It is not often I give a reading from the platform," said she, her face rotating between him and the audience, " but we have friends here to-night, and it may interest them to come in contact with the spirit people. There is a presence building up behind the gentleman with a moustache—the gentleman who sits next to the young lady. Yes, sir, behind you. He is a man of middle size, rather inclined to short-ness. He is old, over sixty, with white hair, curved nose and a white, small beard of the variety that is called goatee. He is no relation, I gather, but a friend. Does that suggest anyone to you, sir ?"

Malone shook his head with some contempt. " It would nearly fit any old man," he whispered to Enid.

" We will try to get a little closer. He has deep lines on his face. I should say he was an irritable man in his life-time. He was quick and nervous in his ways. Does that help you ?"

Again Malone shook his head.

" Rot ! Perfect rot," he muttered.

" Well, he seems very anxious, so we must do what we can for him. He holds up a book. It is a learned book. He opens it and I see diagrams in it. Perhaps he wrote it—

or perhaps he taught from it. Yes, he nods. He taught from it. He was a teacher."

Malone remained unresponsive.

" I don't know that I can help him any more. Ah ! there is one thing. He has a mole over his right eyebrow."

Malone started as if he had been stung.

" One mole ?" he cried.

The spectacles flashed round again.

" Two moles—one large, one small."

" My God !" gasped Malone. " It's Professor Summerlee !"

"'Ah, you've got it. There's a message: ' Greetings to old —— ' It's a long name and begins with a C. I can't get it. Does it mean anything ?"

" Yes."

In an instant she had turned and was describing something or someone else. But she had left a badly-shaken man upon the platform behind her.

It was at this point that the orderly service had a remarkable interruption which surprised the audience as much as it did the two visitors. This was the sudden appearance beside the chairman of a tall, pale-faced bearded man dressed like a superior artisan, who held up his hand with a quietly impressive gesture as one who was accustomed to exert authority. He then half-turned and said a word to Mr. Bolsover.

" This is Mr. Miromar of Dalston," said the chairman. " Mr. Miromar has a message to deliver. We are always glad to hear from Mr. Miromar."

The reporters could only get a half-view of the newcomer's face, but both of them were struck by his noble bearing and by the massive outline of his head which promised very unusual intellectual power. His voice when he spoke rang clearly and pleasantly through the hall.

" I have been ordered to give the message wherever I think that there are ears to hear it. There are some here who are ready for it, and that is why I have come. They wish that the human race should gradually understand the situation so that there shall be the less shock or panic. I am one of several who are chosen to carry the news."

" A lunatic, I'm afraid !" whispered Malone, scribbling hard upon his knee There was a general inclination to smile among the audience. And yet there was something in the man's manner and voice which made them hang on every word.

" Things have now reached a climax. The very idea of progress has been made material. It is progress to go swiftly, to send swift messages, to build new machinery. All this is a diversion of real ambition. There is only one real progress—spiritual progress. Mankind gives it a lip tribute but presses on upon its false road of material science.

" The Central Intelligence recognized that amid all the apathy there was also much honest doubt which had out-grown old creeds and had a right to fresh evidence. There-fore fresh evidence was sent—evidence which made the life after death as clear as the sun in the heavens. It was laughed at by scientists, condemned by the churches, be-came the butt of the newspapers, and was discarded with contempt. That was the last and greatest blunder of humanity."

The audience had their chins up now. General specula-tions were beyond their mental horizon. But this was very clear to their comprehension. There was a murmur of sympathy and applause.

" The thing was now hopeless. It had got beyond all control. Therefore something sterner was needed since Heaven's gift had been disregarded. The blow fell. Ten million young men were laid dead upon the ground. Twice as many were mutilated. That was God's first warning to mankind. But it was vain. The same dull materialism prevailed as before. Years of grace were given, and save the stirrings of the spirit seen in such churches as these, no change was anywhere to be seen. The nations heaped up fresh loads of sin, and sin must ever be atoned for. Russia became a cesspool. Germany was unrepentant of her terrible materialism which had been the prime cause of the war. Spain and Italy were sunk in alternate atheism and superstition. France had no religious ideal. Britain was confused and distracted, full of wooden sects which had nothing of life in them. America had abused her glorious opportunities and, instead of being the loving younger brother to a stricken Europe, she held up all economic reconstruction by her money claims; she dishonoured the signature of her own president, and she refused to join that League of Peace which was the one hope of the future. All have sinned, but some more than others, and their punishment will be in exact proportion.

" And that punishment soon comes. These are the exact words I have been asked to give you. I read them lest I should in any way garble them."

He took a slip of paper from his pocket and read:

" ' What we want is, not that folk should be frightened, but that they should begin to change themselves—to develop themselves on more spiritual lines. We are not trying to make people nervous, but to prepare while there is yet time. The world cannot go on as it has done. It would destroy itself if it did. Above all we must sweep away the dark cloud of theology which has come between mankind and God '."

He folded up the paper and replaced it in his pocket.

" That is what I have been asked to tell you. Spread the news where there seems to be a window in the soul. Say to them, ' Repent ! Reform ! the Time is at hand '."

He had paused and seemed about to turn. The spell was broken. The audience rustled and leaned back in its seats. Then a voice from the back:

" Is this the end of the world, mister ?"

" No," said the stranger, curtly.

" Is it the Second Coming ?" asked another voice.

" Yes."

With quick light steps he threaded his way among the chairs on the platform and stood near the door. When Malone next looked round he was gone.

" He is one of these Second-Coming fanatics," he

whispered to Enid. " There are a lot of them—Christadelphians, Russellites, Bible Students and what-not. But he was impressive."

" Very," said Enid.

" We have, I am sure, been very interested in what our friend has told us," said the chairman. " Mr. Miromar is in hearty sympathy with our movement even though he cannot be said actually to belong to it. I am sure he is always welcome upon our platforms. As to his prophecy, it seems to me the world has had enough trouble without our anticipating any more. If it is as our friend says, we can't do much to mend the matter. We can only go about our daily jobs, do them as well as we can, and await the event in full confidence of help from above. If it's the Day of Judgment to-morrow," he added, smiling, " I mean to look after my provision store at Hammersmith to-day. We shall now continue with the service."

There was a vigorous appeal for money and a great deal about the building-fund from the young secretary. " It's a shame to think that there are more left in the street than in the building on a Sunday night. We all give our services. No one takes a penny. Mrs. Debbs is here for her bare expenses. But we want another thousand pounds before we can start. There is one brother here who mortgaged his house to help us. That's the spirit that wins. Now let us see what you can do for us to-night."

A dozen soup-plates circulated, and a hymn was sung to the accompaniment of much chinking of coin. Enid and Malone conversed in undertones.

" Professor Summerlee died, you know, at Naples last year."

" Yes, I remember him well."

" And ' old C ' was, of course, your father."

" It was really remarkable."

" Poor old Summerlee. He thought survival was an absurdity. And here he is—or here he seems to be."

The soup-plates returned—it was mostly brown soup, unhappily, and they were deposited on the table where the eager eye of the secretary appraised their value. Then the little shaggy man from Australia gave a benediction in the same simple fashion as the opening prayer. It needed no Apostolic succession or laying-on of hands to make one feel that his words were from a human heart and might well go straight to a Divine one. Then the audience rose and sang their final farewell hymn—a hymn with a haunting tune and a sad, sweet refrain of " God keep you safely till we meet once more." Enid was surprised to feel the tears running down her cheeks. These earnest, simple folks with their direct methods had wrought upon her more than all the gorgeous service and rolling music of the cathedral.

Mr. Bolsover, the stout president, was in the waiting-room and so was Mrs. Debbs.

" Well, I expect you are going to let us have it," he laughed. " We are used to it Mr. Malone. We don't mind. But you will see the turn some day. These articles may rise up in judgment."

" I will treat it fairly, I assure you."

" Well, we ask no more."

The medium was leaning with her elbow on the mantel-piece, austere and aloof.

" I am afraid you are tired," said Enid.

" No, young lady, I am never tired in doing the work of the spirit people. They see to that."

" May I ask," Malone ventured, " whether you ever knew Professor Summerlee ?"

The medium shook her head.

" No, sir, no. They always think I know them. I know none of them. They come and I describe them."

" How do you get the message ?"

" Clairaudient. I hear it. I hear them all the time. The poor things all want to come through and they pluck at me and pull me and pester me on the platform. ' Me next—me—me '! That's what I hear. I do my best, but I can't handle them all."

" Can you tell me anything of that prophetic person ?"

asked Malone of the chairman. Mr. Bolsover shrugged his shoulders with a deprecating smile.

" He is an Independent. We see him now and again as a sort of comet passing across us. By the way, it comes back to me that he prophesied the war. I'm a practical man myself. Sufficient for the day is the evil thereof. We get plenty in ready cash without any bills for the future. Well, good night ! Treat us as well as you can."

" Good night," said Enid.

" Good night," said Mrs. Debbs. " By the way, young lady, you are a medium yourself. Good night !"

And so they found themselves in the street once more inhaling long draughts of the night air. It was sweet after that crowded hall. A minute later they were in the rush of the Edgware Road and Malone had hailed a cab to carry them back to Victoria Gardens.

3. *In Which Professor Challenger Gives His Opinion*

ENID had stepped into the cab and Malone was following when his name was called and a man came running down the street. He was tall, middle-aged, handsome and well-dressed, with the clean-shaven, self-confident face of the successful surgeon.

" Hullo, Malone ! Stop !"

" Why, it's Atkinson ! Enid, let me introduce you. This is Mr. Atkinson of St. Mary's about whom I spoke to your father. Can we give you a lift ? We are going towards Victoria."

" Capital !" The surgeon followed them into the cab. " I was amazed to see you at a Spiritualist meeting."

" We were only there professionally. Miss Challenger and I are both on the Press."

" Oh, really ! The *Daily Gazette*, I suppose, as before Well, you will have one more subscriber, for I shall want to see what you made of to-night's show."

"You'll have to wait till next Sunday. It is one of a series."

"Oh, I say, I can't wait as long as that. What *did* you make of it?"

"I really don't know. I shall have to read my notes carefully to-morrow and think it over, and compare impressions with my colleague here. She has the intuition, you see, which goes for so much in religious matters."

"And what is your intuition, Miss Challenger?"

"Good—oh yes, good! But, dear me, what an extraordinary mixture!"

"Yes, indeed. I have been several times and it always leaves the same mixed impression upon my own mind. Some of it is ludicrous, and some of it might be dishonest, and yet again some of it is clearly wonderful."

"But you are not on the Press. Why were *you* there?"

"Because I am deeply interested. You see, I am a student of psychic matters and have been for some years. I am not a convinced one but I am sympathetic, and I have sufficient sense of proportion to realize that while I seem to be sitting in judgment upon the subject it may in truth be the subject which is sitting in judgment upon me."

Malone nodded appreciation.

"It is enormous. You will realize that as you get to close grips with it. It is half a dozen great subjects in one. And it is all in the hands of these good humble folk who, in the face of every discouragement and personal loss, have carried it on for more than seventy years. It is really very like the rise of Christianity. It was run by slaves and underlings until it gradually extended upwards. There were three hundred years between Cæsar's slave and Cæsar getting the light."

"But the preacher!" cried Enid in protest.

Mr. Atkinson laughed.

"You mean our friend from Atlantis. What a terrible bore the fellow was! I confess I don't know what to make of performances like that. Self-deception, I think, and the temporary emergence of some fresh strand of personality which dramatizes itself in this way. The only thing I am quite sure of is that it is not really an inhabitant of Atlantis who arrives from his long voyage with this awful cargo of platitudes. Well, here we are !"

" I have to deliver this young lady safe and sound to her father," said Malone. " Look here, Atkinson, don't leave us. The Professor would really like to see you."

" What at this hour ! Why, he would throw me down the stairs."

" You've been hearing stories," said Enid. " Really it is not so bad as that. Some people annoy him, but I am sure you are not one of them. Won't you chance it ?"

" With that encouragement, certainly." And the three walked down the bright outer corridor to the lift.

Challenger, clad now in a brilliant blue dressing-gown, was eagerly awaiting them. He eyed Atkinson as a fighting bulldog eyes some canine stranger. The inspection seemed to satisfy him, however, for he growled that he was glad to meet him.

" I've heard of your name, sir, and of your rising reputation. Your resection of the cord last year made some stir, I understand. But have you been down among the lunatics also ?"

" Well, if you call them so," said Atkinson with a laugh.

" Good Heavens, what else could I call them ? I remember now that my young friend here " (Challenger had a way of alluding to Malone as if he were a promising boy of ten) " told me you were studying the subject." He roared with offensive laughter. " ' The proper study of mankind is spooks ', eh, Mr. Atkinson ?"

" Dad really knows nothing about it, so don't be offended with him," said Enid. " But I assure you, Dad, you would have been interested." She proceeded to give a sketch of their adventures, though interrupted by a running commentary of groans, grunts and derisive jeers. It was only when the Summerlee episode was reached that Challenger's indignation and contempt could no longer be restrained. The old volcano blew his head off and a torrent of red-hot invective descended upon his listeners.

"The blasphemous rascals!" he shouted. "To think that they can't let poor old Summerlee rest in his grave. We had our differences in his time and I will admit that I was compelled to take a moderate view of his intelligence, but if he came back from the grave he would certainly have something worth hearing to say to us. It is an absurdity— a wicked, indecent absurdity upon the face of it. I object to any friend of mine being made a puppet for the laughter of an audience of fools. They didn't laugh! They must have laughed when they heard an educated man, a man whom I have met upon equal terms, talking such nonsense. I say it *was* nonsense. Don't contradict me, Malone. I won't have it! His message might have been the postscript of a schoolgirl's letter. Isn't that nonsense, coming from such a source? Are you not in agreement, Mr. Atkinson? No! I had hoped better things from you."

"But the description?"

"Good Heavens, where are your brains? Have not the names of Summerlee and Malone been associated with my own in some peculiarly feeble fiction which attained some notoriety? Is it not also known that you two innocents were doing the Churches week by week? Was it not patent that sooner or later you would come to a Spiritualist gathering? Here was a chance for a convert! They set a bait and poor old gudgeon Malone came along and swallowed it. Here he is with the hook still stuck in his silly mouth. Oh, yes, Malone, plain speaking is needed and you shall have it." The Professor's black mane was bristling and his eyes glaring from one member of the company to another.

"Well, we want every view expressed," said Atkinson. "You seem very qualified, sir, to express the negative one. At the same time I would repeat in my own person the words of Thackeray. He said to some objector: 'What you say is natural, but if you had seen what I have seen you might alter your opinion'. Perhaps sometime you will be able to look into the matter, for your high position in the scientific world would give your opinion great weight."

"If I have a high place in the scientific world as you say,

it is because I have concentrated upon what is useful and discarded what is nebulous or absurd. My brain, sir, does not pare the edges. It cuts right through. It has cut right through this and has found fraud and folly." ˙ ˌ

"Both are there at times," said Atkinson, "and yet . . . and yet! Ah, well, Malone, I'm some way from home and it is late. You will excuse me, Professor. I am honoured to have met you."

Malone was leaving also and the two friends had a few minutes' chat before they went their separate ways, Atkinson to Wimpole Street and Malone to South Norwood, where he was now living.

"Grand old fellow!" said Malone, chuckling. "You must never get offended with him. He means no harm. He is splendid."

"Of course he is. But if anything could make me a real out-and-out Spiritualist it is that sort of intolerance. It is very common, though it is generally cast rather in the tone of the quiet sneer than of the noisy roar. I like the latter best. By the way, Malone, if you care to go deeper into this subject I may be able to help you. You've heard of Linden?"

"Linden, the professional medium. Yes, I've been told he is the greatest blackguard unhung."

"Ah, well, they usually talk of them like that. You must judge for yourself. He put his knee-cap out last winter and I put it in again, and that has made a friendly bond between us. It's not always easy to get him, and of course a small fee, a guinea I think, is usual, but if you wanted a sitting I could work it."

"You think him genuine?"

Atkinson shrugged his shoulders.

"I daresay they all take the line of least resistance. I can only say that I have never detected him in fraud. You must judge for yourself."

"I will," said Malone. "I am getting hot on this trail. And there is copy in it, too. When things are more easy I'll write to you, Atkinson, and we can go more deeply into the matter."

4. *Which Describes Some Strange Doings in Hammersmith*

THE article by the Joint Commissioners (such was their glorious title) aroused interest and contention. It had been accompanied by a depreciating leader-ette from the sub-editor which was meant to calm the susceptibilities of his orthodox readers, as who should say: " These things have to be noticed and seem to be true, but of course you and I recognize how pestilential it all is." Malone found himself at once plunged into a huge correspondence, for and against, which in itself was enough to show how vitally the question was in the minds of men. All the previous articles had only elicited a growl here or there from a hide-bound Catholic or from an iron-clad Evangelical, but now his post-bag was full. Most of them were ridiculing the idea that psychic forces existed and many were from writers who, whatever they might know of psychic forces, had obviously not yet learned to spell. The Spiritualists were in many cases not more pleased than the others, for Malone had—even while his account was true—exercised a journalist's privilege of laying an accent on the more humorous sides of it.

One morning in the succeeding week Mr. Malone was aware of a large presence in the small room wherein he did his work at the office. A page-boy, who preceded the stout visitor, had laid a card on the corner of the table which bore the legend 'James Bolsover, Provision Merchant, High Street, Hammersmith.' It was none other than the genial president of last Sunday's congregation. He wagged a paper accusingly at Malone, but his good-humoured face was wreathed in smiles.

" Well, well," said he. " I told you that the funny side would get you."

" Don't you think it a fair account ? "

" Well, yes, Mr. Malone, I think you and the young woman have done your best for us. But, of course, you know nothing and it all seems queer to you. Come to think of it, it would be a deal queerer if all the clever men who leave this earth could not among them find some way of getting a word back to us."

" But it's such a stupid word sometimes."

" Well, there are a lot of stupid people leave the world. They don't change. And then, you know, one never knows what sort of message is needed. We had a clergyman in to see Mrs. Debbs yesterday. He was broken-hearted because he had lost his daughter. Mrs. Debbs got several messages through that she was happy and that only his grief hurt her. ' That's no use ', said he. ' Anyone could say that. That's not my girl '. And then suddenly she said: ' But I wish to goodness you would not wear a Roman collar with a coloured shirt '. That sounded a trivial message, but the man began to cry. ' That's her ', he sobbed. ' She was always chipping me about my collars '. It's the little things that count in this life—just the homely, intimate things, Mr. Malone."

Malone shook his head.

" Anyone would remark on a coloured shirt and a clerical collar."

Mr. Bolsover laughed. " You're a hard proposition. So was I once, so I can't blame you. But I called here with a purpose. I expect you are a busy man and I know that I am, so I'll get down to the brass tacks. First, I wanted to say that all our people that have any sense are pleased with the article. Mr. Algernon Mailey wrote me that it would do good, and if he is pleased we are all pleased."

" Mailey the barrister ?"

" Mailey, the religious reformer. That's how he will be known."

" Well, what else ?"

" Only that we would help you if you and the young lady wanted to go further in the matter. Not for publicity, mind you, but just for your own good—though we don't

76

shrink from publicity, either. I have psychical phenomena ·séances at my own home without a professional medium, and if you would like . . . "

" There's nothing I would like so much."

" Then you shall come—both of you. I don't have many outsiders. I wouldn't have one of those psychic research people inside my doors. Why should I go out of my way to be insulted by all their suspicions and their traps ? They seem to think that folk have no feelings. But you have some ordinary common sense. That's all we ask."

" But I don't believe. Would that not stand in the way ?"

" Not in the least. So long as you are fair-minded and don't disturb the conditions, all is well. Spirits out of the body don't like disagreeable people any more than spirits in the body do. Be gentle and civil, same as you would to any other company."

" Well, I can promise that."

" They are funny sometimes," said Mr. Bolsover, in reminiscent vein. " It is as well to keep on the right side of them. They are not allowed to hurt humans, but we all do things we're not allowed to do, and they are very human themselves. You remember how *The Times* correspondent got his head cut open with the tambourine in one of the Davenport Brothers' séances. Very wrong, of course, but it happened. No friend ever got his head cut open. There was another case down Stepney way. A moneylender went to a séance. Some victim that he had driven to suicide got into the medium. He got the moneylender by the throat and it was a close thing for his life. But I'm off, Mr. Malone. We sit once a week and have done for four years without a break. Eight o'clock Thursdays. Give us a day's notice and I'll get Mr. Mailey to meet you. He can answer questions better than I. Next Thursday ! Very good." And Mr. Bolsover lurched out of the room.

Both Malone and Enid Challenger had, perhaps, been more shaken by their short experience than they had admitted, but both were sensible people who agreed that every possible natural cause should be exhausted—and very thoroughly exhausted—before the bounds of what is possible should be enlarged. Both of them had the utmost respect for the ponderous intellect of Challenger and were affected by his strong views, though Malone was compelled to admit in the frequent arguments in which he was plunged that the opinion of a clever man who has had no experience is really of less value than that of the man in the street who has actually been there.

These arguments, as often as not, were with Mervin, editor of the psychic paper *Dawn*, which dealt with every phase of the occult, from the lore of the Rosicrucians to the strange regions of the students of the Great Pyramid, or of those who uphold the Jewish origin of our blonde Anglo-Saxons. Mervin was a small, eager man with a brain of a high order, which might have carried him to the most lucrative heights of his profession had he not determined to sacrifice worldy prospects in order to help what seemed to him to be a great truth. As Malone was eager for knowledge and Mervin was equally keen to impart it, the waiters at the Literary Club found it no easy matter to get them away from the corner-table in the window at which they were wont to lunch. Looking down at the long, grey curve of the Embankment and the noble river with its vista of bridges, the pair would linger over their coffee, smoking cigarettes and discussing various sides of this most gigantic and absorbing subject, which seemed already to have disclosed new horizons to the mind of Malone.

There was one warning given by Mervin which aroused impatience amounting almost to anger in Malone's mind. He had the hereditary Irish objection to coercion and it seemed to him to be appearing once more in an insidious and particularly objectionable form.

"You are going to one of Bolsover's family séances," said Mervin. "They are, of course, well known among our people, though few have been actually admitted, so you may consider yourself privileged. He has clearly taken a fancy to you."

- - -

" He thought I wrote fairly about them."

" Well, it wasn't much of an article, but still among the dreary, purblind nonsense that assails us it did show some traces of dignity and balance and sense of proportion."

Malone waved a deprecating cigarette.

" Bolsover's séances and others like them are, or course, things of no moment to the real psychic. They are like the rude foundations of a building which certainly help to sustain the edifice, but are forgotten when once you come to inhabit it. It is the higher superstructure with which we have to do. You would think that the physical phenomena were the whole subject—those and a fringe of ghosts and haunted houses—if you were to believe the cheap papers who cater for the sensationalist. Of course, these physical phenomena have a use of their own. They rivet the attention of the inquirer and encourage him to go further. Personally, having seen them all, I would not go across the road to see them again. But I would go across many roads to get high messages from the beyond."

" Yes, I quite appreciate the distinction, looking at it from your point of view. Personally, of course, I am equally agnostic as to the messages and the phenomena."

" Quite so. St. Paul was a good psychic. He makes the point so neatly that even his ignorant translators were unable to disguise the real occult meanings as they have succeeded in doing in so many cases."

" Can you quote it ?"

" I know my New Testament pretty well, but I am not letter-perfect. It is the passage where he says that the gift of tongues, which was an obvious sensational thing, was for the uninstructed, but that prophecies, that is real spiritual messages, were for the elect. In other words that an experienced Spiritualist has no need of phenomena."

" I'll look that passage up."

" You will find it in Corinthians, I think. By the way, there must have been a pretty high average of intelligence among those old congregations if Paul's letters could have been read aloud to them and thoroughly comprehended."

" That is generally admitted, is it not ?'"

" Well, it is a concrete example of it. However, I am down a side-track. What I wanted to say to you is that you must not take Bolsover's little spirit circus too seriously. It is honest as far as it goes, but it goes a mighty short way. It's a disease, this phenomena hunting. I know some of our people, women mostly, who buzz around séance rooms continually, seeing the same thing over and over, sometimes real, sometimes, I fear, imitation. What better are they for that as souls or as citizens or in any other way ? No, when your foot is firm on the bottom rung don't mark time on it, but step up to the next rung and get firm upon that."

" I quite get your point. But I'm still on the solid ground."

" Solid !" cried Mervin. " Good Lord ! But the paper goes to press to-day and I must get down to the printer. With a circulation of ten thousand or so we do things modestly, you know—not like you plutocrats of the daily press. I am practically the staff."

" You said you had a warning."

" Yes, yes, I wanted to give you a warning." Mervin's thin, eager face became intensely serious. " If you have any ingrained religious or other prejudices which may cause you to turn down this subject after you have investigated it, then don't investigate at all—for it is dangerous."

" What do you mean—dangerous ?"

" They don't mind honest doubt, or honest criticism, but if they are badly treated they are dangerous."

" Who are ' they ' ?"

" Ah, who are they ? I wonder. Guides, controls, psychic entities of some kind. Who the agents of vengeance—or I should say justice—are, is really not essential. The point is that they exist."

" Oh, rot, Mervin !"

" Don't be too sure of that."

" Pernicious rot ! These are the old theological bogies of the Middle Ages coming up again. I am surprised at a sensible man like you !"

Mervin smiled—he had a whimsical smile—but his eyes, looking out from under bushy yellow brows, were as serious as ever.

" You may come to change your opinion. There are some queer sides to this question. As a friend I put you wise to this one."

" Well, put me wise, then."

Thus encouraged, Mervin went into the matter. He rapidly sketched the career and fate of a number of men who had, in his opinion, played an unfair game with these forces, become an obstruction, and suffered for it. He spoke of judges who had given prejudiced decisions against the cause, of journalists who had worked up stunt cases for sensational purposes and to throw discredit on the movement; of others who had interviewed mediums to make game of them, or who, having started to investigate, had drawn back alarmed, and given a negative decision when their inner soul knew that the facts were true. It was a formidable list, for it was long and precise, but Malone was not to be driven.

" If you pick your cases I have no doubt one could make such a list about any subject. Mr. Jones said that Raphael was a bungler, and Mr. Jones died of angina pectoris. Therefore it is dangerous to criticize Raphael. That seems to be the argument."

" Well, if you like to think so."

" Take the other side. Look at Morgate. He has always been an enemy, for he is a convinced materialist. But he prospers—look at his professorship."

" Ah, an honest doubter. Certainly. Why not ?"

" And Morgan who at one time exposed mediums."

" If they were really false he did good service."

" And Falconer who has written so bitterly about you ?"

" Ah, Falconer ! Do you know anything of Falconer's private life ? No. Well, take it from me he has got his dues. He doesn't know why. Some day these gentlemen will begin to compare notes and then it may dawn on them. But they get it."

He went on to tell a horrible story of one who had devoted his considerable talents to picking Spiritualism to pieces, though really convinced of its truth, because his worldly ends were served thereby. The end was ghastly —too ghastly for Malone.

" Oh, cut it out, Mervin ! " he cried impatiently. " I'll say what I think, no more and no less, and I won't be scared by you or your spooks into altering my opinions."

" I never asked you to."

" You got a bit near it. What you have said strikes me as pure superstition. If what you say is true you should have the police after you."

" Yes, if we did it. But it is out of our hands. However, Malone, for what it's worth I have given you the warning and you can now go your way. Bye-bye ! You can always ring me up at the office of *Dawn*."

If you want to know if a man is of the true Irish blood there is one infallible test. Put him in front of a swing-door with " Push " or " Pull " printed upon it. The Englishman will obey like a sensible man. The Irishman, with less sense but more individuality, will at once and with vehemence do the opposite. So it was with Malone. Mervin's well-meant warning simply raised a rebellious spirit within him, and when he called for Enid to take her to the Bolsover séance he had gone back several degrees in his dawning sympathy for the subject. Challenger bade them farewell with many gibes, his beard projecting forward and his eyes closed with upraised eyebrows, as was his wont when inclined to be facetious.

" You have your powder-bag, my dear Enid. If you see a particularly good specimen of ectoplasm in the course of the evening don't forget your father. I have a microscope, chemical reagents and everything ready. Perhaps even a small *poltergeist* might come your way. Any trifle would be welcome."

His bull's bellow of laughter followed them into the lift.

The provision merchant's establishment of Mr. Bolsover proved to be a euphemism for an old-fashioned grocer's shop in the most crowded part of Hammersmith. The neighbouring church was chiming out the three-quarters as the taxi drove up, and the shop was full of people. So Enid and Malone walked up and down outside. As they were so engaged another taxi drove up and a large, untidy-looking, ungainly bearded man in a suit of Harris tweed stepped out of it. He glanced at his watch and then began to pace the pavement. Presently he noted the others and came up to them.

" May I ask if you are the journalists who are going to attend the séance? . . . I thought so. Old Bolsover is terribly busy so you were wise to wait. Bless him, he is one of God's saints in his way."

" You are Mr. Algernon Mailey, I presume?"

" Yes. I am the gentleman whose credulity is giving rise to considerable anxiety upon the part of my friends, as one of the rags remarked the other day." His laugh was so infectious that the others were bound to laugh also. Certainly, with his athletic proportions, which had run a little to seed but were still notable, and with his virile voice and strong if homely face, he gave no impression of instability.

" We are all labelled with some stigma by our opponents," said he. " I wonder what yours will be."

" We must not sail under false colours, Mr. Mailey," said Enid. " We are not yet among the believers."

" Quite right. You should take your time over it. It is infinitely the most important thing in the world, so it is worth taking time over. I took many years myself. Folk can be blamed for neglecting it, but no one can be blamed for being cautious in examination. Now I am all out for it, as you are aware, because I *know* it is true. There is such a difference between believing and knowing. I lecture a good deal. But I never want to convert my audience. I don't believe in sudden conversions. They are shallow, superficial things. All I want is to put the thing before the people as clearly as I can. I just tell them the truth and why we know it is the truth. Then my job is done. They can take it or leave it. If they are wise they will explore along the paths that I indicate. If they are unwise they miss their chance. I don't want to press them or to proselytize. It's their affair, not mine."

" Well, that seems a reasonable view," said Enid, who was attracted by the frank manner of their new acquaintance. They were standing now in the full flood of light cast by Bolsover's big plate-glass window. She had a good look at him, his broad forehead, his curious grey eyes, thoughtful and yet eager, his straw-coloured beard which indicated the outline of an aggressive chin. He was solidity personi-fied—the very opposite of the fanatic whom she had imagined. His name had been a good deal in the papers lately as a protagonist in the long battle, and she remem-bered that it had never been mentioned without an answer-ing snort from her father.

" I wonder," she said to Malone, " what would happen if Mr. Mailey were locked up in a room with Dad !"

Malone laughed. " There used to be a schoolboy question as to what would occur if an irresistible force were to strike an invincible obstacle."

" Oh, you are the daughter of Professor Challenger," said Mailey with interest. " He is a big figure in the scien-tific world. What a grand world it would be if it would only realize its own limitations."

" I don't quite follow you."

" It is this scientific world which is at the bottom of much of our materialism. It has helped us in comfort—if comfort is any use to us. Otherwise it has usually been a curse to us, for it has called itself progress and given us a false impression that we are making progress, whereas we are really drifting very steadily backwards."

" Really, I can't quite agree with you there, Mr. Mailey," said Malone, who was getting restive under what seemed to him dogmatic assertion. " Look at wireless. Look at the S.O.S. call at sea. Is that not a benefit to mankind !"

" Oh, it works out all right sometimes. I value my electric reading-lamp, and that is a product of science. It gives us, as I said before, comfort and occasionally safety."

" Why, then, do you depreciate it ?"

" Because it obscures the vital thing—the object of life. We were not put into this planet in order that we should go fifty miles an hour in a motor-car, or cross the Atlantic in an airship, or send messages either with or without wires. These are the mere trimmings and fringes of life. But these men of science have so riveted our attention on these fringes that we forget the central object."

" I don't follow you."

" It is not how fast you go that matters, it is the object of your journey. It is not how you send a message, it is what the value of the message may be. At every stage this so-called progress may be a curse, and yet as long as we use the word we confuse it with real progress and imagine that we are doing that for which God sent us into the world."

" Which is ?"

" To prepare ourselves for the next phase of life. There is mental preparation and spiritual preparation, and we are neglecting both. To be in an old age better men and women, more unselfish, more broadminded, more genial and tolerant, that is what we are for. It is a soul factory, and it is turning out a bad article. But——Hullo !" he burst into his infectious laugh. " Here I am delivering my lecture in the street. Force of habit, you see. My son says that if you press the third button of my waistcoat I automatically deliver a lecture. But here is the good Bolsover to your rescue."

The worthy grocer had caught sight of them through the window and came bustling out, untying his white apron.

" Good evening, all ! I won't have you waiting in the cold. Besides, there's the clock, and time's up. It does not do to keep them waiting. Punctuality for all—that's my motto and theirs. My lads will shut up the shop. This way, and mind the sugar-barrel."

They threaded their way amid boxes of dried fruits and piles of cheese, finally passing between two great casks which hardly left room for the grocer's portly form. A narrow door beyond opened into the residential part of the establishment. Ascending the narrow stair, Bolsover threw open a door and the visitors found themselves in a considerable room in which a number of people were seated round a large table. There was Mrs. Bolsover herself, large, cheerful and buxom like her husband. Three daughters were all of the same pleasing type. There was an elderly woman who seemed to be some relation, and two other colourless females who were described as neighbours and Spiritualists. The only other man was a little grey-headed fellow with a pleasant face and quick, twinkling eyes, who sat at a harmonium in the corner.

"Mr. Smiley, our musician," said Bolsover. "I don't know what we could do without Mr. Smiley. It's vibrations, you know. Mr. Mailey could tell you about that. Ladies, you know Mr. Mailey, our very good friend. And these are the two inquirers—Miss Challenger and Mr. Malone."

The Bolsover family all smiled genially, but the nondescript elderly person rose to her feet and surveyed them with an austere face.

"You're very welcome here, you two strangers," she said. "But we would say to you that we want outward reverence. We respect the shining ones and we will not have them insulted."

"I assure you we are very earnest and fairminded," said Malone.

"We've had our lesson. We haven't forgotten the Meadows' affair, Mr. Bolsover."

"No, no, Mrs. Seldon. That won't happen again. We were rather upset over that," Bolsover added, turning to the visitors. "That man came here as our guest, and when the lights were out he poked the other sitters with his finger so as to make them think it was a spirit hand. Then he wrote the whole thing up as an exposure in the public Press, when the only fraudulent thing present had been himself."

Malone was honestly shocked. "I can assure you we are incapable of such conduct."

The old lady sat down, but still regarded them with a suspicious eye. Bolsover bustled about and got things ready.

"You sit here, Mr. Mailey. Mr. Malone, will you sit between my wife and my daughter? Where would the young lady like to sit?"

Enid was feeling rather nervous. "I think," said she, "that I would like to sit next to Mr. Malone."

Bolsover chuckled and winked at his wife.

"Quite so. Most natural, I am sure." They all settled into their places. Mr. Bolsover had switched off the electric light, but a candle burned in the middle of the table. Malone thought what a picture it would have made for a Rembrandt. Deep shadows draped it in, but the yellow light flickered upon the circle of faces—the strong, homely, heavy features of Bolsover, the solid line of his family circle, the sharp, austere countenance of Mrs. Seldon, the earnest eyes and yellow beard of Mailey, the worn, tired faces of the two Spiritualist women, and finally the firm, noble profile of the girl who sat beside him. The whole world had suddenly narrowed down to that one little group, so intensely concentrated upon its own purpose.

On the table there was scattered a curious collection of objects, which had all the same appearance of tools which had long been used. There was a battered brass speaking-trumpet, very discoloured, a tambourine, a musical-box, and a number of smaller objects. "We never know what they may want," said Bolsover, waving his hand over them. "If Wee One calls for a thing and it isn't there she lets us know all about it—oh, yes, something shocking!"

"She has a temper of her own has Wee One," remarked Mrs. Bolsover.

"Why not, the pretty dear?" said the austere lady. "I expect she has enough to try it with researchers and what-not. I often wonder she troubles to come at all."

"Wee One is our little girl guide," said Bolsover. "You'll hear her presently."

"I do hope she will come," said Enid.

"Well, she never failed us yet, except when that man Meadows clawed hold of the trumpet and put it outside the circle."

"Who is the medium?" asked Malone.

"Well, we don't know ourselves. We all help, I think. Maybe, I give as much as anyone. And mother, she is a help."

"Our family is a co-operative store," said his wife, and everyone laughed.

"I thought one medium was necessary."

"It is usual but not necessary," said Mailey in his deep, authoritative voice. "Crawford showed that pretty clearly in the Gallagher séances when he proved, by weighing chairs, that everyone in the circle lost from half to two pounds at a sitting, though the medium, Miss Kathleen, lost as many as ten or twelve. Here the long series of sittings—— How long, Mr. Bolsover?"

"Four years unbroken."

"The long series has developed everyone to some extent, so that there is a high average output from each, instead of an extraordinary amount from one."

"Output of what?"

"Animal magnetism, ectoplasm—in fact, power. That is the most comprehensive word. The Christ used that word. ' Much power has gone out of me '. It is ' dunamis ' in the Greek, but the translators missed the point and translated it ' virtue '. If a good Greek scholar who was also a profound occult student was to re-translate the New Testament we should get some eye-openers. Dear old Ellis Powell did a little in that direction. His death was a loss to the world."

"Aye, indeed," said Bolsover in a reverent voice. "But now, before we get to work, Mr. Malone, I want you just to note one or two things. You see the white spots on the trumpet and the tambourine? Those are luminous points so that we can see where they are. The table is just our dining-table, good British oak. You can examine it if you like. But you'll see things that won't depend upon the table. Now, Mr. Smiley, out goes the light and we'll ask you for ' The Rock of Ages '."

The harmonium droned in the darkness and the circle sang. They sang very tunefully, too, for the girls had fresh voices and true ears. Low and vibrant, the solemn rhythm became most impressive when no sense but that of hearing was free to act. Their hands, according to instructions, were laid lightly upon the table, and they were warned not to cross their legs. Malone, with his hand touching Enid's, could feel the little quiverings which showed that her nerves were highly strung. The homely, jovial voice of Bolsover relieved the tension.

" That should do it," he said. " I feel as if the conditions were good to-night. Just a touch of frost in the air, too. I'll ask you now to join with me in prayer."

It was effective, that simple, earnest prayer in the darkness—an inky darkness which was only broken by the last red glow of a dying fire.

" Oh, great Father of us all," said the voice. " You who are beyond our thoughts and who yet pervade our lives, grant that all evil may be kept from us this night and that we may be privileged to get in touch, if only for an hour, with those who dwell upon a higher plane than ours. You are our Father as well as theirs. Permit us, for a short space, to meet in brotherhood, that we may have an added knowledge of that eternal life which awaits us, and so be helped during our years of waiting in this lower world." He ended with the " Our Father ", in which we all joined. Then they all sat in expectant silence. Outside was the dull roar of traffic and the occasional ill-tempered squawk of a passing car. Inside there was absolute stillness. Enid and Malone felt every sense upon the alert and every nerve on edge as they gazed out into the gloom.

" Nothing doing, mother," said Bolsover at last. " It's the strange company. New vibrations. They have to tune them in to get harmony. Give us another tune, Mr. Smiley."

Again the harmonium droned. It was still playing when a woman's voice cried: " Stop ! Stop ! They are here !"

Again they waited without result.

"Yes! Yes! I heard Wee One. She is here, right enough. I'm sure of it."

Silence again, and then it came—such a marvel to the visitors, such a matter of course to the circle.

"Gooda evenin'!" cried a voice.

There was a burst of greeting and of welcoming laughter from the circle. They were all speaking at once. "Good evening, Wee One!" "There you are, dear!" "I knew you would come!" "Well done, little girl guide!"

"Gooda evenin', all!" replied the voice. "Wee One so glad see Daddy and Mummy and the rest. Oh, what big man with beard! Mailey, Mister Mailey, I meet him before. He big Mailey, I little femaley. Glad to see you, Mr. Big Man."

Enid and Malone listened with amazement, but it was impossible to be nervous in face of the perfectly natural way in which the company accepted it. The voice was very thin and high—more so than any artificial falsetto could produce. It was the voice of a female child. That was certain. Also that there was no female child in the room unless one had been smuggled in after the light went out. That was possible. But the voice seemed to be in the middle of the table. How could a child get there?

"Easy get there, Mr. Gentleman," said the voice, answering his unspoken thought. "Daddy strong man. Daddy lift Wee One on to table. Now I show what Daddy not able to do."

"The trumpet's up!" cried Bolsover.

The little circle of luminous paint rose noiselessly into the air. Now it was swaying above their heads.

"Go up and hit the ceiling!" cried Bolsover.

Up it went and they heard the metallic tapping above them. Then the high voice came from above:

"Clever Daddy! Daddy got fishing-rod and put trumpet up to ceiling. But how Daddy make the voice, eh? What you say, pretty English Missy? Here is a present from Wee One."

90

Something soft dropped on Enid's lap. She put her hand down and felt it.

"It's a flower—a chrysanthemum. Thank you, Wee One!"

"An apport?" asked Mailey.

"No, no, Mr. Mailey," said Bolsover. "They were in the vase on the harmonium. Speak to her, Miss Challenger. Keep the vibrations going."

"Who are you, Wee One?" asked Enid, looking up at the moving spot above her.

"I am little black girl. Eight-year-old little black girl."

"Oh, come, dear," said mother in her rich, coaxing voice. "You were eight when you came to us first, and that was years ago."

"Years ago to you. All one time to me. I to do my job as eight-year child. When job done then Wee One become Big One all in one day. No time here, same as you have. I always eight-year-old."

"In the ordinary way they grow up exactly as we do here," said Mailey. "But if they have a special bit of work for which a child is needed, then as a child they remain. It's a sort of arrested development."

"That's me. 'Rested envelopment'," said the voice proudly. "I learn good England when big man here."

They all laughed. It was the most genial, free-and-easy association possible. Malone heard Enid's voice whispering in his ear.

"Pinch me from time to time, Edward—just to make me sure that I am not in a dream."

"I have to pinch myself, too."

"What about your song, Wee One?" asked Bolsover.

"Oh, yes, indeeda! Wee One sing to you." She began some simple song, but faded away in a squeak, while the trumpet clattered on to the table.

"Ah, power run down!" said Mailey. "I think a little more music will set us right. 'Lead, Kindly Light', Smiley."

They sang the beautiful hymn together. As the verse

closed an amazing thing happened—amazing, at least, to the novices, though it called for no remark from the circle.

The trumpet still shone upon the table, but two voices, those apparently of a man and a woman, broke out in the air above them and joined very tunefully in the singing. The hymn died away and all was silence and tense expectancy once more.

It was broken by a deep male voice from the darkness. It was an educated English voice, well modulated, a voice which spoke in a fashion to which the good Bolsover could never attain.

" Good evening, friends. The power seems good to-night."

" Good evening, Luke. Good evening !" cried everyone.

" It is our teaching guide," Bolsover explained. " He is a high spirit from the sixth sphere who gives us instruction."

" I may seem high to you," said the voice. " But what am I to those in turn who instruct me ! It is not *my* wisdom. Give me no credit. I do but pass it on."

" Always like that," said Bolsover. " No swank. It's a sign of his height."

" I see you have two inquirers present. Good evening, young lady ! You know nothing of your own powers or destiny. You will find them out. Good evening, sir, you are on the threshold of great knowledge. Is there any subject upon which you would wish me to say a few words ? I see that you are making notes."

Malone had, as a fact, disengaged his hand in the darkness and was jotting down in shorthand the sequence of events.

" What shall I speak of ?"

" Of love and marriage," suggested Mrs. Bolsover, nudging her husband.

" Well, I will say a few words on that. I will not take long, for others are waiting. The room is crowded with spirit people. I wish you to understand that there is one man, and only one, for each woman, and one woman only for each man. When those two meet they fly together and

92

are one through all the endless chain of existence. Until they meet all unions are mere accidents which have no meaning. Sooner or later each couple becomes complete. It may not be here. It may be in the next sphere where the sexes meet as they do on earth. Or it may be further delayed. But every man and every woman has his or her affinity, and will find it. Of earthly marriages perhaps one in five is permanent. The others are accidental. Real marriage is of the soul and spirit. Sex actions are a mere external symbol which mean nothing and are foolish, or even pernicious, when the thing which they should symbolize is wanting. Am I clear?"

" Very clear," said Mailey.

" Some have the wrong mate here. Some have no mate, which is more fortunate. But all will sooner or later get the right mate. That is certain. Do not think that you will not necessarily have your present husband when you pass over."

" Gawd be praised! Gawd be thanked!" cried a voice.

" No. Mrs. Melder, it is love—real love—which unites us here. He goes his way. You go yours. You are on separate planes, perhaps. Some day you will each find your own, when your youth has come back as it will over here."

" You speak of love. Do you mean sexual love?" asked Mailey.

" Where are we gettin' to?" murmured Mrs. Bolsover.

" Children are not born here. That is only on the earth plane. It was this aspect of marriage to which the great Teacher referred when he said: ' There will be neither marriage nor giving in marriage '. No! It is purer, deeper, more wonderful, a unity of souls, a complete merging of interests and knowledge without a loss of individuality. The nearest you ever get to it is the first high passion, too beautiful for physical expression when two high-souled lovers meet upon your plane. They find lower expression afterwards, but they will always in their hearts know that the first delicate, exquisite soul-union was the more lovely. So it is with us. Any question?"

93

" If a woman loves two men equally, what then ?" asked Malone.

" It seldom happens. She nearly always knows which is really nearest to her. If she really did so, then it would be a proof that neither was the real affinity, for he is bound to stand high above all. Of course, if she . . ."

The voice trailed off and the trumpet fell.

" Sing ' Angels are hoverin' around '!" cried Bolsover. " Smiley, hit that old harmonium. The vibrations are at zero."

Another bout of music, another silence, and then a most dismal voice. Never had Enid heard so sad a voice. It was like clods on a coffin. At first it was a deep mutter. Then it was a prayer—a Latin prayer apparently—for twice the word *Domine* sounded and once the word *peccavimus*. There was an indescribable air of depression and desolation in the room. " For God's sake what is it ?" cried Malone.

The circle was equally puzzled.

" Some poor chap out of the lower spheres, I think," said Bolsover. " Orthodox folk say we should avoid them. I say we should hurry up and help them."

" Right, Bolsover !" said Mailey, with hearty approval. " Get on with it, quick !"

"Can we do anything for you, friend ?"

There was silence.

" He doesn't know. He doesn't understand the conditions. Where is Luke ? He'll know what to do."

" What is it, friend ?" asked the pleasant voice of the guide.

" There is some poor fellow here. We want to help him."

" Ah ! yes, yes, he has come from the outer darkness," said Luke in a sympathetic voice. " He doesn't know. He doesn't understand. They come over here with a fixed idea, and when they find the real thing is quite different from anything they have been taught by the Churches, they are helpless. Some adapt themselves and they go on. Others don't, and they just wander on unchanging, like this man. He was a cleric, and a very narrow, bigoted one.

This is the growth of his own mental seed sown upon earth —sown in ignorance and reaped in misery."

" What is amiss with him ?"

" He does not know he is dead. He walks in the mist. It is all an evil dream to him. He has been years so. To him it seems an eternity."

" Why do you not tell him—instruct him ?"

" We cannot. We——"

The trumpet crashed.

" Music, Smiley, music ! Now the vibrations should be better."

" The higher spirits cannot reach earth-bound folk," said Mailey. " They are in very different zones of vibration. It is we who are near them and can help them."

" Yes, you ! you !" cried the voice of Luke.

" Mr. Mailey, speak to him. You know him !" The low mutter had broken out again in the same weary monotone.

" Friend, I would have a word with you," said Mailey in a firm, loud voice. The mutter ceased and one felt that the invisible presence was straining its attention. ' Friend, we are sorry at your condition. You have passed on. You see us and you wonder why we do not see you. You are in the other world. But you do not know it, because it is not as you expected. You have not been received as you imagined. It is because you imagined wrong. Understand that all is well, and that God is good, and that all happiness is awaiting you if you will but raise your mind and pray for help, and above all think less of your own condition and more of those other poor souls who are round you."

There was a silence and Luke spoke again.

" He has heard you. He wants to thank you. He has some glimmer now of his condition. It will grow within him. He wants to know if he may come again."

" Yes ! yes !" cried Bolsover. " We have quite a number who report progress from time to time. God bless you, friend. Come as often as you can." The mutter had ceased and there seemed to be a new feeling of peace in the air. The high voice of Wee One was heard.

" Plenty power still left. Red Cloud here. Show what he can do, if Daddy likes."

" Red Cloud is our Indian control. He is usually busy when any purely physical phenomena have to be done. You there, Red Cloud ?"

Three loud thuds, like a hammer on wood, sounded from the darkness.

" Good evening, Red Cloud !"

A new voice, slow, staccato, laboured, sounded above them.

" Good day, Chief! How the squaw? How the papooses? Strange faces in wigwam to-night."

" Seeking knowledge, Red Cloud. Can you show what you can do ?"

" I try. Wait a little. Do all I can."

Again there was a long hush of expectancy. Then the novices were faced once more with the miraculous.

There came a dull glow in the darkness. It was apparently a wisp of luminous vapour. It whisked across from one side to the other and then circled in the air. By degrees it condensed into a circular disc of radiance about the size of a bull's-eye lantern. It cast no reflection round it and was simply a clean-cut circle in the gloom. Once it approached Enid's face and Malone saw it clearly from the side.

" Why, there is a hand holding it !" he cried, with sudden suspicion.

" Yes, there is a materialized hand," said Mailey. " I can see it clearly."

" Would you like it to touch you, Mr. Malone ?"

" Yes, if it will."

The light vanished and an instant afterwards Malone felt pressure upon his own hand. He turned it palm upwards and clearly felt three fingers laid across it, smooth, warm fingers of adult size. He closed his own fingers and the hand seemed to melt away in his grasp.

" It has gone !" he gasped.

" Yes ! Red Cloud is not very good at materializations.

Perhaps we don't give him the proper sort of power. But his lights are excellent."

Several more had broken out. They were of different types, slow-moving clouds and little dancing sparks like glow-worms. At the same time both visitors were conscious of a cold wind which blew upon their faces. It was no delusion, for Enid felt her hair stream across her forehead.

"You feel the rushing wind," said Mailey. "Some of these lights would pass for tongues of fire, would they not? Pentecost does not seem such a very remote or impossible thing, does it?"

The tambourine had risen in the air, and the dot of luminous paint showed that it was circling round. Presently it descended and touched their heads each in turn. Then with a jingle it quivered down upon the table.

"Why a tambourine? It seems always to be a tambourine," remarked Malone.

"It is a convenient little instrument," Mailey explained. "The only one which shows automatically by its noise where it is flying. I don't know what other I could suggest except a musical-box."

"Our box here flies round somethin' amazin'" said Mrs. Bolsover. "It thinks nothing of winding itself up in the air as it flies. It's a heavy box too."

"Nine pounds," said Bolsover. "Well, we seem to have got to the end of things. I don't think we shall get much more to-night. It has not been a bad sitting—what I should call a fair average sitting. We must wait a little before we turn on the light. Well, Mr. Malone, what do you think of it? Let's have any objections now before we part. That's the worst of you inquirers, you know. You often bottle things up in your own minds and let them loose afterwards, when it would have been easy to settle it at the time. Very nice and polite to our faces, and then we are a gang of swindlers in the report."

Malone's head was throbbing and he passed his hand over his heated brow.

"I am confused," he said, "but impressed. Oh, yes,

97

certainly impressed. I've read of these things, but it is very different when you see them. What weighs most with me is the obvious sincerity and sanity of all you people. No one could doubt that."

"Come. We're gettin' on." said Bolsover.

"I try to think the objections which would be raised by others who were not present. I'll have to answer them. First, there is the oddity of it all. It is so different to our preconceptions of spirit people."

"We must fit our theories to the facts," said Mailey. "Up to now we have fitted the facts to our theories. You must remember that we have been dealing to-night—with all respect to our dear good hosts—with a simple, primitive, earthly type of spirit, who has his very definite uses, but is not to be taken as an average type. You might as well take the stevedore whom you see on the quay as being a representative Englishman."

"There's Luke," said Bolsover.

"Ah, yes, he is, of course, very much higher. You heard him and could judge. What else, Mr. Malone?"

"Well, the darkness! Everything done in darkness. Why should all mediumship be associated with gloom?"

"You mean all physical mediumship. That is the only branch of the subject which needs darkness. It is purely chemical, like the darkness of the photographic room. It preserves the delicate physical substance which, drawn from the human body, is the basis of these phenomena. A cabinet is used for the purpose of condensing this same vaporous substance and helping it to solidify. Am I clear?"

"Yes, but it is a pity all the same. It gives a horrible air of deceit to the whole business."

"We get it now and again in the light, Mr. Malone," said Bolsover. "I don't know if Wee One is gone yet. Wait a bit! Where are the matches?" He lit the candle, which set them all blinking after their long darkness, "Now let us see what we can do."

There was a round wood platter or circle of wood lying among the miscellaneous objects littered over the table to serve as playthings for the strange forces. Bolsover stared at it. They all stared at it. They had risen but no one was within three feet of it.

" Please, Wee One, please !" cried Mrs. Bolsover.

Malone could hardly believe his eyes. The disc began to move. It quivered and then rattled upon the table, exactly as the lid of a boiling pot might do.

" Up with it, Wee One !" They were all clapping their hands.

The circle of wood, in the full light of the candle, rose upon edge and stood there shaking, as if trying to keep its balance.

" Give three tilts, Wee One."

The disc inclined forward three times. Then it fell flat and remained so.

" I am so glad you have seen that," said Mailey. " There is Telekenesis in its simplest and most decisive form."

" I could not have believed it !" cried Enid.

" Nor I," said Malone. " I have extended my knowledge of what is possible. Mr. Bolsover, you have enlarged my views."

" Good, Mr. Malone !"

" As to the power at the back of these things I am still ignorant. As to the thing themselves I have now and henceforward not the slightest doubt in the world. I *know* that they are true. I wish you all good night. It is not likely that Miss Challenger or I will ever forget the evening that we have spent under your roof."

It was like another world when they came out into the frosty air, and saw the taxis bearing back the pleasure-seekers from the theatre or cinema palace. Mailey stood beside them while they waited for a cab.

" I know exactly how you feel," he said, smiling. " You look at all these bustling, complacent people, and you marvel to think how little they know of the possibilities of life. Don't you want to stop them ? Don't you want to tell them ? And yet they would only think you a liar or a lunatic. Funny situation, is it not ?"

" I've lost all my bearings for the moment."

" They will come back to-morrow morning. It is curious how fleeting these impressions are. You will persuade yourselves that you have been dreaming. Well, good-bye— and let me know if I can help your studies in the future."

The friends—one could hardly yet call them lovers— were absorbed in thought during their drive home. When he reached Victoria Gardens Malone escorted Enid to the door of the flat, but he did not go in with her. Somehow the jeers of Challenger which usually rather woke sympathy within him would now get upon his nerves. As it was he heard his greeting in the hall.

" Well, Enid. Where's your spook? Spill him out of the bag on the floor and let us have a look at him."

His evening's adventure ended as it had begun, with a bellow of laughter which pursued him down the lift.

5. *Where Our Commissioners Have a Remarkable Experience*

MALONE sat at the side table of the smoking-room of the Literary Club. He had Enid's impressions of the séance before him—very subtle and observant they were—and he was endeavouring to merge them in his own experience. A group of men were smoking and chatting round the fire. This did not disturb the journalist, who found, as many do, that his brain and his pen worked best sometimes when they were stimulated by the knowledge that he was part of a busy world. Presently, however, some-body who observed his presence brought the talk round to psychic subjects, and then it was more difficult for him to remain aloof. He leaned back in his chair and listened.

Polter, the famous novelist, was there, a brilliant man with a subtle mind, which he used too often to avoid obvious truth and to defend some impossible position for the sake of the empty dialectic exercise. He was holding forth now to an admiring, but not entirely a subservient audience.

" Science," said he, " is gradually sweeping the world clear of all these old cobwebs of superstition. The world was like some old, dusty attic, and the sun of science is bursting in, flooding it with light, while the dust settles gradually to the floor."

" By science," said someone maliciously, " you mean, of course, men like Sir William Crookes, Sir Oliver Lodge, Sir William Barrett, Lombroso, Richet, and so forth."

Polter was not accustomed to be countered, and usually became rude.

" No, sir, I mean nothing so preposterous," he answered, with a glare. " No name, however eminent, can claim to stand for science so long as he is a member of an insignificant minority of scientific men."

" He is, then, a crank," said Pollifex, the artist, who usually played jackal to Polter.

The objector, one Millworthy, a free-lance of journalism, was not to be so easily silenced.

" Then Galileo was a crank in his day," said he. " And Harvey was a crank when he was laughed at over the circulation of the blood."

" It's the circulation of the *Daily Gazette* which is at stake," said Marrible, the humorist of the club. " If they get off their stunt I don't suppose they care a tinker's curse what is truth or what is not."

" Why such things should be examined at all, except in a police court, I can't imagine," said Polter. " It is a dispersal of energy, a misdirection of human thought into channels which lead nowhere. We have plenty of obvious, material things to examine. Let us get on with our job."

Atkinson, the surgeon, was one of the circle, and had sat silently listening. Now he spoke.

" I think the learned bodies should find more time for the consideration of psychic matters."

" Less," said Polter.

" You can't have less than nothing. They ignore them altogether. Some time ago I had a series of cases of telepathic *rapport* which I wished to lay before the Royal

Society. My colleague Wilson, the zoologist, also had a paper which he proposed to read. They went in together. His was accepted and mine rejected. The title of his paper was ' The Reproductive System of the Dung-Beetle '."

There was a general laugh.

" Quite right, too," said Polter. " The humble dung-beetle was at least a fact. All this psychic stuff is not."

" No doubt you have good grounds for your views," chirped the mischievous Millworthy, a mild youth with a velvety manner. " I have little time for solid reading, so I should like to ask you which of Dr. Crawford's three books you consider the best ?"

" I never heard of the fellow."

Millworthy simulated intense surprise.

" Good Heavens, man ! Why, he is *the* authority. If you want pure laboratory experiments those are the books. You might as well lay down the law about zoology and confess that you had never heard of Darwin."

" This is not science," said Polter, emphatically.

" What is really not science," said Atkinson, with some heat, " is the laying down of the law on matters which you have not studied. It is talk of that sort which has brought me to the edge of Spiritualism, when I compare this dogmatic ignorance with the earnest search for truth conducted by the great Spiritualists. Many of them took twenty years of work before they formed their conclusions."

" But their conclusions are worthless because they are upholding a formed opinion."

" But each of them fought a long fight before he formed that opinion. I know a few of them, and there is not one who did not take a lot of convincing."

Polter shrugged his shoulders.

" Well, they can have their spooks if it makes them happier so long as they let me keep my feet firm on the ground."

" Or stuck in the mud," said Atkinson.

" I would rather be in the mud with sane people than in the air with lunatics," said Polter. " I know some of these

Spiritualists people and I believe that you can divide them equally into fools and rogues."

Malone had listened with interest and then with a growing indignation. Now he suddenly took fire.

" Look here, Polter," he said, turning his chair towards the company, " it is fools and dolts like you which are holding back the world's progress. You admit that you have read nothing of this, and I'll swear you have seen nothing. Yet you use the position and the name which you have won in other matters in order to discredit a number of people who, whatever they may be, are certainly very earnest and very thoughtful."

" Oh," said Polter, " I had no idea you had got so far. You don't dare to say so in your articles. You *are* a Spiritualist then. That rather discounts your views, does it not ?"

" I am not a Spiritualist, but I am an honest inquirer, and that is more than you have ever been. You call them rogues and fools, but, little as I know, I am sure that some of them are men and women whose boots you are not worthy to clean."

" Oh, come, Malone !" cried one or two voices, but the insulted Polter was on his feet. " It's men like you who empty this club," he cried, as he swept out. " I shall certainly never come here again to be insulted."

" I say, you've done it, Malone !"

" I felt inclined to help him out with a kick. Why should he ride roughshod over other people's feelings and beliefs ? He has got on and most of us haven't, so he thinks it's a condescension to come among us."

" Dear old Irishman !" said Atkinson, patting his shoulder. " Rest, perturbed spirit, rest ! But I wanted to have a word with you. Indeed, I was waiting here because I did not want to interrupt you."

" I've had interruptions enough !" cried Malone. " How could I work with that damned donkey braying in my ear ?"

" Well, I've only a word to say. I've got a sitting with Linden, the famous medium of whom I spoke to you, at the Psychic College to-night. I have an extra ticket. Would you care to come ?"

" Come ? I should think so !"

" I have another ticket. I should have asked Polter if he had not been so offensive. Linden does not mind sceptics, but objects to scoffers. Who should I ask ?"

" Let Miss Enid Challenger come. We work together, you know."

" Why, of course I will. Will you let her know ?"

" Certainly."

" It's at seven o'clock to-night. The Psychic College. You know the place down at Holland Park."

" Yes, I have the address. Very well, Miss Challenger and I will certainly be there."

Behold the pair, then, upon a fresh psychic adventure. They picked Atkinson up at Wimpole Street, and then traversed that long, roaring rushing, driving belt of the great city which extends through Oxford Street and Bayswater to Notting Hill and the stately Victorian houses of Holland Park. It was at one of these that the taxi drew up, a large, imposing building, standing back a little from the road. A smart maid admitted them, and the subdued light of the tinted hall-lamp fell upon shining linoleum and polished woodwork with the gleam of white marble statuary in the corner. Enid's female perceptions told her of a well-run, well-appointed establishment, with a capable direction at the head. This direction took the shape of a kindly Scottish lady who met them in the hall and greeted Mr. Atkinson as an old friend. She was, in turn, introduced to the journalists as Mrs. Ogilvy. Malone had already heard how her husband and she had founded and run this remarkable institute, which is the centre of psychic experiment in London, at a very great cost, both in labour and in money, to themselves.

" Linden and his wife have gone up," said Mrs. Ogilvy. " He seems to think that the conditions are favourable. The rest are in the drawing-room. Won't you join them for a few minutes ?"

Quite a number of people had gathered for the séance, some of them old psychic students who were mildly interested; others, beginners who looked about them with rather startled eyes, wondering what was going to happen next. A tall man was standing near the door who turned and disclosed the tawny beard and open face of Algernon Mailey. He shook hands with the newcomers.

"Another experience, Mr. Malone? Well, I thought you gave a very fair account of the last. You are still a neophyte, but you are well within the gates of the temple. Are you alarmed, Miss Challenger?"

"I don't think I could be while you were around," she answered.

He laughed.

"Of course, a materialization séance is a little different to any other—more impressive, in a way. You'll find it very instructive, Malone, as bearing upon psychic photography and other matters. By the way, you should try for a psychic picture. The famous Hope works upstairs."

"I always thought that that at least was fraud."

"On the contrary, I should say it was the best established of all phenomena, the one which leaves the most permanent proof. I've been a dozen times under every possible test conditions. The real trouble is, not that it lends itself to fraud, but that it lends itself to exploitation by that villainous journalism which cares only for a sensation. Do you know anyone here?"

"No, we don't."

"The tall, handsome lady is the Duchess of Rossland. Then, there are Lord and Lady Montnoir, the middle-aged couple near the fire. Real, good folk and among the very few of the aristocracy who have shown earnestness and moral courage in this matter. The talkative lady is Miss Badley, who lives for séances, a jaded Society woman in search of new sensations—always visible, always audible, and always empty. I don't know the two men. I heard someone say they were researchers from the university. The stout man with the lady in black is Sir James Smith—

they lost two boys in the war. The tall, dark person, is a weird man named Barclay, who lives, I understand, in one room and seldom comes out save for a séance."

" And the man with the horn glasses ?"

" That is a pompous ass named Weatherby. He is one of those who wander about on the obscure edges of Masonry, talking with whispers and reverence of mysteries where no mystery is. Spiritualism, with its very real and awful mysteries, is, to him, a vulgar thing because it brought consolation to common folk, but he loves to read papers on the Palladian Cultus, ancient and accepted Scottish rites, and Baphometic figures. Eliphas Levi is his prophet."

" It sounds very learned," said Enid.

" Or very absurd. But, hullo ! Here are mutual friends."

The two Bolsovers had arrived, very hot and frowsy and genial. There is no such leveller of classes as Spiritualism, and the charwoman with psychic force is the superior of the millionaire who lacks it. The Bolsovers and the aristocrats fraternized instantly. The Duchess was just asking for admission to the grocer's circle, when Mrs. Ogilvy bustled in.

" I think everyone is here now," she said. " It is time to go upstairs."

The séance room was a large, comfortable chamber on the first floor, with a circle of easy chairs, and a curtain-hung divan which served as a cabinet. The medium and his wife were waiting there. Mr. Linden was a gentle, large-featured man, stoutish in build, deep-chested, clean-shaven, with dreamy, blue eyes and flaxen, curly hair which rose in a pyramid at the apex of his head. He was of middle age. His wife was rather younger, with the sharp, querulous expression of the tired housekeeper, and quick, critical eyes, which softened into something like adoration when she looked at her husband. Her role was to explain matters, and to guard his interests while he was unconscious.

" The sitters had better just take their own places," said the medium. " If you can alternate the sexes it is as well. Don't cross your knees, it breaks the current. If we have a materialization, don't grab at it. If you do, you are liable to injure me."

The two sleuths of the Research Society looked at each other knowingly. Mailey observed it.

"Quite right," he said. "I have seen two cases of dangerous hæmorrhage in the medium brought on by that very cause."

"Why?" asked Malone.

"Because the ectoplasm used is drawn from the medium. It recoils upon him like a snapped elastic band. Where it comes through the skin you get a bruise. Where it comes from mucous membrane you get bleeding."

"And when it comes from nothing, you get nothing," said the researcher with a grin.

"I will explain the procedure in a few words," said Mrs. Ogilvy, when everyone was seated. "Mr. Linden does not enter the cabinet at all. He sits outside it, and as he tolerates red light you will be able to satisfy yourselves that he does not leave his seat. Mrs. Linden sits on the other side. She is there to regulate and explain. In the first place we would wish you to examine the cabinet. One of you will also please lock the door on the inside and be responsible for the key."

The cabinet proved to be a mere tent of hangings, detached from the wall and standing on a solid platform. The researchers ferreted about inside it and stamped on the boards. All seemed solid.

"What is the use of it?" Malone whispered to Mailey.

"It serves as a reservoir and condensing place for the ectoplasmic vapour from the medium, which would otherwise diffuse over the room."

"It has been known to serve other purposes also," remarked one of the researchers, who overheard the conversation.

"That's true enough," said Mailey philosophically. "I am all in favour of caution and supervision."

"Well, it seems fraud-proof on this occasion, if the medium sits outside." The two researchers were agreed on this.

The medium was seated on one side of the little tent, his wife on the other. The light was out, and a small red lamp near the ceiling was just sufficient to enable outlines to be clearly seen. As the eyes became accustomed to it some detail could also be observed.

" Mr. Linden will begin by some clairvoyant readings," said Mrs. Linden. Her whole attitude, seated beside the cabinet with her hands on her lap and the air of a proprietor, made Enid smile, for she thought of Mrs. Jarley and her waxworks.

Linden, who was not in a trance, began to give clairvoyance. It was not very good. Possibly the mixed influence of so many sitters of various types at close quarters was too disturbing. That was the excuse which he gave himself when several of his descriptions were unrecognized. But Malone was more shocked by those which were recognized, since it was so clear that the word was put into the medium's mouth. It was the folly of the sitter rather than the fault of the medium, but it was disconcerting all the same.

" I see a young man with brown eyes and a rather drooping moustache."

" Oh, darling, darling, have you then come back !" cried Miss Badley. " Oh, has he a message ?"

" He sends his love and does not forget."

" Oh, how evidential ! It is so exactly what the dear boy would have said ! My first lover, you know," she added, in a simpering voice to the company. " He never fails to come. Mr. Linden has brought him again and again."

" There is a young fellow in khaki building up on the left. I see a symbol over his head. It might be a Greek cross."

" Jim—it is surely Jim !" cried Lady Smith.

" Yes. He nods his head."

" And the Greek cross is probably a propeller," said Sir James. " He was in the Air Service, you know."

Malone and Enid were both rather shocked. Mailey was also uneasy.

" This is not good," he whispered to Enid. " Wait a bit ! You will get something better."

There were several good recognitions, and then someone resembling Summerlee was described for Malone. This was wisely discounted by him, since Linden might have been in the audience on the former occasion. Mrs. Debbs' exhibition seemed to him far more convincing than that of Linden.

" Wait a bit !" Mailey repeated.

" The medium will now try for materializations," said Mrs. Linden. " If the figures appear I would ask you not to touch them, save by request. Victor will tell you if you may do so. Victor is the medium's control."

The medium had settled down in his chair and he now began to draw long, whistling breaths with deep intakes, puffing the air out between his lips. Finally he steadied down and seemed to sink into a deep coma, his chin upon his breast. Suddenly he spoke, but it seemed that his voice was better modulated and more cultivated than before.

" Good evening, all !" said the voice.

There was a general murmur of " Good evening, Victor."

" I am afraid that the vibrations are not very harmonious. The sceptical element is present, but not, I think, predominant, so that we may hope for results. Martin Lightfoot is doing what he can."

" That is the Indian control," Mailey whispered.

" I think that if you would start the gramophone it would be helpful. A hymn is always best, though there is no real objection to secular music. Give us what you think best, Mrs. Ogilvy."

There was the rasping of a needle which had not yet found its grooves. Then " Lead, Kindly Light " was churned out. The audience joined in in a subdued fashion. Mrs. Ogilvy then changed it to " O, God, our help in ages past ".

" They often change the records themselves," said Mrs. Ogilvy, " but to-night there is not enough power."

" Oh, yes," said the voice. " There *is* enough power, Mrs. Ogilvy, but we are anxious to conserve it all for the materializations. Martin says they are building up very well."

At this moment the curtain in front of the cabinet began to sway. It bellied out as if a strong wind were behind it. At the same time a breeze was felt by all who were in the circle, together with a sensation of cold.

" It is quite chilly," whispered Enid, with a shiver.

" It is not a subjective feeling," Mailey answered. " Mr. Harry Price has tested it with thermometric readings. So did Professor Crawford."

" My God !" cried a startled voice. It belonged to the pompous dabbler in mysteries, who was suddenly faced with a real mystery. The curtains of the cabinet had parted and a human figure had stolen noiselessly out. There was the medium clearly outlined on one side. There was Mrs. Linden, who had sprung to her feet, on the other. And, between them, the little black, hesitating figure, which seemed to be terrified at its own position. Mrs. Linden soothed and encouraged it.

" Don't be alarmed, dear. It is all quite right. No one will hurt you."

" It is someone who has never been through before," she explained to the company. " Naturally it seems very strange to her. Just as strange as if we broke into their world. That's right, dear. You are gaining strength, I can see. Well done !"

The figure was moving forward. Everyone sat spell-bound, with staring eyes. Miss Badley began to giggle hysterically. Weatherby lay back in his chair, gasping with horror. Neither Malone nor Enid felt any fear, but were consumed with curiosity. How marvellous to hear the humdrum flow of life in the street outside and to be face to face with such a sight as that.

Slowly the figure moved round. Now it was close to Enid and between her and the red light. Stooping, she could get the silhouette sharply outlined. It was that of a little, elderly woman, with sharp, clear-cut features.

" It's Susan !" cried Mrs. Bolsover. " Oh, Susan, don't you know me ?"

The figure turned and nodded her head.

"Yes, yes, dear, it is your sister Susie," cried her husband. "I never saw her in anything but black. Susan, speak to us !"

The head was shaken.

"They seldom speak the first time they come," said Mrs. Linden, whose rather blasé, business-like air was in contrast to the intense emotion of the company. "I'm afraid she can't hold together long. Ah, there ! She has gone !"

The figure had disappeared. There had been some backward movement towards the cabinet, but it seemed to the observers that she sank into the ground before she reached it. At any rate, she was gone.

"Gramophone, please !" said Mrs. Linden. Everyone relaxed and sat back with a sigh. The gramophone struck up a lively air. Suddenly the curtains parted, and a second figure appeared.

It was a young girl, with flowing hair down her back. She came forward swiftly and with perfect assurance to the centre of the circle.

Mrs. Linden laughed in a satisfied way.

"Now you will get something good," she said. "Here is Lucille."

"Good evening, Lucille !" cried the Duchess. "I met you last month, you will remember, when your medium came to Maltraver Towers."

"Yes, yes, lady, I remember you. You have a little boy, Tommy, on our side of life. No, no, not dead, lady ! We are far more alive than you are. All the fun and frolic are with us !" She spoke in a high clear voice and perfect English.

"Shall I show you what we do over here ?" She began a graceful, gliding dance, while she whistled as melodiously as a bird. "Poor Susan could not do that. Susan has had no practice. Lucille knows how to use a built-up body."

"Do you remember me, Lucille ?" asked Mailey.

"I remember you, Mr. Mailey. Big man with yellow beard."

For the second time in her life Enid had to pinch herself

hard to satisfy herself that she was not dreaming. Was this graceful creature, who had now sat down in the centre of the circle, a real materialization of ectoplasm, used for the moment as a machine for expression by a soul that had passed, or was it an illusion of the senses, or was it a fraud? There were the three possibilities. An illusion was absurd when all had the same impression. Was it a fraud? But this was certainly not the little old woman. She was inches taller and fair, not dark. And the cabinet was fraud-proof. It had been meticulously examined. Then it was true. But if it were true, what a vista of possibilities opened out. Was it not far the greatest matter which could claim the attention of the world!

Meanwhile, Lucille had been so natural and the situation was so normal that even the most nervous had relaxed. The girl answered most cheerfully to every question, and they rained upon her from every side.

" Where did you live, Lucille? "

" Perhaps I had better answer that," interposed Mrs. Linden. " It will save the power. Lucille was bred in South Dakota in the United States, and passed over at the age of fourteen. We have verified some of her statements."

" Are you glad you died, Lucille? "

" Glad for my own sake. Sorry for mother."

" Has your mother seen you since? "

" Poor mother is a shut box. Lucille cannot open the lid."

" Are you happy? "

" Oh, yes, so gloriously happy."

" Is it right that you can come back? "

" Would God allow it if it were not right? What a wicked man you must be to ask! "

" What religion were you? "

" We were Roman Catholics."

" Is that the right religion? "

" All religions are right if they make you better."

" Then it does not matter."

" It is what people do in daily life, not what they believe."

" Tell us more, Lucille."

" Lucille has little time. There are others who wish to come. If Lucille uses too much power, the others have less. Oh, God is very good and kind ! You poor people on earth do not know how good and kind He is because it is grey down there. But it is grey for your own good. It is to give you your chance to earn all the lovely things which wait for you. But you can only tell how wonderful He is when you get over here."

" Have you seen him ?"

" Seen Him ! How could you see God ? No, no, He is all round us and in us and in everything, but we do not see Him. But I have seen the Christ. Oh, He was glorious, glorious ! Now, good-bye—good-bye !" She backed towards the cabinet and sank into the shadows.

Now came a tremendous experience for Malone. A small, dark, rather broad figure of a woman appeared slowly from the cabinet. Mrs. Linden encouraged her, and then came across to the journalist.

" It is for you. You can break the circle. Come up to her."

Malone advanced and peered, awestruck, into the face of the apparition. There was not a foot between them. Surely that large head, that solid, square outline was familiar ! He put his face still nearer—it was almost touching. He strained his eyes. It seemed to him that the features were semi-fluid, moulding themselves into a shape, as if some unseen hand was modelling them in putty.

" Mother !" he cried. " Mother !"

Instantly the figure threw up both her hands in a wild gesture of joy. The motion seemed to destroy her equilibrium and she vanished.

" She had not been through before. She could not speak," said Mrs. Linden, in her business-like way. " It was your mother."

Malone went back half-stunned to his seat. It is only when these things come to one's own address that one understands their full force. His mother ! Ten years in

113

her grave and yet standing before him. Could he *swear* it was his mother? No, he could not. Was he morally certain that it was his mother? Yes, he was morally certain. He was shaken to the core.

But other wonders diverted his thoughts. A young man had emerged briskly from the cabinet and had advanced to the front of Mailey, where he had halted.

"Hullo, Jock! Dear old Jock!" said Mailey. "My nephew," he explained to the company. "He always comes when I am with Linden."

"The power is sinking," said the lad, in a clear voice. "I can't stay very long. I am so glad to see you, Uncle. You know, we can see quite clearly in this light, even if you can't."

"Yes, I know you can. I say, Jock. I wanted to tell you that I told your mother I had seen you. She said her Church taught her it was wrong."

"I know. And that I was a demon. Oh, it is rotten, rotten, rotten, and rotten things will fall!" His voice broke in a sob.

"Don't blame her Jock, she believes this."

"No, no, I don't blame her! She will know better some day. The day is coming soon when all truth will be manifest and all these corrupt Churches will be swept off the earth with their cruel doctrines and their caricatures of God."

"Why, Jock, you are becoming quite a heretic!"

"Love, Uncle! Love! That is all that counts. What matter what you believe if you are sweet and kind and unselfish as the Christ was of old?"

"Have you seen Christ?" asked someone.

"Not yet. Perhaps the time may come."

"Is he not in Heaven, then?"

"There are many heavens. I am in a very humble one. But it is glorious all the same."

Enid had thrust her head forward during this dialogue. Her eyes had got used to the light and she could see more clearly than before. The man who stood within a few feet of her was not human. Of that she had no doubt whatever, and yet the points were very subtle. Something in his strange, yellow-white colouring as contrasted with the faces of her neighbours. Something, also, in the curious stiffness of his carriage, as of a man in very rigid stays.

" Now, Jock," said Mailey, " give an address to the company. Tell them a few words about your life."

The figure hung his head, exactly as a shy youth would do in life.

" Oh, Uncle, I can't."

" Come, Jock, we love to listen to you."

" Teach the folk what death is," the figure began. " God wants them to know. That is why He lets us come back. It is nothing. You are no more changed than if you went into the next room. You can't believe you are dead. I didn't. It was only when I saw old Sam that I knew, for I was certain that he was dead, anyhow. Then I came back to mother. And "—his voice broke—" she would not receive me."

" Never mind, dear old Jock," said Mailey. " She will learn wisdom."

" Teach them the truth ! Teach it to them ! Oh, it is so much more important than all the things men talk about. If papers for one week gave as much attention to psychic things as they do to football, it would be known to all. It is ignorance which stands——"

The observers were conscious of a sort of flash towards the cabinet, but the youth had disappeared.

" Power run down," said Mailey. " Poor lad, he held on to the last. He always did. That was how he died."

There was a long pause. The gramophone started again. Then there was a movement of the curtains. Something was emerging. Mrs. Linden sprang up and waved the figure back. The medium for the first time stirred in his chair and groaned.

" What is the matter, Mrs. Linden ?"

" Only half-formed," she answered. " The lower face had not materialized. Some of you would have been alarmed. I think that we shall have no more to-night. The power has sunk very low."

So it proved. The lights were gradually turned on. The medium lay with a white face and a clammy brow in his chair, while his wife sedulously watched over him, unbuttoning his collar and bathing his face from a water-glass. The company broke into little groups, discussing what they had seen.

" Oh, wasn't it thrilling ?" cried Miss Badley. " It really was most exciting. But what a pity we could not see the one with the semi-materialized face."

" Thanks, I have seen quite enough," said the pompous mystic, all the pomposity shaken out of him. " I confess that it has been rather too much for my nerves."

Mr. Atkinson found himself near the psychic researchers. " Well, what do you make of it ?" he asked.

" I have seen it better done at Maskelyne's Hall," said one.

" Oh, come, Scott !" said the other. " You've no right to say that. You admitted that the cabinet was fraud-proof."

" Well, so do the committees who go on the stage at Maskelyne's."

" Yes, but it is Maskelyne's own stage. This is not Linden's own stage. He has no machinery."

" *Populus vult decipi*," the other answered, shrugging his shoulders. " I should certainly reserve judgment." He moved away with the dignity of one who cannot be deceived, while his more rational companion still argued with him as they went.

" Did you hear that ?" said Atkinson. " There is a certain class of psychic researcher who is absolutely incapable of receiving evidence. They misuse their brains by straining them to find a way round when the road is quite clear before them. When the human race advances into its new kingdom, these intellectual men will form the absolute rear."

" No, no," said Mailey, laughing. " The bishops are predestined to be the rearguard. I see them all marching

116

in step, a solid body, with their gaiters and cassocks—the last in the whole world to reach spiritual truth."

" Oh, come," said Enid, " that is too severe. They are all good men."

" Of course they are. It's quite physiological. They are are a body of elderly men, and the elderly brain is sclerosed and cannot record new impressions. It's not their fault, but the fact remains. You are very silent, Malone."

But Malone was thinking of a little, squat, dark figure which waved its hands in joy when he spoke to it. It was with that image in his mind that he turned from this room of wonders and passed down into the street.

6. *In Which the Reader is Shown the Habits of a Notorious Criminal*

WE will now leave that little group with whom we have made our first exploration of these grey and ill-defined, but immensely important, regions of human thought and experiences. From the researchers we will turn to the researched. Come with me and we will visit Mr. Linden at home, and will examine the lights and shades which make up the life of a professional medium.

To reach him we will pass down the crowded thoroughfare of Tottenham Court Road, where the huge furniture emporia flank the way, and we will turn into a small street of drab houses which leads eastwards towards the British Museum. Tullis Street is the name and 40 the number. Here it is, one of a row, flat-faced, dull-coloured and commonplace, with railed steps leading up to a discoloured door, and one front-room window, in which a huge gilt-edged Bible upon a small round table reassures the timid visitor. With the universal pass-key of imagination we open the dingy door, pass down a dark passage and up a narrow stair. It is nearly ten o'clock in the morning and yet it is in his bedroom that we must seek the famous worker of miracles. The fact is that he has had, as we have seen, an

exhausting sitting the night before, and that he has to conserve his strength in the mornings.

At the moment of our inopportune, but invisible, visit
he was sitting up, propped by the pillows, with a breakfast-
tray upon his knees. The vision he presented would have
amused those who have prayed with him in the humble
Spiritualist temples, or had sat with awe at the séances
where he had exhibited the modern equivalents of the gifts
of the Spirit. He looked unhealthily pallid in the dim
morning light, and his curly hair rose up in a tangled pyramid above his broad, intellectual brow. The open collar
of his nightshirt displayed a broad, bull's neck, and the
depth of his chest and spread of his shoulders showed that
he was a man of considerable personal strength. He was
eating his breakfast with avidity while he conversed with
the little, eager, dark-eyed wife who was seated on the side
of the bed.

" And you reckon it a good meeting, Mary ?"

" Fair to middling, Tom. There was two of them researchers raking round with their feet and upsetting everybody. D'ye think those folk in the Bible would have got
their phenomena if they had chaps of that sort on the
premises? 'Of one accord ', that's what they say in the Book."

" Of course !" cried Linden heartily. " Was the Duchess
pleased ?"

" Yes, I think she was very pleased. So was Mr. Atkinson, the surgeon. There was a new man there called Malone
of the Press. Then Lord and Lady Montnoir got evidence,
and so did Sir James Smith and Mr. Mailey."

" I wasn't satisfied with the clairvoyance," said the
medium. " The silly idiots kept on putting things into my
mind. 'That's surely my Uncle Sam', and so forth. It
blurs me so that I can see nothing clear."

" Yes, and they think they are helping ! Helping to
muddle you and deceive themselves. I know the kind."

" But I went under nicely and I am glad there were some
fine materializations. It took it out of me, though. I'm
a rag this morning."

" They work you too hard, dear. I'll take you to Margate and build you up."

" Well, maybe at Easter we could do a week. It would be fine. I don't mind readings and clairvoyance, but the physicals do try you. I'm not as bad as Hallows. They say he just lies white and gasping on the floor after them."

" Yes," cried the woman bitterly. " And then they run to him with whisky, and so they teach him to rely on the bottle and you get another case of a drunken medium. I know them. You keep off it, Tom !"

" Yes, one of our trade should stick to soft drinks. If he can stick to vegetables, too, he's all the better, but I can't preach that while I am wolfin' up ham and eggs. By Gosh, Mary ! it's past ten and I have a string of them comin' this morning. I'm going to make a bit to-day."

" You give it away as quick as you make it, Tom."

" Well, some hard cases come my way. So long as we can make both ends meet what more do we want ? I expect *they* will look after us all right."

" They have let down a lot of other poor mediums who did good work in their day."

" It's the rich folk that are to blame not the Spirit-people," said Tom Linden hotly. " It makes me see red when I remember these folk, Lady This and Countess That, declaring all the comfort they have had, and then leaving those who gave it to die in the gutter or rot in the workhouse. Poor old Tweedy and Soames and the rest all living on old-age pensions and the papers talking of the money that mediums make, while some damned conjuror makes more than all of us put together by a rotten imitation with two tons of machinery to help him."

" Don't worry, dear," cried the medium's wife, putting her thin hand caressingly upon the tangled mane of her man. " It all comes level in time and everybody pays the price for what they have done."

Linden laughed loudly. " It's my Welsh half that comes out when I flare up. Let the conjurors take their dirty money and let the rich folk keep their purses shut. I wonder what they think money is for. Paying death duties is about the only fun some of them seem to get out of it. If I had their money . . ."

There was a knock at the door.

" Please, sir, your brother Silas is below."

The two looked at each other with some dismay.

" More trouble," said Mrs. Linden sadly.

Linden shrugged his shoulders. " All right, Susan !" he cried. " Tell him I'll be down. Now, dear, you keep him going and I'll be with you in a quarter of an hour."

In less time than he named he was down in the front-room—his consulting room—where his wife was evidently having some difficulty in making agreeable conversation with their visitor. He was a big, heavy man, not unlike his elder brother, but with all the genial chubbiness of the medium coarsened into pure brutality. He had the same pile of curly hair, but he was clean-shaven with a heavy, obstinate jowl. He sat by the window with his huge freckled hands upon his knees. A very important part of Mr. Silas Linden lay in those hands, for he had been a formidable professional boxer, and at one time was fancied for the welter-weight honours of England. Now, as his stained tweed suit and frayed boots made clear, he had fallen on evil days, which he endeavoured to mitigate by cadging on his brother.

" Mornin', Tom," he said in a husky voice. Then as the wife left the room: " Got a drop of Scotch about ? I've a head on me this morning. I met some of the old set last night down at ' The Admiral Vernon '. Quite a reunion it was—chaps I hadn't seen since my best ring days."

" Sorry, Silas," said the medium, seating himself behind his desk. " I keep nothing in the house."

" Spirits enough, but not the right sort," said Silas. " Well, the price of a drink will do as well. If you've got a Bradbury about you I could do with it, for there's nothing coming my way."

Tom Linden took a pound note from his desk.

" Here you are, Silas. So long as I have any you have

your share. But you had two pounds last week. Is it gone ?"

"Gone! I should say so!" He put the note in his pocket. "Now, look here, Tom, I want to speak to you very serious as between man and man."

"Yes, Silas, what is it ?"

"You see that !" He pointed to a lump on the back of his hand. "That's a bone ! See ? It will never be right. It was when I hit Curly Jenkins third round and outed him at the N.S.C. I outed myself for life that night. I can put up a show fight and exhibition bout, but I'm done for the real thing. My right has gone west."

"It's a hard case, Silas."

"Damned hard ! But that's neither here nor there. What matters is that I've got to pick up a living and I want to know how to do it. An old scrapper don't find many openings. Chucker-out at a pub with free drinks. Nothing doing there. What I want to know, Tom, is what's the matter with my becoming a medium ?"

"A medium ?"

"Why the devil should you stare at me ! If it's good enough for you it's good enough for me."

"But you are *not* a medium."

"Oh, come ! Keep that for the newspapers. It's all in the family, and between you an' me, how d'ye do it ?"

"I don't do it. I do nothing."

"And get four or five quid a week for it. That's a good yarn. Now you can't fool me. Tom, I'm not one o' those duds that pay you a thick 'un for an hour in the dark. We're on the square, you an' me. How d'ye do it ?"

"Do what ?"

"Well, them raps, for example. I've seen you sit there at your desk, as it might be, and raps come answerin' questions over yonder on the bookshelf. It's damned clever —fair puzzles 'em every time. How d'ye get them ? "

"I tell you I don't. It's outside myself."

"Rats ! You can tell me, Tom. I'm Griffiths, the safe man. It would set me up for life if I could do it."

For the second time in one morning the medium's Welsh strain took control.

"You're an impudent, blasphemous rascal, Silas Linden. It's men like you who come into our movement and give it a bad name. You should know me better than to think that I am a cheat. Get out of my house, you ungrateful rascal!"

"Not too much of your lip," growled the ruffian.

"Out you go, or I'll put you out, brother or no brother."

Silas doubled his great fists and looked ugly for a moment. Then the anticipation of favours to come softened his mood.

"Well, well, no harm meant," he growled, as he made for the door. "I expect I can make a shot at it without your help." His grievance suddenly overcame his prudence as he stood in the doorway. "You damned, canting, hypocritical box-of-tricks. I'll be even with you yet."

The heavy door slammed behind him.

Mrs. Linden had rushed in to her husband.

"The hulking blackguard!" she cried. "I 'eard 'im. What did 'e want?"

"Wanted me to put him wise to mediumship. Thinks it's a trick of some sort that I could teach him."

"The foolish lump! Well, it's a good thing, for he won't dare show his face here again."

"Oh, won't he?"

"If he does I'll slap it for him. To think of his upsettin' you like this. Why, you're shakin' all over!"

"I suppose I wouldn't be a medium if I wasn't high strung. Someone said we were poets, only more so. But it's bad just when work is beginning."

"I'll give you healing."

She put her little work-worn hands over his high forehead and held them there in silence.

"That's better!" said he. "Well done, Mary. I'll have a cigarette in the kitchen. That will finish it."

"No, there's someone here." She had looked out of the window. "Are you fit to see her? It's a woman."

"Yes, yes. I am all right now. Show her in."

An instant later a woman entered, a pale, tragic figure in black, whose appearance told its own tale. Linden motioned her to a chair away from the light. Then he looked through his papers.

"You are Mrs. Blount, are you not? You had an appointment?"

"Yes—I wanted to ask——"

"Please ask me nothing. It confuses me."

He was looking at her with the medium's gaze in his light grey eyes—that gaze which looks round and through a thing rather than at it.

"You have been wise to come, very wise. There is someone beside you who has an urgent message which could not be delayed. I get a name . . . Francis . . . yes, Francis."

The woman clasped her hands.

"Yes, yes, it is the name."

"A dark man, very sad, very earnest—oh, so earnest. He will speak. He must speak! It is urgent. He says, 'Tink-a-bell'. Who is Tink-a-bell?"

"Yes, yes, he called me so. Oh, Frank, Frank, speak to me! Speak!"

"He is speaking. His hand is on your head. "Tink-a-bell', he says, 'If you do what you purpose doing it will make a gap that it will take many years to cross'. Does that mean anything?"

She sprang from her chair. "It means everything. Oh, Mr. Linden, this was my last chance. If this had failed—if I found that I had really lost him I meant to go and seek him. I would have taken poison this night."

"Thank God that I have saved you. It is a terrible thing, madame, to take one's life. It breaks the law of Nature, and Nature's laws cannot be broken without punishment. I rejoice that he has been able to save you. He has more to say to you. His message is, 'If you will live and do your duty I will for ever be by your side, far closer to you than ever I was in life. My presence will surround you and guard both you and our three babes.'"

It was marvellous the change! The pale, worn woman.

who had entered the room was now standing with flushed cheeks and smiling lips. It is true that tears were pouring down her face, but they were tears of joy. She clapped her hands. She made little convulsive movements as if she would dance.

" He's not dead ! He's not dead ! How can he be dead if he can speak to me and be closer to me than ever ? Oh, it's glorious ! Oh, Mr. Linden, what can I do for you ? You have saved me from shameful death ! You have restored my husband to me ! Oh, what a God-like power you have !"

The medium was an emotional man and his own tears were moist upon his cheeks.

" My dear lady, say no more. It is not I. I do nothing. You can thank God Who in His mercy permits some of His mortals to discern a spirit or to carry a message. Well, well, a guinea is my fee, if you can afford it. Come back to me if ever you are in trouble."

" I am content now," she cried, drying her eyes, " to await God's will and to do my duty in the world until such time as it shall be ordained that we unite once more."

The widow left the house walking on air. Tom Linden also felt that the clouds left by his brother's visit had been blown away by this joyful incident, for there is no happiness like giving happiness and seeing the beneficient workings of one's own power. He had hardly settled down in his chair, however, before another client was ushered in. This time it was a smartly-dressed, white-spatted, frock-coated man of the world, with a bustling air as of one to whom minutes are precious.

Mr. Linden, I believe ? I have heard, sir, of your powers. I am told that by handling an object you can often get some clue as to the person who owned it ?"

" It happens sometimes. I cannot command it."

" I should like to test you. I have a letter here which I received this morning. Would you try your powers upon that ?"

The medium took the folded letter, and, leaning back

in his chair, he pressed it upon his forehead. He sat with his eyes closed for a minute or more. Then he returned the paper.

"I don't like it," he said. "I get a feeling of evil. I see a man dressed all in white. He has a dark face. He writes at a bamboo table. I get a sensation of heat. The letter is from the tropics."

"Yes, from Central America."

"I can tell you no more."

"Are the spirits so limited? I thought they knew everything."

"They do not know everything. Their power and knowledge are as closely limited as ours. But this is not a matter for the spirit people. What I did then was psychometry, which, so far as we know, is a power of the human soul."

"Well, you are right as far as you have gone. This man, my correspondent, wants me to put up the money for the half-share in an oil boring. Shall I do it?"

Tom Linden shook his head.

"These powers are given to some of us, sir, for the consolation of humanity and for a proof of immortality. They were never meant for worldly use. Trouble always comes of such use, trouble to the medium and trouble to the client. I will not go into the matter."

"Money's no object," said the man, drawing a wallet from his inner pocket.

"No, sir, nor to me. I am poor, but I have never ill-used my gift."

"A fat lot of use the gift is, then!" said the visitor, rising from his chair. "I can get all the rest from the parsons who are licensed, and you are not. There is your guinea, but I have not had the worth of it."

"I am sorry, sir, but I cannot break a rule. There is a lady beside you—near your left shoulder—an elderly lady . . ."

"Tut! tut!" said the financier, turning towards the door.

"She wears a large gold locket with an emerald cross upon her breast."

The man stopped, turned and stared.

" Where did you pick that up ?"

" I see it before me, now."

" Why, dash it, man, that is what my mother always wore ! D'you tell me you can see her ?"

" No, she is gone."

" What was she like ? What was she doing ?"

" She *was* your mother. She said so. She was weeping."

" Weeping ! My mother ! Why, she is in heaven if ever a woman was. They don't weep in heaven !"

" Not in the imaginary heaven. They do in the real heaven. It is only we who ever make them weep. She left a message."

" Give it to me !"

" The message was: ' Oh, Jack ! Jack ! you are drifting ever further from my reach '."

The man made a contemptuous gesture.

" I was a damned fool to let you have my name when I made the appointment. You have been making inquiries. You don't take me in with your tricks. I've had enough of it—more than enough !"

For the second time that morning the door was slammed by an angry visitor.

" He didn't like his message." Linden explained to his wife. " It was his poor mother, She is fretting over him. Lord ! If folk only knew these things it would do them more good than all the forms and ceremonies."

" Well, Tom, it's not your fault if they don't," his wife answered. " There are two women waiting to see you. They have not an introduction but they seem in great trouble."

" I've a bit of a headache. I haven't got over last night. Silas and I are the same in that. Our night's work finds us out next morning. I'll just take these and no more, for it is bad to send anyone sorrowin' away if one can help it."

The two women were shown in, both of them austere figures dressed in black, one a stern-looking person of fifty, the other about half that age.

126

"I believe your fee is a guinea," said the elder, putting that sum upon the table.

" To those who can afford it," Linden answered. As a matter of fact, the guinea often went the other way.

" Oh yes, I can afford it," said the woman. " I am in sad trouble and they told me maybe you could help me."

" Well, I will if I can. That's what I am for."

" I lost my poor husband in the war—killed at Ypres he was. Could I get in touch with him ?"

" You don't seem to bring any influence with you. I get no impression. I am sorry but we can't command these things. I get the name Edmund. Was that his name ?"

" No."

" Or Albert ?"

" No."

" I am sorry, but it seems confused—cross vibrations, perhaps, and a mix-up of messages like crossed telegraph wires."

" Does the name Pedro help you ?"

" Pedro ! Pedro ! No, I get nothing. Was Pedro an elderly man ?"

" No, not elderly."

" I can get no impression."

" It was about this girl of mine that I really wanted advice. My husband would have told me what to do. She has got engaged to a young man, a fitter by trade, but there are one or two things against it and I want to know what to do."

" Do give us some advice," said the young woman, looking at the medium with a hard eye.

" I would if I could, my dear. Do you love this man ?"

" Oh yes, he's all right."

" Well, if you don't feel more than that about him, I should leave him alone. Nothing but unhappiness comes of such a marriage."

" Then you see unhappiness waiting for her ?"

" I see a good chance of it. I think she should be careful."

" Do you see anyone else coming along ?"

"Everyone, man or woman, meets their mate sometime somewhere."

"Then she will get a mate ?"

"Most certainly she will."

"I wonder if I should have any family ?" asked the girl.

"Nay, that's more than I can say."

"And money—will she have money ? We are downhearted, Mr. Linden, and we want a little——"

At this moment there came a most surprising interruption. The door flew open and little Mrs. Linden rushed into the room with pale face and blazing eyes.

"They are policewomen, Tom. I've had a warning about them. It's only just come. Get out of this house, you pair of snivelling hypocrites. Oh, what a fool ! What a fool I was not to recognize what you were."

The two women had risen.

"Yes, you are rather late, Mrs. Linden," said the senior. "The money has passed."

"Take it back ! Take it back ! It's on the table."

"No, no, the money has passed. We have had our fortune told. You will hear more of this, Mr. Linden."

"You brace of frauds ! You talk of frauds when it is you who are the frauds all the time ! He would not have seen you if it had not been for compassion."

"It is no use scolding us," the woman answered. "We do our duty and we did not make the law. So long as it is on the Statute Book we have to enforce it. We must report the case at headquarters."

Tom Linden seemed stunned by the blow, but, when the policewomen had disappeared, he put his arm round his weeping wife and consoled her as best he might.

"The typist at the police office sent down the warning," she said. "Oh, Tom, it is the second time !" she cried. "It means gaol and hard labour for you."

"Well, dear, so long as we are conscious of having done no wrong and of having done God's work to the best of our power, we must take what comes with a good heart."

" But where were they ? How could they let you down
so ? Where was your guide ?"

" Yes, Victor," said Tom Linden, shaking his head at the
air above him, " where were you ? I've got a crow to pick
with you. You know, dear," he added, " just as a doctor
can never treat his own case, a medium is very helpless when
things come to his own address. That's the law. And yet
I should have known. I was feeling in the dark. I had
no inspiration of any sort. It was just a foolish pity and
sympathy that led me on when I had no sort of a real message. Well, dear Mary, we will take what's coming to us
with a brave heart. Maybe they have not enough to make
a case, and maybe the beak is not as ignorant as most of
them. We'll hope for the best."

In spite of his brave words the medium was shaking and
quivering at the shock. His wife had put her hands upon
him and was endeavouring to steady him, when Susan,
the maid, who knew nothing of the trouble, admitted a
fresh visitor into the room. It was none other than Edward
Malone.

" He can't see you," said Mrs. Linden, " the medium is
ill. He will see no one this morning."

But Linden had recognized his visitor.

"This is Mr. Malone, my dear, of the *Daily Gazette*. He was
with us last night. We had a good sitting, had we not, sir ?"

" Marvellous !" said Malone. " But what is amiss ?"

Both husband and wife poured out their sorrows.

" What a dirty business !" cried Malone, with disgust.
" I am sure the public does not realize how this law is en-
forced, or there would be a row. This agent-provocateur
business is quite foreign to British justice. But in any case,
Linden, you are a *real* medium. The law was made to sup-
press false ones."

" There are no real mediums in British law," said Linden,
ruefully. " I expect the more real you are the greater the
offence. If you are a medium at all and take money you
are liable. But how can a medium live if he does not take
money ? It's a man's whole work and needs all his strength.

129

You can't be a carpenter all day and a first-class medium in the evening."

" What a wicked law ! It seems to be deliberately stifling all physical proofs of spiritual power."

" Yes, that is just what it is. If the Devil passed a law it would be just that. It is supposed to be for the protection of the public and yet no member of the public has ever been known to complain. Every case is a police trap. And yet the police know as well as you or I that every Church charity garden-party has got its clairvoyante or its fortune-teller."

" It does seem monstrous. What will happen now ?"

" Well, I expect a summons will come along. Then a police court case. Then fine or imprisonment. It's the second time, you see."

" Well, your friends will give evidence for you and we will have a good man to defend you."

Linden shrugged his shoulders.

" You never know who are your friends. They slip away like water when it comes to the pinch."

" Well, I won't, for one," said Malone, heartily. " Keep me in touch with what is going on. But I called because I had something to ask you."

" I am sorry, but I am really not fit." Linden held out a quivering hand.

" No, no, nothing psychic. I simply wanted to ask you whether the presence of a strong sceptic would stop all your phenomena ?"

" Not necessarily. But, of course, it makes everything more difficult. If they will be quiet and reasonable we can get results. But they know nothing, break every law, and ruin their own sittings. There was old Sherbank, the doctor, the other day. When the raps came on the table he jumped up, put his hand on the wall, and cried, ' Now then, put a rap on the palm of my hand within five seconds '. Because he did not get it he declared it was all humbug and stamped out of the room. They will not admit that there are fixed laws in this as in everything else."

" Well, I must confess that the man I am thinking of
might be quite as unreasonable. It is the great Professor
Challenger."

" Oh, yes, I've heard he is a hard case."

" Would you give him a sitting ?"

" Yes, if you desired it."

" He won't come to you or to any place you name. He
imagines all sorts of wires and contrivances. You might
have to come down to his country house."

" I would not refuse if it might convert him."

" And when ?"

" I can do nothing until this horrible affair is over. It
will take a month or two."

" Well, I will keep in touch with you till then. When
all is well again we shall make our plans and see if we can
bring these facts before him, as they have been brought
before me. Meanwhile, let me say how much I sympathize.
We will form a committee of your friends and all that can
will surely be done."

7. *In Which the Notorious Criminal gets what the British Law Considers to be His Deserts*

BEFORE we pursue further the psychic adventures of
our hero and heroine, it would be well to see how the
British law dealt with that wicked man, Mr. Tom
Linden.

The two policewomen returned in triumph to Bardley
Square Station where Inspector Murphy, who had sent
them, was waiting for their report. Murphy was a jolly-
looking, red-faced, black-moustached man who had a
cheerful, fatherly way with women which was by no means
justified by his age or virility. He sat behind his official
table, his papers strewn in front of him.

" Well, girls," he said as the two women entered, " what
luck ?"

" I think it's a go, Mr. Murphy," said the elder policewoman. " We have the evidence you want."

The Inspector took up a written list of questions from his desk.

" You ran it on the general lines that I suggested ?" he asked.

" Yes. I said my husband was killed at Ypres."

" What did he do ?"

" Well, he seemed sorry for me."

" That, of course, is part of the game. He'll be sorry for himself before he is through with it. He didn't say, ' You are a single woman and never had a husband ?' "

" No."

" Well, that's one up against his spirits, is it not ? That should impress the Court. What more ?"

" He felt round for names. They were all wrong."

" Good !"

" He believed me when I said that Miss Bellinger here was my daughter."

" Good again ! Did you try the Pedro stunt ?"

" Yes, he considered the name, but I got nothing."

" Ah, that's a pity. But, anyhow, he did not know that Pedro was your Alsatian dog. He considered the name. That's good enough. Make the jury laugh and you have your verdict. Now about fortune-telling ? Did you do what I suggested ?"

" Yes, I asked about Amy's young man. He did not give much that was definite."

" Cunning devil ! He knows his business."

" But he did say that she would be unhappy if she married him."

" Oh, he did, did he ? Well, if we spread that a little we have got all we want. Now sit down and dictate your report while you have it fresh. Then we can go over it together and see how we can put it best. Amy must write one, also."

" Very good, Mr. Murphy."

" Then we shall apply for the warrant. You see, it all depends upon which magistrate it comes before. There was Mr. Dalleret who let a medium off last month. He is no

132

use to us. And Mr. Lancing has been mixed up with these people. Mr. Melrose is a stiff materialist. We could depend on him, and have timed the arrest accordingly. It would never do to fail to get our conviction."

" Couldn't you get some of the public to corroborate ?"

The inspector laughed.

" We are supposed to be protecting the public, but between you and me none of the public have ever yet asked to be protected. There are no complaints. Therefore it is left to us to uphold the law as best we can. As long as it is there we have got to enforce it. Well, good-bye, girls ! Let me have the report by four o'clock."

" Nothing for it, I suppose ?" said the elder woman, with a smile.

" You wait, my dear. If we get twenty-five pounds fine it has got to go somewhere—Police Fund, of course, but there may be something over. Anyhow, you go and cough it up and then we shall see."

Next morning a scared maid broke into Linden's modest study. " Please sir, it's an officer."

The man in blue followed hard at her heels.

" Name of Linden ?" said he, and handing a folded sheet of foolscap he departed.

The stricken couple who spent their lives in bringing comfort to others were sadly in need of comfort themselves. She put her arm round his neck while they read the cheerless document:

To THOMAS LINDEN of 40, Tullis Street, N.W.

Information has been laid this day by Patrick Murphy, Inspector of Police, that you the said Thomas Linden on the 10th day of November at the above dwelling did profess to Henrietta Dresser and to Amy Bellinger to tell fortunes to deceive and impose on certain of His Majesty's subjects, to wit those above mentioned. You are therefore summoned to appear before the Magistrate of the Police Court in Bardsley Square on Wednesday next, the 17th, at the hour of 11 in the forenoon to answer to the said information.

Dated the 10th day of November.

(Signed) B. J. WITHERS.

On the same afternoon Mailey called upon Malone and they sat in consultation over this document. Then they went together to see Summerway Jones, an acute solicitor and an earnest student of psychic affairs. Incidentally, he was a hard rider to hounds, a good boxer, and a man who carried a fresh-air flavour into the mustiest law chambers. He arched his eyebrows over the summons.

"The poor devil has not an earthly !" said he. "He's lucky to have a summons. Usually they act on a warrant. Then the man is carted right off, kept in the cells all night, and tried next morning with no one to defend him. The police are cute enough, of course, to choose either a Roman Catholic or a materialist as the magistrate. Then, by the beautiful judgment of Chief Justice Lawrence—the first judgment, I believe, that he delivered in that high capacity —the profession of mediumship or wonder-working is in itself a legal crime, whether it be genuine or no, so that no defence founded upon good results has a look in. It's a mixture of religious persecution and police blackmail. As to the public, they don't care a damn ! Why should they ? If they don't want their fortune told, they don't go. The whole thing is the most absolute bilge and a disgrace to our legislature."

"I'll write it up," said Malone, glowing with Celtic fire. "What do you call the Act ?"

"Well, there are two Acts, each more putrid than the other, and both passed long before Spiritualism was ever heard of. There is the Witchcraft Act dating from George the Second. That has become too absurd, so they only use it as a second string. Then there is the Vagrancy Act of 1824. It was passed to control the wandering gipsy folk on the roadside, and was never intended, of course, to be used like this." He hunted among his papers. "Here is the beastly thing. 'Every person professing to tell fortunes or using any subtle craft, means or device to deceive and impose on any of His Majesty's subjects shall be deemed a rogue and a vagabond', and so on and so forth. The two Acts together would have roped in the whole Early

Christian movement just as surely as the Roman persecution did."

" Lucky there are no lions now," said Malone.

" Jackasses !" said Mailey. " That's the modern substitute. But what are we to do ?"

" I'm damned if I know !" said the solicitor, scratching his head. " It's perfectly hopeless !"

" Oh, dash it all !" cried Malone, " we can't give it up so easily. We know the man is an honest man."

Mailey turned and grasped Malone's hand.

" I don't know if you call yourself a Spiritualist yet," he said, " but you are the kind of chap we want. There are too many white-livered folk in our movement who fawn on a medium when all is well, and desert him at the first breath of an accusation. But, thank God ! there are a few stalwarts. There is Brookes and Rodwin and Sir James Smith. We can put up a hundred or two among us."

" Right-o !" said the solicitor, cheerily. " If you feel like that we will give you a run for your money."

" How about a K.C. ?"

" Well, they don't plead in police courts. If you'll leave it in my hands I fancy I can do as well as anyone, for I've had a lot of these cases. It will keep the costs down, too."

" Well, we are with you. And we will have a few good men at our back."

" If we do nothing else we shall ventilate it," said Malone. " I believe in the good old British public. Slow and stupid, but sound at the core. They will not stand for injustice if you can get the truth into their heads."

" They damned well need trepanning before you can get it there," said the solicitor. " Well, you do your bit and I'll do mine and we will see what comes of it."

The fateful morning arrived and Linden found himself in the dock facing a spruce, middle-aged man with rat-trap jaws, Mr. Melrose, the redoubtable police magistrate. Mr. Melrose had a reputation for severity with fortune-tellers and all who foretold the future, though he spent the intervals in his court by reading up the sporting prophets, for he was an ardent follower of the Turf, and his trim, fawn-coloured coat and rakish hat were familiar objects at every race meeting which was within his reach. He was in no particularly good humour this morning as he glanced at the charge-sheet and then surveyed the prisoner. Mrs. Linden had secured a position below the dock, and occasionally extended her hand to pat that of the prisoner which rested on the edge. The court was crowded and many of the prisoner's clients had attended to show their sympathy.

"Is this case defended?" asked Mr. Melrose.

"Yes, your worship," said Summerway Jones. "May I, before it opens, make an objection?"

"If you think it worth while, Mr. Jones."

"I beg to respectfully request your ruling before the case is proceeded with. My client is not a vagrant, but a respectable member of the community, living in his own house, paying rates and taxes, and on the same footing as every other citizen. He is now prosecuted under the fourth section of the Vagrancy Act of 1824, which is styled, 'An Act for punishing idle and disorderly persons, and rogues and vagabonds'. The Act was intended, as the words imply, to restrain lawless gipsies and others, who at that time infested the country. I ask your worship to rule that my client is clearly not a person within the purview of this Act or liable to its penalties."

The magistrate shook his head.

"I fear, Mr. Jones, that there have been too many precedents for the Act to be now interpreted in this limited fashion. I will ask the solicitor prosecuting on behalf of the Commissioner of Police to put forward his evidence."

A little bull of a man with side-whiskers and a raucous voice sprang to his feet.

"I call Henrietta Dresser."

The elder policewoman popped up in the box with the alacrity of one who is used to it. She held an open notebook in her hand.

"You are a policewoman, are you not?"

136

" Yes, sir."

" I understand that you watched the prisoner's home the day before you called on him ?"

" Yes, sir."

" How many people went in ?"

" Fourteen, sir."

" Fourteen people. And I believe the prisoner's average fee is ten and sixpence."

" Yes."

" Seven pounds in one day ! Pretty good wages when many an honest man is content with five shillings."

" These were the tradespeople !" cried Linden.

" I must ask you not to interrupt. You are already very efficiently represented," said the magistrate severely.

" Now, Henrietta Dresser," continued the prosecutor, wagging his pince-nez. " Let's hear what occurred when you and Amy Bellinger visited the prisoner."

The policewoman gave an account which was in the main true, reading it from her book. She was not a married woman, but the medium had accepted her statement that she was. He had fumbled with several names and had seemed greatly confused. The name of a dog—Pedro—had been submitted to him, but he had not recognized it as such. Finally, he had answered questions as to the future of her alleged daughter, who was, in fact, no relation to her, and had foretold that she would be unhappy in her marriage.

" Any questions, Mr. Jones ?" asked the magistrate.

" Did you come to this man as one who needed consolation ? And did he attempt to give it ?"

" I suppose you might put it so."

" You professed deep grief, I understand."

" I tried to give that impression."

" You do not consider that to be hypocrisy ?"

" I did what was my duty."

" You saw no signs of psychic power, or anything abnormal ?" asked the prosecutor.

" No, he seemed a very nice, ordinary sort of man."

Amy Bellinger was the next witness. She appeared with her notebook in her hand.

" May I ask, your worship, whether it is in order that these witnesses should read their evidence?" asked Mr. Jones.

" Why not ?" queried the magistrate. " We desire the exact facts, do we not ?"

" *We* do. Possibly Mr. Jones does not," said the prosecuting solicitor.

" It is clearly a method of securing that the evidence of these two witnesses shall be in accord," said Jones. " I submit that these accounts are carefully prepared and collated."

" Naturally, the police prepare their case," said the magistrate. " I do not see that you have any grievance, Mr. Jones. Now, witness, let us hear your evidence."

It followed on the exact lines of the other.

" You asked questions about your fiancé ? You had no fiancé," said Mr. Jones.

" That is so."

" In fact, you both told a long sequence of lies ?"

" With a good object in view."

" You thought the end justified the means ?"

" I carried out my instructions."

" Which were given you beforehand ?"

" Yes, we were told what to ask."

" I think," said the magistrate, " that the policewomen have given their evidence very fairly and well. Have you any witnesses for the defence, Mr. Jones ?"

" There are a number of people in court, your worship, who have received great benefit from the mediumship of the prisoner. I have subpœnaed one woman who was, by her own account, saved from suicide that very morning by what he told her. I have another man who was an atheist, and had lost all belief in future life. He was completely converted by his experience of psychic phenomena. I can produce men of the highest eminence in science and literature who will testify to the real nature of Mr. Linden's powers."

The magistrate shook his head.

" You must know, Mr. Jones, that such evidence would be quite beside the question. It has been clearly laid down by the ruling of the Lord Chief Justice and others that the law of this country does not recognize supernatural power of any sort whatever, and that a pretence of such power where payment is involved constitutes a crime in itself. Therefore your suggestion that you should call witnesses could not possibly lead to anything save a wasting of the time of the court. At the same time, I am, of course, ready to listen to any observations which you may care to make after the solicitor for the prosecution has spoken."

" Might I venture to point out, your worship," said Jones, " that such a ruling would mean the condemnation of any sacred or holy person of whom we have any record, since even holy persons have to live, and have therefore to receive money."

" If you refer to Apostolic times, Mr. Jones," said the magistrate sharply, " I can only remind you that the Apostolic age is past and also that Queen Anne is dead. Such an argument is hardly worthy of your intelligence. Now, sir, if you have anything to add . . ."

Thus encouraged the prosecutor made a short address, stabbing the air at intervals with his pince-nez as if every stab punctured afresh all claims of the spirit. He pictured the destitution among the working-classes, and yet charlatans, by advancing wicked and blasphemous claims, were able to earn a rich living. That they had real powers was, as had been observed, beside the question, but even that excuse was shattered by the fact that these policewomen, who had discharged an unpleasant duty in a most exemplary way, had received nothing but nonsense in return for their money. Was it likely that other clients fared any better ? These parasites were increasing in number, trading upon the finer feelings of bereaved parents, and it was high time that some exemplary punishment should warn them that they would be wise to turn their hands to some more honest trade.

Mr. Summerway Jones replied as best he might. He began by pointing out that the Acts were being used for a purpose for which they were never intended. (" That point has already been considered !" snapped the magistrate.) The whole position was open to criticism. The convictions were secured by evidence from agents-provocateurs, who, if any crime had been committed, were obviously inciters to it and also participants. The fines obtained were often deflected for purposes in which the police had a direct interest.

" Surely, Mr. Jones, you do not mean to cast a reflection upon the honesty of the police !"

The police were human, and were naturally inclined to stretch a point where there own interests were affected. All these cases were artificial. There was no record at any time of any real complaint from the public or any demand for protection. There were frauds in every profession, and if a man deliberately invested and lost a guinea in a false medium he had no more right to protection than the man who invested his money in a bad company on the stock market. Whilst the police were wasting time upon such cases, and their agents were weeping crocodile tears in the character of forlorn mourners, many of her branches of real crime received far less attention than they deserved. The law was quite arbitrary in its action. Every big garden-party, even, as he had been informed, every police fête was incomplete without its fortune-teller or palmist.

Some years ago the *Daily Mail* had raised an outcry against fortune-tellers. That great man, the late Lord Northcliffe, had been put in the box by the defence, and it had been shown that one of his other papers was running a palmistry column, and that the fees received were divided equally between the palmist and the proprietors. He mentioned this in no spirit which was derogatory to the memory of this great man, but merely as an example of the absurdity of the law as it was now administered. Whatever might be the individual opinion of members of that court, it was incontrovertible that a large number of intelligent

140

and useful citizens regarded this power of mediumship as a remarkable manifestation of the power of spirit, making for the great improvement of the race. Was it not a most fatal policy in these days of materialism to crush down by law that which in its higher manifestation might work for the regeneration of mankind? As to the undoubted fact that information received by the policewomen was incorrect and that their lying statements were not detected by the medium, it was a psychic law that harmonious conditions were essential for true results, and that deceit on one side produced confusion on the other. If the court would for a moment adopt the Spiritualistic hypothesis, they would realize how absurd it would be to expect that angelic hosts would descend in order to answer the questions of two mercenary and hypocritical inquirers.

Such, in a short synopsis, was the general line of Mr. Summerway Jones's defence which reduced Mrs. Linden to tears and threw the magistrate's clerk into a deep slumber. The magistrate himself rapidly brought the matter to a conclusion.

" Your quarrel, Mr. Jones, seems to be with the law, and that is outside my competence. I administer it as I find it, though I may remark that I am entirely in agreement with it. Such men as the defendant are the noxious fungi which collect on a corrupt society, and the attempt to compare their vulgarities with the holy men of old, or to claim similar gifts, must be reprobated by all right-thinking men.

" As to you, Linden," he added, fixing his stern eyes upon the prisoner, " I fear that you are a hardened offender since a previous conviction has not altered your ways. I sentence you, therefore, to two months' hard labour without the option of a fine."

There was a scream from Mrs. Linden.

" Good-bye, dear, don't fret," said the medium, glancing over the side of the dock. An instant later he had been hurried down to the cell.

Summerway Jones, Mailey and Malone met in the hall, and Mailey volunteered to escort the poor stricken woman home.

141

" What had he ever done but bring comfort to all ?" she moaned. " Is there a better man living in the whole great City of London ?"

" I don't think there is a more useful one," said Mailey. " I'll venture to say that the whole of Crockford's Directory with the Archbishops at their head could not prove the things of religion as I have seen Tom Linden prove them, or convert an atheist as I have seen Linden convert him."

" It's a shame !" A damned shame !" said Malone, hotly.

" The touch about vulgarity was funny," said Jones. " I wonder if he thinks the Apostles were very cultivated people. Well, I did my best. I had no hopes, and it has worked out as I thought. It is a pure waste of time."

" Not at all," Malone answered. " It has ventilated an evil. There were reporters in court. Surely some of them have some sense. They will note the injustice."

" Not they," said Mailey. " The Press is hopeless. My God, what a responsibility these people take on themselves, and how little they guess the price that each will pay ! I know. I have spoken with them while they were paying it."

" Well, I for one will speak out," said Malone, " and I believe others will also. The Press is more independent and intelligent than you seem to think."

But Mailey was right, after all. When he had left Mrs. Linden in her lonely home and had reached Fleet Street once more, Malone bought a *Planet*. As he opened it a scare head-line met his eye:

IMPOSTOR IN THE POLICE COURT.

Dog Mistaken for Man.
Who Was Pedro ?
Exemplary Sentence.

He crumpled the paper up in his hand.

" No wonder these Spiritualists feel bitterly," he thought " They have good cause."

Yes, poor Tom Linden had a bad Press. He went down into his miserable cell amid universal objurgation. The *Planet*, an evening paper which depended for its circulation upon the sporting forecasts of Captain Touch-and-go, remarked upon the absurdity of forecasting the future. *Honest John*, a weekly journal which had been mixed up with some of the greatest frauds of the century, was of opinion that the dishonesty of Linden was a public scandal. A rich country rector wrote to *The Times* to express his indignation that anyone should profess to sell the gifts of the spirit. The *Churchman* remarked that such incidents arose from the growing infidelity, while the *Freethinker* saw in them a reversion to superstition. Finally Mr. Maskelyne showed the public, to the great advantage of his box office, exactly how the swindle was perpetrated. So for a few days Tom Linden was what the French call a " succés d'execration." Then the world moved on and he was left to his fate.

8. *In Which Three Investigators Come Upon a Dark Soul*

LORD ROXTON had returned from a Central African heavy game shooting, and had at once carried out a series of Alpine ascents which had satisfied and surprised everyone except himself.

" Top of the Alps is becomin' a perfect bear-garden," said he. " Short of Everest there don't seem to be any decent privacy left."

His advent into London was acclaimed by a dinner given in his honour at the 'Travellers' by the Heavy Game Society. The occasion was private and there were no reporters, but Lord Roxton's speech was fixed *verbatim* in the minds of all his audience and has been imperishably preserved. He writhed for twenty minutes under the flowery and eulogistic periods of the president, and rose himself in the state of confused indignation which the Briton feels when he is publicly approved. " Oh, I say ! By Jove ! What !" was his oration, after which he resumed his seat and perspired profusely.

Malone was first aware of Lord Roxton's return through McArdle, the crabbed old red-headed news editor, whose bald dome projected further and further from its ruddy fringe as the years still found him slaving at the most grinding of tasks. He retained his keen scent of what was good copy, and it was this sense of his which caused him one winter morning to summon Malone to his presence. He removed the long glass tube which he used as a cigarette-holder from his lips, and he blinked through his big round glasses at his subordinate.

" You know that Lord Roxton is back in London ?"

" I had not heard."

" Aye, he's back. Dootless you've heard that he was wounded in the war. He led a small column in East Africa and made a wee war of his own till he got an elephant bullet through his chest. Oh, he's done fine since then, or he couldn't be climbin' these mountains. He's a deevil of a man and aye stirring up something new."

" What is the latest ?" asked Malone, eyeing a slip of paper which McArdle was waving between his finger and thumb.

" Well, that's where he impinges on you. I was thinking maybe you could hunt in couples and, there would be copy in it. There's a leaderette in the *Evening Standard.*" He handed it over. It ran thus:

" A quaint advertisement in the columns of a contemporary shows that the famous Lord John Roxton, third son of the Duke of Pomfret, is seeking fresh worlds to conquer. Having exhausted the sporting adventures of this terrestrial globe, he is now turning to those of the dim, dark and dubious regions of psychic research. He is in the market apparently for any genuine specimen of a haunted house, and is open to receive information as to any violent or dangerous manifestation which called for investigation. As Lord John Roxton is a man of resolute character and one of the best revolver shots in England, we would warn any practical joker that he would be well-advised to stand aside and leave this matter to those who are said to be as impervious to bullets as their supporters are to common sense."

144

McArdle gave his dry chuckle at the concluding words.

" I'm thinking they are getting pairsonal there, friend Malone, for if you are no a supporter, you're well on the way. But are you no of the opeenion that this chiel and you between you might put up a spook and get two racy columns off him ?"

" Well, I can see Lord Roxton," said Malone. " He's still, I suppose, in his old rooms in the Albany. I would wish to call in any case, so I can open this up as well."

Thus it was that in the late afternoon just as the murk of London broke into dim circles of silver, the pressman found himself once more walking down Vigo Street and accosting the porter at the dark entrance of the old-fashioned chambers. Yes, Lord John Roxton was in, but a gentleman was with him. He would take a card. Presently he returned with word that in spite of the previous visitor, Lord Roxton would see Malone at once. An instant later, he had been ushered into the old luxurious rooms with their trophies of war and of the chase. The owner of them with outstretched hand was standing at the door, long, thin, austere, with the same gaunt, whimsical, Don Quixote face as of old. There was no change save that he was more aquiline, and his eyebrows jutted more thickly over his reckless, restless eyes.

" Hullo, young fellah !" he cried. " I was hopin' you'd draw this old covert once more. I was comin' down to the office to look you up. Come in ! Come in ! Let me introduce you to the Reverend Charles Mason."

A very tall, thin clergyman, who was coiled up in a large basket chair, gradually unwound himself and held out a bony hand to the newcomer. Malone was aware of two very earnest and human grey eyes looking searchingly into his, and of a broad, welcoming smile which disclosed a double row of excellent teeth. It was a worn and weary face, the tired face of the spiritual fighter, but it was very kindly and companionable, none the less. Malone had heard of the man, a Church of England vicar, who had left his model parish and the church which he had built himself in order to preach freely the doctrines of Christianity, with the new psychic knowledge super-added.

"Why, I never seem to get away from the Spiritualists!" he exclaimed.

"You never will, Mr. Malone," said the lean clergyman, chuckling. "The world never will until it has absorbed this new knowledge which God has sent. You can't get away from it. It is too big. At the present moment, in this great city there is not a place where men or women meet that it does not come up. And yet you would not know it from the Press."

"Well, you can't level that reproach at the *Daily Gazette*," said Malone. "Possibly you may have read my own descriptive articles."

"Yes, I read them. They are at least better than the awful sensational nonsense which the London Press usually serves up, save when they ignore it altogether. To read a paper like *The Times* you would never know that this vital movement existed at all. The only editorial allusion to it that I can ever remember was in a leading article when the great paper announced that it would believe in it when it found it could, by means of it, pick out more winners on a race-card than by other means."

"Doosed useful, too," said Lord Roxton. "It's just what I should have said myself. What!"

The clergyman's face was grave and he shook his head. "That brings me back to the object of my visit," he said. He turned to Malone. "I took the liberty of calling upon Lord Roxton in connection with his advertisement to say that if he went on such a quest with a good intention, no better work could be found in the world, but if he did it out of a love of sport, following some poor earth-bound soul in the same spirit as he followed the white rhinoceros of the Lido, he might be playing with fire."

"Well, padre, I've been playin' with fire all my life and that's nothin' new. What I mean—if you want me to look at this ghost business from the religious angle, there's nothin' doin', for the Church of England that I was brought up in fills my very modest need. But if it's got a spice of danger, as you say, then it's worth while. What !"

The Rev. Charles Mason smiled his kindly, toothsome grin.

" Incorrigible, is he not ?" he said to Malone. " Well, I can only wish you a fuller comprehension of the subject." He rose as if to depart.

" Wait a bit, padre !" cried Lord Roxton, hurriedly. " When I'm explorin', I begin by ropin' in a friendly native. I expect you're just the man. Won't you come with me ?"

" Where to ?"

" Well, sit down and I'll tell you." He rummaged among a pile of letters on his desk. " Fine selection of spooks !" he said. " I got on the track of over twenty by the first post. This is an easy winner, though. Read it for yourself. Lonely house, man driven mad, tenants boltin' in the night, horrible spectre. Sounds all right—what !"

The clergyman read the letter with puckered brows. " It seems a bad case," said he.

" Well, suppose you come along. What ! Maybe you can help clear it up."

The Rev. Mason pulled out a pocket-almanac. " I have a service for ex-Service men on Wednesday, and a lecture the same evening."

" But we could start to-day."

" It's a long way."

" Only Dorsetshire. Three hours."

" What is your plan ?"

" Well, I suppose a night in the house should do it."

" If there is any poor soul in trouble it becomes a duty. Very well, I will come."

" And surely there is room for me," pleaded Malone.

" Of course there is, young fellah ! What I mean—I expect that old, red-headed bird at the office sent you round with no other purpose. Ah, I thought so. Well, you can write an adventure that is not perfect bilge for a change— what ! There's a train from Victoria at eight o'clock. We can meet there, and I'll have a look in at old man Challenger as I pass."

147

They dined together in the train and after dinner reassembled in their first-class carriage, which is the snuggest mode of travel which the world can show. Roxton, behind a big black cigar, was full of his visit to Challenger.

" The old dear is the same as ever. Bit my head off once or twice in his own familiar way. Talked unadulterated tripe. Says I've got brain-softenin', if I could think there was such a thing as a real spook. ' When you're dead you're dead '. That's the old man's cheery slogan. Surveyin' his contemporaries, he said, extinction was a doosed good thing ! ' It's the only hope of the world ', said he.' ' Fancy the awful prospect if they survived '. Wanted to give me a bottle of chlorine to chuck at the ghost. I told him that if my automatic was not a spook-stopper, nothin' else would serve. Tell me, padre, is this the first time you've been on safari after this kind of game ?"

" You treat the matter too lightly, Lord John," said the clergyman gravely. " You have clearly had no experience of it. In answer to your question I may say that I have several times tried to help in similar cases."

" And you take it seriously ?" asked Malone, making notes for his article.

" Very, very seriously."

" What do you think these influences are ?"

" I am no authority upon the general question. You know Algernon Mailey, the barrister, do you not ? He could give you facts and figures. I approach the subject rather perhaps from the point of view of instinct and emotion. I remember Mailey lecturing on Professor Bozzano's book on ghosts where over five hundred well-authenticated instances were given, every one of them sufficient to establish an *à priori* case. There is Flammarion, too. You can't laugh away evidence of that kind."

" I've read Bozzano and Flammarion, too," said Malone, " but it is your own experience and conclusions that I want."

" Well, if you quote me, remember that I do not look on myself as a great authority on psychic research. Wiser brains than mine may come along and give some other explanation. Still, what I have seen has led me to certain conclusions. One of them is to think that there is some truth in the theosophical idea of shells."

" What is that ?"

" They imagined that all spirit bodies near the earth were empty shells or husks from which the real entity had departed. Now, of course, we know that a general statement of that sort is nonsense, for we could not get the glorious communications which we do get from anything but high intelligences. But we also must beware of generalizations. They are not *all* high intelligences. Some are so low that I think the creature is purely external and is an appearance rather than a reality."

" But why should it be there ?"

" Yes, that is the question. It is usually allowed that there is the natural body, as St. Paul called it, which is dissolved at death, and the etheric or spiritual body which survives and functions upon an etheric plane. Those are the essential things. But we may really have as many coats as an onion and there may be a mental body which may shed itself at any spot where great mental or emotional strain has been experienced. It may be a dull automatic simulacrum and yet carry something of our appearance and thoughts."

" Well," said Malone, " that would to some extent get over the difficulty, for I could never imagine that a murderer or his victim could spend whole centuries re-acting the old crime. What would be the sense of it ?"

" Quite right, young fellah," said Lord Roxton. " There was a pal of mine, Archie Soames, the gentleman Jock, who had an old place in Berkshire. Well, Nell Gwynne had lived there once, and he was ready to swear he met her a dozen times in the passage. Archie never flinched at the big jump at the Grand National, but, by Jove ! he flinched at those passages after dark. Doosed fine woman she was and all that, but dash it all ! What I mean—one has to draw the line—what !"

149

" Quite so !" the clergyman answered. " You can't imagine that the real soul of a vivid personality like Nell could spend centuries walking those passages. But if by chance she had ate her heart out in that house, brooding and fretting, one could think that she might have cast a shell and left some thought-image of herself behind her."

" You said you had experiences of your own."

" I had one before ever I knew anything of Spiritualism. I hardly expect that you will believe me, but I assure you it is true. I was a very young curate up in the north. There was a house in the village which had a poltergeist, one of those very mischievous influences which cause so much trouble. I volunteered to exorcize it. We have an official form of exorcism in the Church, you know, so I thought that I was well-armed. I stood in the drawing-room which was the centre of the disturbances, with all the family on their knees beside me, and I read the service. What do you think happened ?"

Mason's gaunt face broke into a sweetly humorous laugh. " Just as I reached Amen, when the creature should have been slinking away abashed, the big bearskin hearthrug stood up on end and simply enveloped me. I am ashamed to say that I was out of that house in two jumps. It was then that I learned that no formal religious proceeding has any effect at all."

" Then what has ?"

" Well, kindness and reason may do something. You see, they vary greatly. Some of these earthbound or earth-interested creatures are neutral, like these simulacra or shells that I speak of. Others are essentially good like these monks of Glastonbury, who have manifested so wonderfully of late years and are recorded by Bligh Bond. They are held to earth by a pious memory. Some are mischievous children like the poltergeists. And some—only a few, I hope—are deadly beyond words, strong, malevolent creatures too heavy with matter to rise above our earth plane—so heavy with matter that their vibrations may be low enough to affect the human retina and to become visible. If they have been cruel, cunning brutes in life, they are cruel and cunning still with more power to hurt. It is evil monsters of this kind who are let loose by our system of capital punishment, for they die with unused vitality which may be expended upon revenge."

" This Dryfont spook has a doosed bad record," said Lord Roxton.

" Exactly. That is why I disapprove of levity. He seems to me to be the very type of the creature I speak of. Just as an octopus may have his den in some ocean cave, and come floating out a silent image of horror to attack a swimmer, so I picture such a spirit lurking in the dark of the house which he curses by his presence, and ready to float out upon all whom he can injure."

Malone's jaw began to drop.

" I say !" he exclaimed, " have we no protection ?"

" Yes, I think we have. If we had not, such a creature could devastate the earth. Our protection is that there are white forces as well as dark ones. We may call them ' guardian angels ' as the Catholics do, or ' guides ' or ' controls ', but whatever you call them, they really do exist and they guard us from evil on the spiritual plane."

" What about the chap who was driven mad, padre ? Where was your guide when the spook put the rug round you ? What !"

" The power of our guides may depend upon our own worthiness. Evil may always win for a time. Good wins in the end. That's my experience in life."

Lord Roxton shook his head.

" If good wins, then it runs a doosed long waitin' race, and most of us never live to see the finish. Look at those rubber devils that I had a scrap with up the Putomayo River. Where are they ? What ! Mostly in Paris havin' a good time. And the poor niggers they murdered. What about them ?"

" Yes, we need faith sometimes. We have to remember that we don't see the end. ' To be continued in our next ' is the conclusion of every life-story. That's where the enormous value of the other world accounts come in. They give us at least one chapter more."

"Where can I get that chapter?" asked Malone.

"There are many wonderful books, though the world has not yet learned to appreciate them—records of the life beyond. I remember one incident—you may take it as a parable, if you like—but it is really more than that. The dead rich man pauses before the lovely dwelling. His sad guide draws him away. 'It is not for you. It is for your gardener'. He shows him a wretched shack. 'You gave us nothing to build with. It was the best that we could do'. That may be the next chapter in the story of our rubber millionaires."

Roxton laughed grimly.

"I gave some of them a shack that was six foot long and two foot deep," said he. "No good shakin' your head, padre. What I mean—I don't love my neighbour as myself, and never shall. I hate some of 'em like poison."

"Well, we should hate sin, and, for my own part, I have never been strong enough to separate sin from the sinner. How can I preach when I am as human and weak as anyone?"

"Why, that's the only preachin' I could listen to," said Lord Roxton. "The chap in the pulpit is over my head. If he comes down to my level I have some use for him. Well, it strikes me we won't get much sleep to-night. We've just an hour before we reach Dryfont. Maybe we had better use it."

It was past eleven o'clock of a cold, frosty night when the party reached their destination. The station of the little watering-place was almost deserted, but a small, fat man in a fur overcoat ran forward to meet them, and greeted them warmly.

"I am Mr. Belchamber, owner of the house. How do you do, gentlemen? I got your wire, Lord Roxton, and everything is in order. It is indeed kind of you to come down. If you can do anything to ease my burden I shall indeed be grateful."

Mr. Belchamber led them across to the little Station Hotel where they partook of sandwiches and coffee, which he had thoughtfully ordered. As they ate he told them something of his troubles.

"It isn't as if I was a rich man, gentlemen. I am a retired grazier and all my savings are in three houses. That is one of them, the Villa Maggiore. Yes, I got it cheap, that's true. But how could I think there was anything in this story of the mad doctor?"

"Let's have the yarn," said Lord Roxton, munching at a sandwich.

"He was there away back in Queen Victoria's time. I've seen him myself. A long, stringy, dark-faced kind of man, with a round back and a queer, shuffling way of walking. They say he had been in India all his life, and some thought he was hiding from some crime, for he would never show his face in the village and seldom came out till after dark. He broke a dog's leg with a stone, and there was some talk of having him up for it, but the people were afraid of him, and no one would prosecute. The little boys would run past, for he would sit glowering and glooming in the front window. Then one day he didn't take the milk in, and the same the next day, and so they broke the door open, and he was dead in his bath—but it was a bath of blood, for he opened the veins of his arm. Tremayne was his name. No one here forgets it."

"And you bought the house?"

"Well, it was re-papered and painted and fumigated, and done up outside. You'd have said it was a new house. Then, I let it to Mr. Jenkins of the Brewery. Three days he was in it. I lowered the rent, and Mr. Beale, the retired grocer, took it. It was he who went mad—clean mad— after a week of it. And I've had it on my hands ever since —sixty pounds out of my income, and taxes to pay on it, into the bargain. If you gentlemen can do anything, for God's sake do it! If not, it would pay me to burn it down."

The Villa Maggiore stood about half a mile from the town on the slope of a low hill. Mr. Belchamber conducted them so far, and even up to the hall door. It was certainly a depressing place, with a huge, gambrel roof which came down over the upper windows and nearly obscured them. There was a half-moon, and by its light they could see that the garden was a tangle of scraggy, winter vegetation, which had, in some places, almost overgrown the path. It was all very still, very gloomy and very ominous.

"The door is not locked," said the owner. "You will find some chairs and a table in the sitting-room on the left of the hall. I had a fire lit there, and there is a bucketful of coals. You will be pretty comfortable, I hope. You won't blame me for not coming in, but my nerves are not so good as they were." With a few apologetic words, the owner slipped away, and they were alone with their task.

Lord Roxton had brought a strong electric torch. On opening the mildewed door, he flashed a tunnel of light down the passage, uncarpeted and dreary, which ended in a broad, straight, wooden staircase leading to the upper floor. There were doors on either side of the passage. That on the right led into a large, cheerless, empty room, with a derelict lawn-mower in one corner and a pile of old books and journals. There was a corresponding room upon the left which was a much more cheery apartment. A brisk fire burned in the grate, there were three comfortable chairs, and a deal table with a water carafe, a bucket of coals, and a few other amenities. It was lit by a large oil-lamp. The clergyman and Malone drew up to the fire, for it was very cold, but Lord Roxton completed his preparations. From a little hand-bag he extracted his automatic pistol, which he put upon the mantelpiece. Then he produced a packet of candles, placing two of them in the hall. Finally he took a ball of worsted and tied strings of it across the back passage and across the opposite door.

"We will have one look round," said he, when his preparations were complete. "Then we can wait down here and take what comes."

The upper passage led at right angles to left and right

from the top of the straight staircase. On the right were two large, bare, dusty rooms, with the wallpaper hanging in strips and the floor littered with scattered plaster. On the left was a single large room in the same derelict condition. Out of it was the bathroom of tragic memory, with the high, zinc bath still in position. Great blotches of red lay within it, and though they were only rust stains, they seemed to be terrible reminders from the past. Malone was surprised to see the clergyman stagger and support himself against the door. His face was ghastly white and there was moisture on his brow. His two comrades supported him down the stairs, and he sat for a little, as one exhausted, before he spoke.

"Did you two really feel nothing?" he asked. "The fact is that I am mediumistic myself and very open to psychic impressions. This particular one was horrible beyond description."

"What did you get, padre?"

"It is difficult to describe these things. It was a sinking of my heart, a feeling of utter desolation. All my senses were affected. My eyes went dim. I smelt a terrible odour of putrescence. The strength seemed to be sapped out of me. Believe me, Lord Roxton, it is no light thing which we are facing to-night."

The sportsman was unusually grave. "So I begin to think," said he. "Do you think you are fit for the job?"

"I am sorry to have been so weak," Mr. Mason answered. "I shall certainly see the thing through. The worse the case, the more need for my help. I am all right now," he added, with his cheery laugh, drawing an old charred briar from his pocket. "This is the best doctor for shaken nerves. I'll sit here and smoke till I'm wanted."

"What shape do you expect it to take?" asked Malone of Lord Roxton.

"Well, it is something you can see. That's certain."

"That's what I cannot understand, in spite of all my reading," said Malone. "These authorities are all agreed that there is a material basis, and that this material basis

155

is drawn from the human body. Call it ectoplasm, or what you like, it is human in origin, is it not ?"

" Certainly," Mason answered.

" Well, then, are we to suppose that this Dr. Tremayne builds up his own appearance by drawing stuff from me and you ?"

" I think, so far as I understand it, that in most cases a spirit does so. I believe that when the spectator feels that he goes cold, that his hair rises and the rest of it, he is really conscious of this draft upon his own vitality which may be enough to make him faint or even to kill him. Perhaps he was drawing on me then."

" Suppose we are not mediumistic ? Suppose we give out nothing ?"

" There is a very full case that I read lately," Mr. Mason answered. " It was closely observed—reported by Professor Neillson of Iceland. In that case the evil spirit used to go down to an unfortunate photographer in the town, draw his supplies from him, and then come back and use them. He would openly say, ' Give me time to get down to So-and-so. Then I will show you what I can do '. He was a most formidable creature and they had great difficulty in mastering him."

" Strikes me, young fellah, we have taken on a larger contract than we knew," said Lord Roxton. " Well, we've done what we could. The passage is well lit. No one can come at us except down the stair without breaking the worsted. There is nothing more we can do except just to wait."

So they waited. It was a weary time. A carriage clock had been placed on the discoloured wooden mantelpiece, and slowly its hands crept on from one to two and from two to three. Outside an owl was hooting most dismally in the darkness. The villa was on a by-road, and there was no human sound to link them up with life. The padre lay dozing in his chair. Malone smoked incessantly. Lord Roxton turned over the pages of a magazine. There were the occasional strange tappings and creakings which come in the silence of the night. Nothing else until . . .

Someone came down the stair.

There could not be a doubt of it. It was a furtive, and yet a clear footstep. Creak! Creak! Creak! Then it had reached the level. Then it had reached their door. They were all sitting erect in their chairs, Roxton grasping his automatic. Had it come in? The door was ajar, but had not further opened. Yet all were aware of a sense that they were not alone, that they were being observed. It seemed suddenly colder, and Malone was shivering. An instant later the steps were retreating. They were low and swift—much swifter than before. One could imagine that a messenger was speeding back with intelligence to some great master who lurked in the shadows above.

The three sat in silence, looking at each other.

" By Jove !" said Lord Roxton at last. His face was pale but firm. Malone scribbled some notes and the hour. The clergyman was praying.

" Well, we are up against it," said Roxton after a pause. " We can't leave it at that. We have to go through with it. I don't mind tellin' you, padre, that I've followed a wounded tiger in thick jungle and never had quite the feelin' I've got now. If I'm out for sensations, I've got them. But I'm going upstairs."

" We will go, too," cried his comrades, rising from their chairs.

" Stay here, young fellah ! And you, too, padre. Three of us make too much noise. I'll call you if I want you. My idea is just to steal out and wait quiet on the stair. If that thing, whatever it was, comes again, it will have to pass me."

All three went into the passage. The two candles were throwing out little circles of light, and the stair was deeply illuminated, with heavy shadows at the top. Roxton sat down half-way up the stair, pistol in hand. He put his finger to his lips and impatiently waved his companions back to the room. Then they sat by the fire, waiting, waiting.

Half an hour, three-quarters—and then, suddenly it

came. There was a sound as of rushing feet, the reverberation of a shot, a scuffle and a heavy fall, with a loud cry for help. Shaking with horror, they rushed into the hall. Lord Roxton was lying on his face amid a litter of plaster and rubbish. He seemed half dazed as they raised him, and was bleeding where the skin had been grazed from his cheek and hands. Looking up the stair, it seemed that the shadows were blacker and thicker at the top.

" I'm all right," said Roxton, as they led him to his chair. "Just give me a minute to get my wind and I'll have another round with the devil—for if this is not the devil, then none ever walked the earth."

" You shan't go alone this time," said Malone.

" You never should," added the clergyman. " But tell us what happened."

" I hardly know myself. I sat, as you saw, with my back to the top landing. Suddenly I heard a rush. I was aware of something dark right on the top of me. I half-turned and fired. The next instant I was chucked down as if I had been a baby. All that plaster came showering down after me. That's as much as I can tell you."

" Why should we go further in the matter ?" said Malone. " You are convinced that this is more than human, are you not ?"

" There is no doubt of that."

" Well, then, you have had your experience. What more can you want ?"

" Well, I, at least, want something more," said Mr. Mason. " I think our help is needed."

" Strikes me that *we* shall need the help," said Lord Roxton, rubbing his knee. " We shall want a doctor before we get through. But I'm with you, padre. I feel that we must see it through. If you don't like it, young fellah——"

The mere suggestion was too much for Malone's Irish blood.

" I am going up alone !" he cried, making for the door.

" No, indeed. I am with you." The clergyman hurried after him.

"And you don't go without me!" cried Lord Roxton, limping in the rear.

They stood together in the candle-lit, shadow-draped passage. Malone had his hand on the balustrade and his foot on the lower step, when it happened.

What was it? They could not tell themselves. They only knew that the black shadows at the top of the staircase had thickened, had coalesced, had taken a definite, batlike shape. Great God! They were moving! They were rushing swiftly and noiselessly downwards! Black, black as night, huge, ill-defined, semi-human and altogether evil and damnable. All three men screamed and blundered for the door. Lord Roxton caught the handle and threw it open. It was too late; the thing was upon them. They were conscious of a warm, glutinous contact, of a purulent smell, of a half-formed, dreadful face and of entwining limbs. An instant later all three were lying half-dazed and horrified, hurled outwards on to the gravel of the drive. The door had shut with a crash.

Malone whimpered and Roxton swore, but the clergyman was silent as they gathered themselves together, each of them badly shaken and bruised, but with an inward horror which made all bodily ill seem insignificant. There they stood in a little group in the light of the sinking moon, their eyes turned upon the black square of the door.

"That's enough," said Roxton, at last.

"More than enough," said Malone. "I wouldn't enter that house again for anything Fleet Street could offer."

"Are you hurt?"

"Defiled, degraded—oh, it was loathsome!"

"Foul!" said Roxton! "Did you get the reek of it? And the purulent warmth?"

Malone gave a cry of disgust. "Featureless—save for the dreadful eyes! Semi-materialized! Horrible!"

"What about the lights?"

"Oh, damn the lights! Let them burn. I am not going in again!"

" Well, Belchamber can come in the morning. Maybe he is waiting for us now at the inn."

" Yes, let us go to the inn. Let us get back to humanity."

Malone and Roxton turned away, but the clergyman stood fast. He had drawn a crucifix from his pocket.

" You can go," said he. " I am going back."

" What ! Into the house ?"

" Yes, into the house."

" Padre, this is madness ! It will break your neck. We were all like stuffed dolls in its clutch."

" Well, let it break my neck. I am going."

" You are not ! Here, Malone, catch hold of him !"

But it was too late With a few quick steps, Mr. Mason had reached the door, flung it open, passed in and closed it behind him. As his comrades tried to follow, they heard a creaking clang upon the further side. The padre had bolted them out. There was a great slit where the letter-box had been. Through it Lord Roxton entreated him to return.

" Stay there !" said the quick, stern voice of the clergyman. " I have my work to do. I will come when it is done."

A moment later he began to speak. His sweet, homely, affectionate accents rang through the hall. They could only hear snatches outside, bits of prayer, bits of exhortation, bits of kindly greeting. Looking through the narrow opening, Malone could see the straight, dark figure in the candlelight, its back to the door, its face to the shadows of the stair, the crucifix held aloft in its right hand.

His voice sank into silence and then there came one more of the miracles of this eventful night. A voice answered him. It was such a sound as neither of the auditors had heard before—a guttural, rasping, croaking utterance, indescribably menacing. What it said was short, but it was instantly answered by the clergyman, his tone sharpened to a fine edge by emotion. His utterance seemed to be exhortation and was at once answered by the ominous voice from beyond. Again and again, and yet again came the speech and the answer, sometimes shorter, sometimes longer, varying in every key of pleading, arguing, praying, soothing, and everything save upbraiding. Chilled to the marrow, Roxton and Malone crouched by the door, catching snatches of that inconceivable dialogue. Then, after what seemed a weary time, though it was less than an hour, Mr. Mason, in a loud, full, exultant tone, repeated the " Our Father." Was it fancy, or echo, or was there really some accompanying voice in the darkness beyond him ? A moment later the light went out in the left-hand window, the bolt was drawn, and the clergyman emerged carrying Lord Roxton's bag. His face looked ghastly in the moonlight, but his manner was brisk and happy.

" I think you will find everything here," he said, handing over the bag.

Roxton and Malone took him by either arm and hurried him down to the road.

" By Jove ! You don't give us the slip again !" cried the nobleman. " Padre, you should have a row of Victoria Crosses."

" No, no, it was my duty. Poor fellow, he needed help so badly. I am but a fellow-sinner and yet I was able to give it."

" You did him good ?"

" I humbly hope so. I was but the instrument of the higher forces. The house is haunted no longer. He promised. But I will not speak of it now. It may be easier in days to come."

The landlord and the maids stared at the three adventurers in amazement when, in the chill light of the winter dawn, they presented themselves at the inn once more. Each of them seemed to have aged five years in the night. Mr. Mason, with the re-action upon him, threw himself down upon the horsehair sofa in the humble coffee-room and was instantly asleep.

" Poor chap ! He looks pretty bad !" said Malone. Indeed, his white, haggard face and long, limp limbs might have been those of a corpse.

" We will get a cup of hot tea into him," Lord Roxton answered, warming his hands at the fire, which the maid

161

had just lit. "By Jove! We shall be none the worse for some ourselves. Well, young fellah, we've got what we came for. I've had my sensation, and you've had your copy."

"And he has had the saving of a soul. Well, we must admit that our objects seem very humble compared to his."

They caught the early train to London, and had a carriage to themselves. Mason had said little and seemed to be lost in thought. Suddenly he turned to his companions.

"I say, you two, would you mind joining me in prayer?"

Lord Roxton made a grimace. "I warn you, padre, I am rather out of practice."

"Please kneel down with me. I want your aid."

They knelt down, side by side, the padre in the middle. Malone made a mental note of the prayer.

"Father, we are all Your children, poor, weak, helpless creatures, swayed by Fate and circumstance. I implore You that You will turn eyes of compassion upon the man, Rupert Tremayne, who wandered far from You, and is now in the dark. He has sunk deep, very deep, for he had a proud heart which would not soften, and a cruel mind, which was filled with hate. But now he would turn to the light, and so I beg help for him and for the woman, Emma, who, for the love of him, has gone down into the darkness. May she raise him, as she had tried to do. May they both break the bonds of evil memory which tie them to earth. May they, from to-night, move up towards that glorious light which sooner or later shines upon even the lowest."

They rose from their knees.

"That's better!" cried the padre, thumping his chest with his bony hand, and breaking out into his expansive, toothsome grin. "What a night! Good Lord, what a night!"*

* *Vide* Appendix.

9. Which Introduces Some Very Physical Phenomena

MALONE seemed destined to be entangled in the affairs of the Linden family, for he had hardly seen the last of the unfortunate Tom before he became involved in a very much more unpleasant fashion with his unsavoury brother.

The episode began by a telephone ring in the morning and the voice of Algernon Mailey at the far end of the wire.

." Are you clear for this afternoon ?"

" At your service."

" I say, Malone, you are a hefty man. You played Rugger for Ireland, did you not ? You don't mind a possible rough-and-tumble, do you ?"

Malone grinned over the receiver.

" You can count me in."

" It may be really rather formidable. We shall have possibly to tackle a prize-fighter."

" Right-o !" said Malone, cheerfully.

" And we want another man for the job. Do you know any fellow who would come along just for the sake of the adventure. If he knows anything about psychic matters, all the better."

Malone puzzled for a moment. Then he had an inspiration.

" There is Roxton," said he. " He's not a chicken, but he is a useful man in a row. I think I could get him. He has been keen on your subject since his Dorsetshire experience."

" Right ! Bring him along ! If he can't come, we shall have to tackle the job ourselves. Forty-one, Belshaw Gardens, S.W. Near Earl's Court Station. Three p.m. Right !"

Malone at once rang up Lord Roxton, and soon heard the familiar voice.

"What's that, young fellah? . . . A scrap? Why, certainly. What . . . I mean I had a golf match at Richmond Deer Park, but this sounds more attractive. . . . What? Very good. I'll meet you there."

And so it came about that at the hour of three, Mailey, Lord Roxton and Malone found themselves seated round the fire in the comfortable drawing-room of the barrister. His wife, a sweet and beautiful woman, who was his helpmate in his spiritual as well as in his material life, was there to welcome them.

"Now, dear, you are not on in this act," said Mailey. "You will retire discreetly into the wings. Don't worry if you hear a row."

"But I do worry, dear. You'll get hurt."

Mailey laughed.

"I think your furniture may possibly get hurt. You have nothing else to fear, dear. And it's all for the good of the Cause. That always settles it," he explained, as his wife reluctantly left the room. "I really think she would go to the stake for the Cause. Her great, loving, womanly heart knows what it would mean for this grey earth if people could get away from the shadow of death, and realize the great happiness that is to come. By Jove! she is an inspiration to me. . . . Well," he went on with a laugh, "I must not get on to that subject. We have something very different to think of—something as hideous and vile as she is beautiful and good. It concerns Tom Linden's brother."

"I've heard of the fellow," said Malone. "I used to box a bit and I am still a member of the N.S.C. Silas Linden was very nearly champion in the Welters."

"That's the man. He is out of a job and thought he would take up mediumship. Naturally I and other Spiritualists took him seriously, for we all love his brother, and these powers often run in families, so that his claim seemed reasonable. So we gave him a trial last night."

"Well, what happened?"

" I suspected the fellow from the first. You understand that it is hardly possible for a medium to deceive an experienced Spiritualist. When there is deception it is at the expense of outsiders. I watched him carefully from the first, and I seated myself near the cabinet. Presently he emerged clad in white. I broke the contact by prearrangement with my wife who sat next me, and I felt him as he passed me. He was, of course, in white. I had a pair of scissors in my pocket and snipped off a bit from the edge."

Mailey drew a triangular piece of linen from his pocket.

" There it is, you see. Very ordinary linen. I have no doubt the fellow was wearing his night-gown."

" Why did you not have a show-up at once ?" asked Lord Roxton.

" There were several ladies there, and I was the only really able-bodied man in the room."

" Well, what do you propose ?"

" I have appointed that he come here at three-thirty. He is due now. Unless he has noticed the small cut in his linen, I don't think he has any suspicion why I want him."

" What will you do ?"

" Well, that depends on him. We have to stop him at any cost. That is the way our Cause gets bemired. Some villain who knows nothing about it comes into it for money and so the labours of the honest mediums get discounted. The public very naturally brackets them all together. With your help I can talk to this fellow on equal terms which I certainly could not do if I were alone. By Jove, here he is !"

There was a heavy step outside. The door was opened and Silas Linden, fake medium and ex-prize-fighter, walked in. His small, piggy grey eyes under their shaggy brows looked round with suspicion at the three men. Then he forced a smile and nodded to Mailey.

" Good day, Mr. Mailey. We had a good evening last night, had we not ?"

" Sit down, Linden," said Mailey, indicating a chair. " It's about last night that I want to talk to you. You cheated us."

Silas Linden's heavy face flushed red with anger.

" What's that ?" he cried, sharply.

" You cheated us. You dressed up and pretended to be a spirit."

" You are a damned liar !" cried Linden. " I did nothing of the sort."

Mailey took the rag of linen from his pocket and spread it on his knee.

" What about that ?" he asked.

" Well, what about it ?"

" It was cut out of the white gown you wore. I cut it out myself as you stood in front of me. If you examine the gown you will find the place. It's no use, Linden. The game is up. You can't deny it."

For a moment the man was completely taken aback. Then he burst into a stream of horrible profanity.

" What's the game ?" he cried, glaring round him. " Do you think I am easy and that you can play me for a sucker ? Is it a frame-up, or what ? You've chose the wrong man for a try-on of that sort."

" There is no use being noisy or violent, Linden," said Mailey quietly, " I could bring you up in the police court to-morrow. I don't want any public scandal, for your brother's sake. But you don't leave this room until you have signed a paper that I have here on my desk."

" Oh, I don't, don't I ? Who will stop me ?"

" We will."

The three men were between him and the door.

" You will ! Well, try that !" He stood before them with rage in his eyes and his great hands knotted. " Will you get out of the way ?"

They did not answer, but they all three gave the fighting snarl which is perhaps the oldest of all human expressions. The next instant Linden was upon them, his fists flashing out with terrific force. Mailey, who had boxed in his youth, stopped one blow, but the next beat in his guard and he fell with a crash against the door. Lord Roxton was hurled to one side, but Malone, with a footballer's instinct, ducked his head and caught the prize-fighter round the knees. If a man is too good for you on his feet, then put him on his back, for he cannot be scientific there. Over went Linden, crashing through an armchair before he reached the ground. He staggered to one knee and got in a short jolt to the chin, but Malone had him down again and Roxton's bony hand had closed upon his throat. Silas Linden had a yellow streak in him and he was cowed.

"Let up!" he cried. "That's enough!"

He lay now spreadeagled upon his back. Malone and Roxton were bending over him. Mailey had gathered himself together, pale and shaken after his fall.

"I'm all right!" he cried, in answer to a feminine voice at the other side of the door. "No, not yet, dear, but we shall soon be ready for you. Now, Linden, there's no need for you to get up, for you can talk very nicely where you are. You've got to sign this paper before you leave the room."

"What is the paper?" croaked Linden, as Roxton's grip upon his throat relaxed.

"I'll read it to you."

Mailey took it from the desk and read aloud.

"'I, Silas Linden, hereby admit that I have acted as a rogue and a scoundrel by simulating to be a spirit, and I swear that I will never again in my life pretend to be a medium. Should I break this oath, then this signed confession may be used for my conviction in the police court.'

"Will you sign that?"

"No, I am damned if I will!"

"Shall I give him another squeeze?" asked Lord Roxton. "Perhaps I could choke some sense into him—what!"

"Not at all," said Mailey. "I think that his case now would do good in the police court, for it would show the public that we are determined to keep our house clean. I'll give you one minute for consideration, Linden, and then I ring up the police."

But it did not take a minute for the impostor to make up his mind.

167

" All right," said he in a sulky voice, " I'll sign."

He was allowed to rise with a warning that if he played any tricks he would not get off so lightly the second time. But there was no kick left in him and he scrawled a big, coarse " Silas Linden " at the bottom of the paper without a word. The three men signed as witnesses.

" Now, get out !" said Mailey, sharply. " Find some honest trade in future and leave sacred things alone !"

" Keep your damned cant to yourself !" Linden answered, and so departed, grumbling and swearing, into the outer darkness from which he had come. He had hardly passed before Mrs. Mailey had rushed into the room to reassure herself as to her husband. Once satisfied as to this she mourned over her broken chair, for like all good women she took a personal pride and joy in every detail of her little *ménage.*

" Never mind, dear. It's a cheap price to pay in order to get that blackguard out of the movement. Don't go away, you fellows. I want to talk to you."

" And tea is just coming in."

" Perhaps something stronger would be better," said Mailey, and indeed, all three were rather exhausted, for it was sharp while it lasted. Roxton, who had enjoyed the whole thing immensely, was full of vitality, but Malone was shaken and Mailey had narrowly escaped serious injury from that ponderous blow.

" I have heard," said Mailey, as they all settled down round the fire, " that this blackguard has sweated money out of poor Tom Linden for years. It was a form of black-mail, for he was quite capable of denouncing him. By Jove !" he cried, with sudden inspiration, " that would account for the police raid. Why should they pick Linden out of all the mediums in London ? I remember now that Tom told me the fellow had asked to be taught to be a medium, and that he had refused to teach him."

" Could he teach him ?" asked Malone.

Mailey was thoughtful over this question. " Well, per-haps he could," he said at last. " But Silas Linden as a false medium would be very much less dangerous than Silas Linden as a true medium."

"I don't follow you."

"Mediumship can be developed," said Mrs. Mailey. "One might almost say it was catching."

"That was what the laying-on of hands meant in the early Church," Mailey explained. "It was the conferring of thaumaturgic powers. We can't do it now as rapidly as that. But if a man or woman sits with the desire of development, and especially if that sitting is in the presence of a real medium, the chance is that powers will come."

"But why do you say that would be worse than false mediumship?"

"Because it could be used for evil. I assure you, Malone, that the talk of black magic and of evil entities is not an invention of the enemy. Such things do happen and centre round the wicked medium. You can get down into a region which is akin to the popular idea of witchcraft, It is dishonest to deny it."

"Like attracts like," explained Mrs. Mailey, who was quite as capable an exponent as her husband. "You get what you deserve. If you sit with wicked people you get wicked visitors."

"Then there *is* a dangerous side to it?"

"Do you know anything on earth which has not a dangerous side if it is mishandled and exaggerated? This dangerous side exists quite apart from orthodox Spiritualism, and our knowledge is the surest way to counteract it. I believe that the witchcraft of the Middle Ages was a very real thing, and that the best way to meet such practices is to cultivate the higher powers of the spirit. To leave the thing entirely alone is to abandon the field to the forces of evil."

Lord Roxton interposed in an unexpected way.

"When I was in Paris last year," said he, "there was a fellah called La Paix who dabbled in the black magic business. He held circles and the like. What I mean, there was no great harm in the thing, but it wasn't what you would call very spiritual, either."

"It's a side that I as a journalist would like to see something of, if I am to report impartially upon the subject," said Malone.

"Quite right!" Mailey agreed. "We want all the cards on the table."

"Well, young fellah, if you would give me a week of your time and come to Paris, I'll introduce you to La Paix," said Roxton.

"It is a curious thing, but I also had a Paris visit in my mind for our friend here," said Mailey. "I have been asked over by Dr. Maupuis of the Institut Métapsychique to see some of the experiments which he is conducting upon a Galician medium. It is really the religious side of this matter which interests me, and that is conspicuously wanting in the minds of these scientific men of the Continent; but for accurate, careful examination of the psychic facts they are ahead of anyone except poor Crawford of Belfast, who stood in a class by himself. I promised Maupuis to run across and he has certainly been having some wonderful—in some respects, some rather alarming results."

"Why alarming?"

"Well, his materializations lately have not been human at all. That is confirmed by photographs. I won't say more, for it is best that, if you go, you should approach it with an open mind."

"I shall certainly go," said Malone. "I am sure my chief would wish it."

Tea had arrived to interrupt the conversation in the irritating way that our bodily needs intrude upon our higher pursuits. But Malone was too keen to be thrown off his scent.

"You speak of these evil forces. Have you ever come in contact with them?"

Mailey looked at his wife and smiled.

"Continually," he said. "It is part of our job. We specialize on it."

"I understood that when there was an intrusion of that kind you drove it away."

" Not necessarily. If we can help any lower spirit we do so, and we can only do it by encouraging it to tell us its troubles. Most of them are not wicked. They are poor, ignorant, stunted creatures who are suffering the effects of the narrow and false views which they have learned in this world. We try to help them—and we do."

" How do you know that you do ?"

" Because they report to us afterwards and register their progress. Such methods are often used by our people. They are called ' rescue circles '."

" I have heard of rescue circles. Where could I attend one ? This thing attracts me more and more. Fresh gulfs seem always opening. I would take it as a great favour if you would help me to see this fresh side of it."

Mailey became thoughtful.

" We don't want to make a spectacle of these poor creatures. On the other hand, though we can hardly claim you yet as a Spiritualist, you have treated the subject with some understanding and sympathy." He looked enquiringly at his wife, who smiled and nodded.

" Ah, you have permission. Well then, you must know that we run our own little rescue circle, and that at five o'clock to-day we have our weekly sitting. Mr. Terbane is our medium. We don't usually have anyone else except Mr. Charles Mason, the clergyman. But if you both care to have the experience, we shall be very happy if you will stay. Terbane should be here immediately after tea. He is a railway-porter, you know, so his time is not his own. Yes, psychic power in its varied manifestations is found in humble quarters, but surely that has been its main characteristic from the beginning—fishermen, carpenters, tent-makers, camel drivers, these were the prophets of old. At this moment some of the highest psychic gifts in England lie in a miner, a cotton operative, a railway-porter, a barge-man and a charwoman. Thus does history repeat itself, and that foolish beak, with Tom Linden before him, was but Felix judging Paul. The old wheel goes round."

10. *De Profundis*

THEY were still having tea when Mr. Charles Mason was ushered in. Nothing draws people together into such intimate soul-to-soul relationship as psychic quest, and thus it was that Roxton and Malone, who had only known him in the one episode, felt more near to this man than to others with whom they had associated for years. This close vital comradeship is one of the outstanding features of such communion. When his loosely-built, straggling, lean clerical figure appeared, with that gaunt, worn face illuminated by its human grin and dignified by its earnest eyes, through the doorway, they both felt as if an old friend had entered. His own greeting was equally cordial.

" Still exploring !" he cried, as he shook them by the hand. " We will hope your new experiences will not be so nerve-racking as our last."

" By Jove, padre !" said Roxton. " I've worn out the brim of my hat taking it off to you since then."

" Why, what did he do ?" asked Mrs. Mailey.

" No, no !" cried Mason. " I tried in my poor way to guide a darkened soul. Let us leave it at that. But that is exactly what we are here for now, and what these dear people do every week of their lives. It was from Mr. Mailey here that I learned how to attempt it."

" Well, certainly we have plenty of practice," said Mailey. " You have seen enough of it, Mason, to know that."

" But I can't get the focus of this at all !" cried Malone. " Could you clear my mind a little on the point ? I accept, for the moment, your hypothesis that we are surrounded by material earth-bound spirits who find themselves under strange conditions which they don't understand, and who want counsel and guidance. That more or less expresses it, does it not ?"

The Maileys both nodded their agreement.

"Well, their dead friends and relatives are presumably on the other side and cognizant of their benighted condition. They know the truth. Could they not minister to the wants of these afflicted ones far better than we can?"

"It is a most natural question," Mailey answered. "Of course we put that objection to them and we can only accept their answer. They appear to be actually anchored to the surface of this earth, too heavy and gross to rise. The others are, presumably, on a spiritual level and far separated from them. They explain that they are much nearer to us and that they are cognizant of us, but not of anything higher. Therefore it is we who can reach them best."

"There was one poor dear dark soul——"

"My wife loves everybody and everything," Mailey explained. "She is capable of talking of the poor dear devil."

"Well, surely they are to be pitied and loved!" cried the lady. "This poor fellow was nursed along by us, week by week. He had really come from the depths. Then one day he cried in rapture, 'My mother has come! My mother is here!' We naturally said, 'But why did she not come before?' 'How could she', said he, 'when I was in so dark a place that she could not see me?'"

"That's very well," said Malone, "but so far as I can follow your methods it is some guide or control or higher spirit who regulates the whole matter and brings the sufferer to you. If he can be cognizant, one would think other higher spirits could also be."

"No, for it is his particular mission." said Mailey. "To show how marked the divisions are I can remember one occasion when we had a dark soul here. Our own people came through and did not know he was there until we called their attention to it. When we said to the dark soul, 'Don't you see our friends beside you?' he answered, 'I can see a light but nothing else'."

At this point the conversation was interrupted by the arrival of Mr. John Terbane from Victoria Station, where

173

his mundane duties lay. He was dressed now in civil garb and appeared as a pale, sad-faced, clean-shaven, plump-featured man with dreamy, thoughtful eyes, but no other indication of the remarkable uses to which he was put.

" Have you my record ?" was his first question.

Mrs. Mailey, smiling, handed him an envelope. " We kept it all ready for you but you can read it at home. You see," she explained, " poor Mr. Terbane is in trance and knows nothing of the wonderful work of which he is the instrument, so after each sitting my husband and I draw up an account for him."

" Very much astonished I am when I read it," said Terbane.

" And very proud, I should think," added Mason.

" Well, I don't know about that," Terbane answered humbly. " I don't see that the tool need to be proud because the worker happens to use it. Yet it is a privilege, of course."

" Good old Terbane !" said Mailey, laying his hand affectionately on the railwayman's shoulder. " The better the medium the more unselfish. That is my experience. The whole conception of a medium is one who gives himself up for the use of others, and that is incompatible with selfishness. Well, I suppose we had better get to work or Mr. Chang will scold us."

" Who is he ?" asked Malone.

" Oh, you will soon make the acquaintance of Mr. Chang! We need not sit round the table. A semi-circle round the fire does very well. Lights half-down. That is all right. You'll make yourself comfortable, Terbane. Snuggle among the cushions."

The medium was in the corner of a comfortable sofa, and had fallen at once into a doze. Both Mailey and Malone sat with notebooks upon their knees awaiting developments.

They were not long in coming. Terbane suddenly sat up, his dreamy self transformed into a very alert and masterful individuality. A subtle change had passed over his face. An ambiguous smile fluttered upon his lips, his eyes

- - -

174

seemed more oblique and less open, his face projected. The two hands were thrust into the sleeves of his blue lounge jacket.

" Good evening," said he, speaking crisply and in short staccato sentences. " New faces ! Who these ?"

" Good evening, Chang," said the master of the house. " You know Mr. Mason. This is Mr. Malone who studies our subject. This is Lord Roxton who has helped me to-day."

As each name was mentioned, Terbane made a sweeping, Oriental gesture of greeting, bringing his hand down from his forehead. His whole bearing was superbly dignified and very different from the humble little man who had sat down a few minutes before.

" Lord Roxton !" he repeated. " An English milord ! I knew Lord—Lord Macart——— No—I—I cannot say it. Alas ! I called him ' foreign devil ' then. Chang, too, had much to learn."

" He is speaking of Lord Macartney. That would be over a hundred years ago. Chang was a great living philosopher then," Mailey explained.

" Not lose time !" cried the control. " Much to do to-day. Crowd waiting. Some new, some old. I gather strange folk in my net. Now I go." He sank back among the cushions.

A minute elapsed, then he suddenly sat up.

" I want to thank you," he said, speaking perfect English. " I came two weeks ago. I have thought over all you said. The path is lighter."

" Were you the spirit who did not believe in God ?"

" Yes, yes ! I said so in my anger. I was so weary— so weary. Oh, the time, the endless time, the grey mist, the heavy weight of remorse ! Hopeless ! Hopeless ! And you brought me comfort, you and this great Chinese spirit. You gave me the first kind words I have had since I died."

" When was it that you died ?"

" Oh ! It seems an eternity. We do not measure as you do. It is a long, horrible dream without change or break."

175

" Who was king in England ?"

" Victoria was queen. I had attuned my mind to matter and so it clung to matter. I did not believe in a future life. Now I know that I was all wrong, but I could not adapt my mind to new conditions."

" Is it bad where you are ?"

" It is all—all grey. That is the awful part of it. One's surroundings are so horrible."

" But there are many more. You are not alone."

" No, but they know no more than I. They, too, scoff and doubt and are miserable."

" You will soon get out."

" For God's sake, help me to do so !"

" Poor soul !" said Mrs. Mailey in her sweet, caressing voice, a voice which could bring every animal to her side. " You have suffered much. But do not think of yourself. Think of these others. Try to bring one of them up and so you will best help yourself."

." Thank you, lady, I will. There is one here whom I brought. He has heard you. We will go on together. Perhaps some day we may find the light."

" Do you like to be prayed for ?"

" Yes, yes, indeed I do !"

" I will pray for you," said Mason. " Could you say the ' Our Father ' now ?" He uttered the old universal prayer, but before he had finished Terbane had collapsed again among the cushions. He sat up again as Chang.

" He come on well," said the control. " He give up time for others who wait. That is good. Now I have hard case. Ow !"

He gave a comical cry of disapprobation and sank back.

Next moment he was up, his face long and solemn, his hands palm to palm.

" What is this ?" he asked in a precise and affected voice. " I am at a loss to know what right this Chinese person has to summon me here. Perhaps you can enlighten me."

" It is that we may perhaps help you."

" When I desire help, sir, I ask for it. At present I do

not desire it. The whole proceeding seems to me to be a very great liberty. So far as this Chinaman can explain it, I gather that I am the involuntary spectator of some sort of religious service."

" We are a spiritualistic circle."

" A most pernicious sect. A most blasphemous proceeding. As a humble parish priest I protest against such desecrations."

" You are held back, friend, by those narrow views. It is you who suffer. We want to relieve you."

" Suffer ? What do you mean, sir ?"

" You realize that you have passed over ?"

" You are talking nonsense !"

" Do you realize that you are dead ?"

" How can I be dead when I am talking to you ?"

" Because you are using this man's body."

" I have certainly wandered into an asylum."

" Yes, an asylum for bad cases. I fear you are one of them. Are you happy where you are ?"

" Happy ? No, sir. My present surroundings are perfectly inexplicable to me."

" Have you any recollection of being ill ?"

" I was very ill indeed."

" So ill that you died."

" You are certainly out of your senses."

" How do you know you are not dead ?"

" Sir, I must give you some religious instruction. When one dies and has led an honourable life, one assumes a glorified body and one associates with the angels. I am now in exactly the same body as in life, and I am in a very dull, drab place. Such companions as I have are not such as I have been accustomed to associate with in life, and certainly no one could describe them as angels. Therefore your absurd conjecture may be dismissed."

" Do not continue to deceive yourself. We wish to help you. You can never progress until you realize your position."

" Really, you try my patience too far. Have I not said——?"

The medium fell back among the cushions. An instant later the Chinese control, with his whimsical smile and his hands tucked away in his sleeves, was talking to the circle.

"He good man—fool man—learn sense soon. Bring him again. Not waste more time. Oh, my God! My God! Help! Mercy! Help!"

He had fallen full length upon the sofa, face upwards, and his cries were so terrible that the little audience all sprang to their feet. "A saw! A saw! Fetch a saw!" yelled the medium. His voice sank into a moan.

Even Mailey was agitated. The rest were horrified.

"Someone has obsessed him. I can't understand it. It may be some strong evil entity."

"Shall I speak to him?" asked Mason.

"Wait a moment! Let it develop. We shall soon see."

The medium writhed in agony. "Oh, my God! Why don't you fetch a saw!" he cried. "It's here across my breast-bone. It is cracking! I feel it! Hawkin! Hawkin! Pull me from under! Hawkin! Push up the beam! No, no, that's worse! And it's on fire! Oh, horrible! Horrible!"

His cries were blood-curdling. They were all chilled with horror. Then in an instant the Chinaman was blinking at them with his slanting eyes.

"What you think of that, Mister Mailey?"

"It was terrible, Chang. What was it?"

"It was for him," nodding towards Malone. "He want newspaper story, I give him newspaper story. He will understand. No time 'splain now. Too many waiting. Sailor man come next. Here he come!"

The Chinaman was gone, and a jovial, puzzled grin passed over the face of the medium. He scratched his head.

"Well, damn me," said he. "I never thought I would take orders from a Chink, but he says ' hist!' and by crums you've got to hist and no back talk either. Well, here I am. What did you want?"

"We wanted nothing."

"Well, the Chink seemed to think you did, for he slung me in here."

178

" It was you that wanted something. You wanted know-ledge."

" Well, I've lost my bearings, that's true. I know I am dead 'cause I've seen the gunnery lootenant, and he was blown to bits before my eyes. If he's dead I'm dead and all the rest of us, for we are over to the last man. But we've got the laugh on our sky-pilot, for he's as puzzled as the rest of us. Damned poor pilot, I call him. We're all taking our own soundings now."

" What was your ship ?"

" The *Monmouth*."

" She that went down in battle with the German ?"

" That's right. South American waters. It was clean hell. Yes, it was hell." There was a world of emotion in his voice. " Well," he added more cheerfully, " I've heard our mates got level with them later. That is so, sir, is it not ?"

" Yes, they all went to the bottom."

" We've seen nothing of them this side. Just as well, maybe. We don't forget nothing."

" But you must," said Mailey. " That's what is the matter with you. That is why the Chinese control brought you through. We are here to teach you. Carry our message to your mates."

" Bless your heart, sir, they are all here behind me."

" Well, then, I tell you and them that the time for hard thoughts and worldly strife is over. Your faces are to be turned forward, not back. Leave this earth which still holds you by the ties of thought and let all your desire be to make yourself unselfish and worthy of a higher, more peaceful, more beautiful life. Can you understand ?"

" I hear you, sir. So do they. We want steering, sir, for, indeed, we've had wrong instructions, and we never expected to find ourselves cast away like this. We had heard of heaven and we had heard of hell, but this don't seem to fit in with either. But this Chinese gent. says time is up, and we can report again next week. I thank you, sir, for self and company. I'll come again."

There was silence.

"What an incredible conversation!" gasped Malone.

"If I were to put down that man's sailor talk and slang as emanating from a world of spirits, what would the public say?"

Mailey shrugged his shoulders.

"Does it matter what the public says? I started as a fairly sensitive person, and now a tank takes as much notice of small shot as I do of newspaper attacks. They honestly don't even interest me. Let us just stick fast to truth as near as we can get it, and leave all else to find its own level."

"I don't pretend to know much of these things," said Roxton, "but what strikes me most is that these folk are very decent ordinary people. What? Why should they be wanderin' about in the dark, and hauled up here by this Chinaman when they've done no partic'lar harm in life?"

"It is the strong earth tie and the absence of any spiritual nexus in each case," Mailey explained. "Here is a clergyman with his mind entangled with formulas and ritual. Here is a materialist who has deliberately attuned himself to matter. Here is a seaman brooding over revengeful thoughts. They are there by the million million."

"Where?" asked Malone.

"Here," Mailey answered. "Actually on the surface of the earth. Well, you saw it for yourself, I understand, when you went down to Dorsetshire. That was on the surface, was it not? That was a very gross case, and that made it more visible and obvious, but it did not change the general law. I believe that the whole globe is infested with the earth-bound, and that when a great cleansing comes, as is prophesied, it will be for their benefit as much as for that of the living."

Malone thought of the strange visionary Miromar and his speech at the Spiritualistic Church on the first night of his quest.

"Do you, then, believe in some impending event?" he asked.

Mailey smiled. "That is rather a large subject to open

180

up," he said. " I believe—— But here is Mr. Chang again !"

The control joined in the conversation.

" I heard you. I sit and listen," said he. " You speak now of what is to come. Let it be ! Let it be ! The Time is not yet. You will be told when it is good that you know. Remember this. All is best. Whatever come all is best. God makes no mistakes. Now others here who wish your help, I leave you."

Several spirits came through in quick succession. One was an architect who said that he had lived at Bristol. He had not been an evil man, but had simply banished all thoughts of the future. Now he was in the dark and needed guidance. Another had lived in Birmingham. He was an educated man but a materialist. He refused to accept the assurances of Mailey, and was by no means convinced that he was really dead. Then came a very noisy and violent man of a crudely-religious and narrow, intolerant type, who spoke repeatedly of " the blood ".

" What is this ribald nonsense ?" he asked several times.

" It is not nonsense. We are here to help," said Mailey.

" Who wants to be helped by the devil ?"

" Is it likely that the devil would wish to help souls in trouble ?"

" It is part of his deceit. I tell you it is of the devil ! Be warned ! I will take no further part in it."

The placid, whimsical Chinaman was back like a flash. " Good man. Foolish man," he repeated once more. " Plenty time. He learn better some day. Now I bring bad case—very bad case. Ow !"

He reclined his head in the cushion and did not raise it as the voice, a feminine voice, broke out:

" Janet ! Janet !"

There was a pause.

" Janet, I say ! Where is the morning tea ? Janet ! This is intolerable ! I have called you again and again ! Janet !" The figure sat up, blinking and rubbing his eyes.

" What is this ?" cried the voice. " Who are you ?

What right have you here? Are you aware that this is my house?"

" No, friend, this is my house."

" Your house! How can it be your house when this is my bedroom? Go away this moment!"

" No, friend. You do not understand your position."

" I will have you put out. What insolence! Janet! Janet! Will no one look after me this morning?"

" Look round you, lady. Is this your bedroom?"

Terbane looked round with a wild stare.

" It is a room I never saw in my life. Where am I? What is the meaning of it? You look like a kind lady. Tell me, for God's sake, what is the meaning of it? Oh, I am so terrified, so terrified! Where are John and Janet?"

" What do you last remember?"

" I remember speaking severely to Janet. She is my maid, you know. She has become so very careless. Yes, I was very angry with her. I was so angry that I was ill. I went to bed feeling very ill. They told me that I should not get excited. How can one help getting excited? Yes, I remember being breathless. That was after the light was out. I tried to call Janet. But why should I be in another room?"

" You passed over in the night."

" Passed over? Do you mean I died?"

" Yes, lady, you died."

There was a long silence. Then there came a shrill scream. " No, no, no! It is a dream! A nightmare! Wake me! Wake me! How can I be dead? I was not ready to die? I never thought of such a thing. If I am dead, why am I not in heaven or hell? What is this room? This room is a real room."

" Yes, lady, you have been brought here and allowed to use this man's body——"

" A man?" She convulsively felt the coat and passed her hand over the face. " Yes, it is a man. Oh, I am dead, I am dead! What shall I do?"

" You are here that we may explain to you. You have

182

been, I judge, a worldly woman—a society woman. You have lived always for material things."

" I went to church. I was at St. Saviour's every Sunday."

" That is nothing. It is the inner daily life that counts. You were material. Now you are held down to the world. When you leave this man's body you will be in your own body once more and in your old surroundings. But no one will see you. You will remain there unable to show yourself. Your body of flesh will be buried. You will still persist, the same as ever."

" What am I to do ? Oh, what can I do ?"

" You will take what comes in a good spirit and understand that it is for your cleansing. We only clear ourselves of matter by suffering. All will be well. We will pray for you."

" Oh, do ! I need it so ! Oh my God ! . . ." The voice trailed away.

" Bad case," said the Chinaman, sitting up. " Selfish woman ! Bad woman ! Live for pleasure. Hard on those around her. She have much to suffer. But you put her feet on the path. Now my medium tired. Plenty waiting, but no more to-day."

" Have we done good, Chang ?"

" Plenty good. Plenty good."

" Where are all these people, Chang ?"

" I tell you before."

" Yes, but I want these gentlemen to hear."

" Seven spheres round the world, heaviest below, lightest above. First sphere is on the earth. These people belong to that sphere. Each sphere is separate from the other. Therefore it is easier for you to speak with these people than for those in any other sphere."

" And easier for them to speak to us ?"

" Yes. That why you should be plenty careful when you do not know to whom you talk. Try the spirits."

" What sphere do you belong to, Chang ?"

" I come from Number Four sphere."

" Which is the first really happy sphere ?"

"Number Three. Summerland. Bible book called it the third heaven. Plenty sense in Bible book, but people do not understand."

"And the seventh heaven ?"

"Ah! That is where the Christs are. All come there at last—you, me, everybody."

"And after that ?"

"Too much question, Mr. Mailey. Poor old Chang not know so much as that. Now good-bye! God bless you! I go."

It was the end of the sitting of the rescue circle. A few minutes later Terbane was sitting up smiling and alert, but with no apparent recollection of anything which had occurred. He was pressed for time and lived afar, so that he had to make his departure, unpaid save by the blessing of those who he had helped. Modest little unvenal man, where will he stand when we all find our real places in the order of creation upon the further side ?

The circle did not break up at once. The visitors wanted to talk, and the Maileys to listen.

"What I mean," said Roxton, "it's doosed interestin' and all that, but there is a sort of variety-show element in it. What! Difficult to be sure it's really real, if you take what I mean."

"That is what I feel also," said Malone. "Of course on its face value it is simply unspeakable. It is a thing so great that all ordinary happenings become commonplace. That I grant. But the human mind is very strange. I've read that case Moreton Prince examined, and Miss Beauchamp and the rest; also the results of Charcot, the great Nancy hypnotic school. They could turn a man into anything. The mind seems to be like a rope which can be unravelled into its various threads. Then each thread is a different personality which may take dramatic form, and act and speak as such. That man is honest, and he could not normally produce these effects. But how do we know that he is not self-hypnotized, and that under those conditions one strand of him becomes Mr. Chang and another becomes a sailor and another a society lady, and so forth ?"

Mailey laughed. "Every man his own Cinquevalli," said he, "but it is a rational objection and has to be met."

"We have traced some of the cases," said Mrs. Mailey. "There is not a doubt of it—names, addresses, everything."

"Well, then, we have to consider the question of Terbane's normal knowledge. How can you possibly know what he has learned ? I should think a railway-porter is particularly able to pick up such information."

"You have seen one sitting," Mailey answered. "If you had been present at as many as we and noted the cumulative effect of the evidence you would not be sceptical."

"That is very possible," Malone answered. "And I daresay my doubts are very annoying to you. And yet one is bound to be brutally honest in a case like this. Anyhow, whatever the ultimate cause, I have seldom spent so thrilling an hour. Heavens ! If it only *is* true, and if you had a thousand circles instead of one, what regeneration would result ?"

"That will come," said Mailey in his patient, determined fashion. "We shall live to see it. I am sorry the thing has not forced conviction upon you. However, you must come again."

But it so chanced that a further experience became unnecessary. Conviction came in a full flood and in a strange fashion that very evening. Malone had hardly got back to the office, and was seated at his desk drawing up some sort of account from his notes of all that had happened in the afternoon, when Mailey burst into the room, his yellow beard bristling with excitement. He was waving an *Evening News* in his hand. Without a word he seated himself beside Malone and turned the paper over. Then he began to read:

ACCIDENT IN THE CITY.

This afternoon shortly after five o'clock, an old house, said to date from the fifteenth century, suddenly collapsed. It was situated between Lesser Colman Street and Elliot Square, and next door to the Veterinary Society's Headquarters. Some

. . -

185

preliminary crackings warned the occupants and most of them had time to escape. Three of them, however, James Beale, William Moorson, and a woman whose name has not been ascertained, were caught by the falling rubbish. Two of these seem to have perished at once, but the third, James Beale, was pinned down by a large beam and loudly demanded help. A saw was brought, and one of the occupants of the house, Samuel Hawkin, showed great gallantry in an attempt to free the unfortunate man. Whilst he was sawing the beam, however, a fire broke out among the débris around him, and though he persevered most manfully, and continued until he was himself badly scorched, it was impossible for him to save Beale, who probably died from suffocation. Hawkin was removed to the London Hospital, and it is reported to-night that he is in no immediate danger.

" That's that !" said Mailey, folding up the paper. " Now Mr. Thomas Didymus, I leave you to your conclusions," and the enthusiast vanished out of the office as precipitately as he had entered.

For the incidents recorded in this chapter *vide* Appendix.

11.   *Where Silas Linden Comes into His Own*

SILAS LINDEN, prize-fighter and fake-medium, had had some good days in his life—days crowded with incidents for good or evil. There was the time when he had backed Rosalind at 100 to 1 in the Oaks and had spent twenty-four hours of brutal debauchery on the strength of it. There was the day also when his favourite right upper-cut had connected in most accurate and rhythmical fashion with the protruded chin of Bull Wardell of Whitechapel, whereby Silas put himself in the way of a Lonsdale Belt and a try for the championship. But never in all his varied career had he such a day as this supreme one, so it is worth our while to follow him to the end of it. Fanatical believers have urged that it is dangerous to cross the path of spiritual things when the heart is not clean. Silas Linden's name might be added to their list of examples, but his cup of sin was full and overflowing before the judgment fell.

He emerged from the room of Algernon Mailey with every

reason to know that Lord Roxton's grip was as muscular as ever. In the excitement of the struggle he had hardly realized his injuries, but now he stood outside the door with his hand to his bruised throat and a hoarse stream of oaths pouring through it. His breast was aching also where Malone had planted his knee, and even the successful blow which had struck Mailey down had brought retribution, for it had jarred that injured hand of which he had complained to his brother. Altogether, if Silas Linden was in a most cursed temper, there was a very good reason for his mood.

"I'll get you one at a time," he growled, looking back with his angry pigs' eyes at the outer door of the flats. "You wait my lads, and see!" Then with sudden purpose he swung off down the street.

It was to the Bardsley Square Police Station that he made his way, and he found the jovial, rubicund, black-moustached Inspector Murphy seated at his desk.

"Well, what do *you* want?" asked the inspector in no very friendly voice.

"I hear you got that medium right and proper."

"Yes, we did. I learn he was your brother."

"That's neither here not there. I don't hold with such things in any man. But you got your conviction. What is there for me in it?"

"Not a shilling!"

"What? Wasn't it I that gave the information? Where would you have been if I had not given you the office?"

"If there had been a fine we might have allowed you something. We would have got something, too. Mr. Melrose sent him to gaol. There is nothing for anybody."

"So say you. I'm damned sure you and those two women got something out of it. Why the hell should I give away my own brother for the sake of the likes of you? You'll find your own bird next time."

Murphy was a choleric man with a sense of his own importance. He was not to be bearded thus in his own seat of office. He rose with a very red face.

" I'll tell you what, Silas Linden, I could find my own bird and never move out of this room. You had best get out of this quick, or you may chance to stay here longer than you like. We've had complaints of your treatment of those two children of yours, and the children's protection folk are taking an interest. Look out that we don't take an interest, too."

Silas Linden flung out of the room with his temper hotter than ever, and a couple of rum-and-waters on his way home did not help to appease him. On the contrary, he had always been a man who grew more dangerous in his cups. There were many of his trade who refused to drink with him.

Silas lived in one of a row of small brick houses named Bolton's Court, lying at the back of Tottenham Court Road. His was the end house of a cul-de-sac, with the side wall of a huge brewery beyond. These dwellings were very small, which was probably the reason why the inhabitants, both adults and children, spent most of their time in the street. Several of the elders were out now, and as Silas passed under the solitary lamp-post, they scowled at his thick-set figure, for though the morality of Bolton's Court was of no high order, it was none the less graduated and Silas was at zero. A tall Jewish woman, Rebecca Levi, thin, aquiline and fierce-eyed, lived next to the prize-fighter. She was standing at her door now, with a child holding her apron.

" Mr. Linden," she said as he passed, " them children of yours want more care than they get. Little Margery was in here to-day. That child don't get enough to eat."

" You mind your own business, curse you !" growled Silas. " I've told you before now not to push that long, sheeny beak of yours into my affairs. If you was a man I'd know better how to speak to you."

" If I was a man maybe you wouldn't dare to speak to me so. I say it's a shame, Silas Linden, the way them children is treated. If it's a police-court case, I'll know what to say."

" Oh, go to hell !" said Silas, and kicked open his own

unlatched door. A big, frowsy woman with a shock of dyed hair and some remains of a florid beauty, now long over-ripe, looked out from the sitting-room door.

" Oh, it's you, is it ?" said she.

" Who did you think it was ? The Dook of Wellington ?"

" I thought it was a mad bullock maybe got strayin' down the lane, and buttin' down our door."

" Funny, ain't you?"

" Maybe I am, but I hain't got much to be funny about. Not a shilling in the 'ouse, nor so much as a pint o' beer, and these damned children of yours for ever upsettin' me."

" What have they been a-doin' of?" asked Silas with a scowl. When this worthy pair could get no change out of each other, they usually united their forces against the children. He had entered the sitting-room and flung himself down in the wooden armchair.

" They've been seein' Number One again."

" How d'ye know that ?"

" I 'eard 'im say somethin' to 'er about it. ' Mother was there ', 'e says. Then afterwards 'e 'ad one 'o them sleepy fits."

" It's in the family."

" Yes, it is," retorted the woman. " If you 'adn't sleepy fits you'd get some work to do, like other men."

" Oh, shut it, woman ! What I mean is, that my brother Tom gets them fits, and this lad o' mine is said to be the livin' image of his uncle. So he had a trance, had he ? What did you do ?"

The woman gave an evil grin.

" I did what you did."

" What, the sealin'-wax again ?"

" Not much of it. Just enough to wake 'im. It's the only way to break 'im of it."

Silas shrugged his shoulders.

" 'Ave a care, my lass ! There is talk of the p'lice, and if they see those burns, you and I may be in the dock together."

189

" Silas Linden, you are a fool ! Can't a parent c'rect 'is own child ?"

" Yes, but it ain't *your* own child, and stepmothers has a bad name, see ? There's that Jew woman next door. She saw you when you took the clothes' rope to little Margery last washin'-day. She spoke to me about it and again to-day about the food."

" What's the matter with the food ? The greedy little bastards ! They had a 'unch of bread each when I 'ad my dinner. A bit of real starvin' would do them no 'arm, and I would 'ave less sauce."

" What, has Willie sauced you ?"

" Yes, when 'e woke up."

" After you'd dropped the hot sealin'-wax on him ?"

" Well, I did it for 'is good, didn't I ? It was to cure 'im of a bad 'abit."

" Wot did he say ?"

" Cursed me good and proper, 'e did. All about his mother—wot 'is mother would do to me. I'm dam' well sick of 'is mother !"

" Don't say too much about Amy. She was a good woman."

" So you say now, Silas Linden, but by all accounts you 'ad a queer way of showin' it when she was alive."

" Hold your jaw, woman ! I've had enough to vex me to-day without you startin' your tantrums. You're jealous of the grave. That's wot's the matter with you."

" And her brats can insult me as they like—me that 'as cared for you these five years."

" No, I didn't say that. If he insulted you, it's up to me to deal with him. Where's that strap ? Go, fetch him in !"

The woman came across and kissed him.

" I've only you, Silas."

" Oh hell ! don't muck me about. I'm not in the mood. Go and fetch Willie in. You can bring Margery also. It takes the sauce out of her also, for I think she feels it more than he does."

The woman left the room but was back, in a moment. " 'E's off again !" said she. " It fair gets on my nerves to see him. Come 'ere, Silas ! 'Ave a look !"

They went together into the back kitchen. A small fire was smouldering in the grate. Beside it, huddled up in a chair, sat a fair-haired boy of ten. His delicate face was upturned to the ceiling. His eyes were half-closed, and only the whites visible. There was a look of great peace upon his thin, spiritual features. In the corner a poor little cowed mite of a girl, a year or two younger, was gazing with sad, frightened eyes at her brother.

" Looks awful, don't 'e ?" said the woman. " Don't seem to belong to this world. I wish to God 'e'd make a move for the other. 'E don't do much good 'ere."

" Here, wake up !" cried Silas. " None of your foxin' ! Wake up ! D'ye hear ?" He shook him roughly by the shoulder, but the boy still slumbered on. The backs of his hands, which lay upon his lap, were covered with bright scarlet blotches.

" My word, you've dropped enough hot wax on him. D'you mean to tell me, Sarah, it took all that to wake him ?"

" Maybe I dropped one or two extra for luck. 'E does aggravate me so that I can 'ardly 'old myself. But you wouldn't believe 'ow little 'e can feel when 'e's like that. You can 'owl in 'is ear. It's all lost on 'im. See 'ere !"

She caught the lad by the hair and shook him violently. He groaned and shivered. Then he sank back into his serene trance.

" Say !" cried Silas, stroking his stubbled chin as he looked thoughtfully at his son, " I think there is money in this if it is handled to rights. Wot about a turn on the halls, eh ? ' The Boy Wonder or How is it Done ?' There's a name for the bills. Then folk know his uncle's name, so they will be able to take him on trust."

" I thought you was going into the business yourself."

" That's a wash-out," snarled Silas. " Don't you talk of it. It's finished."

" Been caught out already ?"

" I tell you not to talk about it, woman !" the man shouted. " I'm just in the mood to give you the hidin' of your life, so don't you get my goat, or you'll be sorry." He stepped across and pinched the boy's arm with all his force. " By Cripes, he's a wonder ! Let us see how far it will go."

He turned to the sinking fire and with the tongs he picked out a half-red ember. This he placed on the boy's head. There was a smell of burning hair, then of roasting flesh, and suddenly, with a scream of pain, the boy came back to his senses.

" Mother ! Mother !" he cried. The girl in the corner took up the cry. They were like two lambs bleating together.

" Damn your mother !" cried the woman, shaking Margery by the collar of her frail black dress. " Stop squallin', you little stinker !" She struck the child with her open hand across the face. Little Willie ran at her and kicked her shins until a blow from Silas knocked him into the corner. The brute picked up a stick and lashed the two cowering children, while they screamed for mercy, and tried to cover their little bodies from the cruel blows.

" You stop that !" cried a voice in the passage.

" It's that blasted Jewess !" said the woman. She went to the kitchen door. " What the 'ell are you doing in our 'ouse ? 'Op it, quick, or it will be the worse for you !"

" If I hear them children cry out once more, I'm off for the police."

" Get out of it ! 'Op it, I tell you !" The frowsy step-mother bore down in full sail, but the lean, lank Jewess stood her ground. Next instant they met. Mrs. Silas Linden screamed, and staggered back with blood running down her face where four nails had left as many red furrows. Silas, with an oath, pushed his wife out of the way, seized the intruder round the waist, and slung her bodily through the door. She lay in the roadway with her long gaunt limbs sprawling about like some half-slain fowl. Without rising,

192

she shook her clenched hands in the air and screamed curses at Silas, who slammed the door and left her, while neighbours ran from all sides to hear particulars of the fray. Mrs. Linden, staring through the front blind, saw with some relief that her enemy was able to rise and to limp back to her own door, whence she could be heard delivering a long shrill harangue as to her wrongs. The wrongs of a Jew are not lightly forgotten, for the race can both love and hate.

" She's all right, Silas. I thought maybe you 'ad killed 'er."

" It's what she wants, the damned canting sheeny. It's bad enough to have her in the street without her daring to set foot inside my door. I'll cut the hide off that young Willie. He's the cause of it all. Where is he ?"

" They ran up to their room. I heard them lock the door."

" A lot of good that will do them."

" I wouldn't touch 'em now, Silas. The neighbours is all up and about and we needn't ask for trouble."

" You're right !" he grumbled. " It will keep till I come back."

" Where are you goin' ?"

" Down to the 'Admiral Vernon'. There's a chance of a job as sparrin' partner to Long Davis. He goes into training on Monday and needs a man of my weight."

" Well, I'll expect you when I see you. I get too much of that pub of yours. I know what the 'Admiral Vernon' means."

" It means the only place in God's earth where I get any peace or rest," said Silas.

" A fat lot I get—or ever 'ave 'ad since I married you."

" That's right. Grouse away !" he growled. " If grousin' made a man happy, you'd be the champion."

He picked up his hat and slouched off down the street, his heavy tread resounding upon the great wooden flap which covered the cellars of the brewery.

Up in a dingy attic two little figures were seated on the

side of a wretched straw-stuffed bed, their arms enlacing each other, their cheeks touching, their tears mingling. They had to cry in silence, for any sound might remind the ogre downstairs of their existence. Now and again one would break into an uncontrollable sob, and the other would whisper, " Hush ! Hush ! Oh hush !" Then suddenly they heard the slam of the outer door and that heavy tread booming over the wooden flap. They squeezed each other in their joy. Perhaps when he came back he might kill them, but for a few short hours at least they were safe from him. As to the woman, she was spiteful and vicious, but she did not seem so deadly as the man. In a dim way they felt that he had hunted their mother into her grave and might do as much for them.

The room was dark save for the light which came through the single dirty window. It cast a bar across the floor, but all round was black shadow. Suddenly the little boy stiffened, clasped his sister with a tighter grip, and stared rigidly into the darkness.

" She's coming !" he muttered. " She's coming !"

Little Margery clung to him.

" Oh, Willie, is it mother ?"

" It is a light—a beautiful yellow light. Can you not see it, Margery ?"

But the little girl, like all the world, was without vision. To her all was darkness.

" Tell me, Willie," she whispered, in a solemn voice. She was not really frightened, for many times before had the dead mother returned in the watches of the night to comfort her stricken children.

" Yes. Yes, she is coming now. Oh, mother ! Mother !"

" What does she say, Willie ?"

" Oh, she is beautiful. She is not crying. She is smiling. It is like the picture we saw of the angel. She looks so happy. Dear, dear mother ! Now she is speaking. ' It is over ', she says. ' It is all over '. She says it again. Now she beckons with her hand. We are to follow. She has moved to the door."

" Oh, Willie, I dare not."

" Yes, yes, she nods her head. She bids us fear nothing. Now she has passed through the door. Come, Margery, come, or we shall lose her."

The two little mites crept across the room and Willie unlocked the door. The mother stood at the head of the stair beckoning them onwards. Step by step they followed her down into an empty kitchen. The woman seemed to have gone out. All was still in the house. The phantom still beckoned them on."

" We are to go out."

" Oh, Willie, we have no hats."

" We must follow, Madge. She is smiling and waving."

" Father will kill us for this."

" She shakes her head. She says we are to fear nothing. Come !"

They threw open the door and were in the street. Down the deserted court they followed the gleaming gracious presence, and through a tangle of low streets, and so out into the crowded rush of Tottenham Court Road. Once or twice amid all that blind torrent of humanity, some man or woman, blessed with the precious gift of discernment, would start and stare as if they were aware of an angel presence and of two little white-faced children who followed behind, the boy with fixed, absorbed gaze, the girl glancing ever in terror over her shoulder. Down the long street they passed, then again amid humbler dwellings, and so at last to a quiet drab line of brick houses. On the step of one the spirit had halted.

" We are to knock," said Willie.

" Oh, Willie, what shall we say ? We don't know them."

" We are to knock," he repeated, stoutly. Rat-tat ! " It's all right, Madge. She is clapping her hands and laughing."

So it was that Mrs. Tom Linden, sitting lonely in her misery and brooding over her martyr in gaol, was summoned suddenly to the door, and found two little apologetic figures outside it. A few words, a rush of woman's instinct, and her arms were round the children. These battered little skiffs, who had started their life's voyage so sadly, had found a harbour of peace where no storm should vex them more.

There were some strange happenings in Bolton's Court that night. Some folk thought they had no relation to each other. One or two thought they had. The British Law saw nothing and had nothing to say.

In the second last house, a keen, hawklike face peered from behind a window-blind into the darkened street. A shaded candle was behind that fearful face, dark as death, remorseless as the tomb. Behind Rebecca Levi stood a young man whose features showed that he sprang from the same Oriental race. For an hour—for a second hour—the woman had sat without a word, watching, watching . . . At the entrance to the court there was a hanging lamp which cast a circle of yellow light. It was on this pool of radiance that her brooding eyes were fixed.

Then suddenly she saw what she had waited for. She started and hissed out a word. The young man rushed from the room and into the street. He vanished through a side door into the brewery.

Drunken Silas Linden was coming home. He was in a gloomy, sulken state of befuddlement. A sense of injury filled his mind. He had not gained the billet he sought. His injured hand had been against him. He had hung about the bar waiting for drinks and had got some, but not enough. Now he was in a dangerous mood. Woe to the man, woman or child, who crossed his path! He thought savagely of the Jewess who lived in that darkened house. He thought savagely of all his neighbours. They would stand between him and his children, would they? He would show them. The very next morning he would take them both out into the street and strap them within an inch of their lives. That would show them all what Silas Linden thought of their opinions. Why should he not do it now? If he were to waken the neighbours up with the

196

shrieks of his children, it would show them once for all that they could not defy him with impunity. The idea pleased him. He stepped more briskly out. He was almost at his door when . . .

It was never quite clear how it was that the cellar-flap was not securely fastened that night. The jury were inclined to blame the brewery, but the coroner pointed out that Linden was a heavy man, that he might have fallen on it if he were drunk, and that all reasonable care had been taken. It was an eighteen-foot fall upon jagged stones, and his back was broken. They did not find him till next morning, for, curiously enough, his neighbour, the Jewess, never heard the sound of the accident. The doctor seemed to think that death had not come quickly. There were horrible signs that he had lingered. Down in the darkness, vomiting blood and beer, the man ended his filthy life with a filthy death.

One need not waste words or pity over the woman whom he had left. Relieved from her terrible mate, she returned to that music-hall stage from which he, by force of his virility and bull-like strength, had lured her. She tried to regain her place with:

"Hi! Hi! Hi! I'm the *dernier cri*,
The girl with the cart-wheel hat."

which was the ditty which had won her her name. But it became too painfully evident that she was anything but the *dernier cri*, and that she could never get back. Slowly she sank from big halls to small halls, from small halls to pubs, and so ever deeper and deeper, sucked into the awful silent quicksands of life which drew her down and down until that vacuous painted face and frowsy head were seen no more.

197

12. *There are Heights and there are Depths*

THE Institut Métapsychique was an imposing stone building in the Avenue Wagram with a door like a baronial castle. Here it was that the three friends presented themselves late in the evening. A footman showed them into a reception-room where they were presently welcomed by Dr. Maupuis in person. The famous authority on psychic science was a short, broad man with a large head, a clean-shaven face, and an expression in which worldly wisdom and kindly altruism were blended. His conversation was in French with Mailey and Roxton, who both spoke the language well, but he had to fall back upon broken English with Malone, who could only utter still more broken French in reply. He expressed his pleasure at their visit, as only a graceful Frenchman can, said a few words as to the wonderful qualities of Panbek, the Galician medium, and finally led the way downstairs to the room in which the experiments were to be conducted. His air of vivid intelligence and penetrating sagacity had already shown the strangers how preposterous were those theories which tried to explain away his wonderful results by the supposition that he was a man who was the easy victim of impostors.

Descending a winding stair they found themselves in a large chamber which looked at first glance like a chemical laboratory, for shelves full of bottles, retorts, test-tubes, scales and other apparatus lined the walls. It was more elegantly furnished, however, than a mere workshop, and a large massive oak table occupied the centre of the room with a fringe of comfortable chairs. At one end of the room was a large portrait of Professor Crookes, which was flanked by a second of Lombroso, while between them was a remarkable picture of one of Eusapia Palladino's séances. Round the table there was gathered a group of men who were talking in low tones, too much absorbed in their own conversation to take much notice of the newcomers.

" Three of these are distinguished visitors like yourselves,"
·said Dr. Maupuis. " Two others are my laboratory assist-
ants, Dr. Sauvage and Dr. Buisson. The others are Parisians
of note. The Press is represented to-day by Mr. Forte, sub-
editor of the *Matin*. The tall, dark man who looks like a
retired general you probably know. . . . Not? That is
Professor Charles Richet, our honoured doyen, who has
shown great courage in this matter, though he has not
quite reached the same conclusions as you, Monsieur Mailey.
But that also may come. You must remember that we have
to show policy, and that the less we mix this with religion,
the less trouble we shall have with the Church, which is
still very powerful in this country. The distinguished-
looking man with the high forehead is the Count de Gram-
mont. The gentleman with the head of a Jupiter and the
white beard is Flammarion, the astronomer. Now, gentlemen," he added, in a louder voice, " if you will take your
places we shall get to work."

They sat at random round the long table, the three
Britons keeping together. At one end a large photographic
camera was reared aloft. Two zinc buckets also occupied
a prominent position upon a side table. The door was
locked and the key given to Professor Richet. Dr. Maupuis
sat at one end of the table with a small middle-aged man,
moustached, bald-headed and intelligent, upon his right.

" Some of you have not met Monsieur Panbek," said the
doctor. " Permit me to present him to you. Monsieur
Panbek, gentlemen, has placed his remarkable powers at
our disposal for scientific investigation, and we all owe him
a debt of gratitude. He is now in his forty-seventh year,
a man of normal health, of a neuro-arthritic disposition.
Some hyper-excitability of his nervous system is indicated,
and his reflexes are exaggerated, but his blood-pressure
is normal. The pulse is now at seventy-two, but rises to
one hundred under trance conditions. There are zones of
marked hyper-æsthesia on his limbs. His visual field and
pupillary reaction is normal. I do not know that there is
anything to add."

" I might say," remarked Professor Richet, " that the hyper-sensibility is moral as well as physical. Panbek is impressionable and full of emotion, with the temperament of the poet and all those little weaknesses, if we may call them so, which the poet pays as a ransom for his gifts. A great medium is a great artist and is to be judged by the same standards."

" He seems to me, gentlemen, to be preparing you for the worst," said the medium with a charming smile, while the company laughed in sympathy.

" We are sitting in the hopes that some remarkable materializations which we have recently had may be renewed in such a form that we may get a permanent record of them." Dr. Maupuis was talking in his dry, unemotional voice. " These materializations have taken very unexpected forms of late, and I would beg the company to repress any feelings of fear, however strange these forms may be, as a calm and judicial atmosphere is most necessary. We shall now turn out the white light and begin with the lowest degree of red light until the conditions will admit of further illumination."

The lamps were controlled from Dr. Maupuis' seat at the table. For a moment they were plunged in utter darkness. Then a dull red glow came in the corner, enough to show the dim outlines of the men round the table. There was no music and no religious atmosphere of any sort. The company conversed in whispers.

" This is different to your English procedure," said Malone.

" Very," Mailey answered. " It seems to me that we are wide open to anything which may come. It's all wrong. They don't realize the danger."

" What danger can there be ?"

" Well, from my point of view, it is like sitting at the edge of a pond which may have harmless frogs in it, or may have man-eating crocodiles. You can't tell what may come."

Professor Richet, who spoke excellent English, overheard the words.

" I know your views, Mr. Mailey," said he. " Don't think that I treat them lightly. Some things which I have seen make me appreciate your comparison of the frog and the crocodile. In this very room I have been conscious of the presence of creatures which could, if moved to anger, make our experiments seem rather hazardous. I believe with you that evil people here might bring an evil reflection into our circle."

" I am glad, sir, that you are moving in our direction," said Mailey, for like everyone else he regarded Richet as one of the world's great men.

" Moving, perhaps, and yet I cannot claim to be altogether with you yet. The latent powers of the human incarnate spirit may be so wonderful that they may extend to regions which seem at present to be quite beyond their scope. As an old materialist, I fight every inch of the ground, though I admit that I have lost several lines of trenches. My illustrious friend Challenger still holds his front intact, as I understand."

" Yes, sir," said Malone, " and yet I have some hopes—"

" Hush !" cried Maupuis in an eager voice.

There was dead silence. Then there came a sound of uneasy movement with a strange flapping vibration.

" The bird !" said an awestruck whisper.

There was silence and then once again came the sound of movement and an impatient flap.

" Have you all ready, René ?" asked the doctor.

" All is ready."

" Then shoot !"

The flash of the luminant mixture filled the room, while the shutter of the camera fell. In that sudden glare of light the visitors had a momentary glimpse of a marvellous sight. The medium lay with his head upon his hands in apparent insensibility. Upon his rounded shoulders there was perched a huge bird of prey—a large falcon or an eagle. For one instant the strange picture was stamped upon their retinas even as it was upon the photographic plate. Then the darkness closed down again, save for the two red lamps, like the eyes of some baleful demon lurking in the corner.

" My word ! " gasped Malone. " Did you see it ? "

" A crocodile out of the pond," said Mailey.

" But harmless," added Professor Richet. " the bird has been with us several times. He moves his wings, as you have heard, but otherwise is inert. We may have another and a more dangerous visitor."

The flash of the light had, of course, dispelled all ectoplasm. It was necessary to begin again. The company may have sat for a quarter of an hour when Richet touched Mailey's arm.

" Do you smell anything, Monsieur Mailey ? "

Mailey sniffed the air.

" Yes, surely, it reminds me of our London Zoo."

" There is another more ordinary analogy. Have you been in a warm room with a wet dog ? "

" Exactly," said Mailey. " That is a perfect description. But where is the dog ? "

" It is not a dog. Wait a little ! Wait ! "

The animal smell became more pronounced. It was overpowering. Then suddenly Malone became conscious of something moving round the table. In the dim red light he was aware of a mis-shapen figure, crouching, ill-formed, with some resemblance to man. He silhouetted it against the dull radiance. It was bulky, broad, with a bullet-head, a short neck, heavy, clumsy shoulders. It slouched slowly round the circle. Then it stopped, and a cry of surprise, not unmixed with fear, came from one of the sitters.

" Do not be alarmed," said Dr. Maupuis' quiet voice. " It is the Pithecanthropus. He is harmless." Had it been a cat which had strayed into the room the scientist could not have discussed it more calmly.

" It has long claws. It laid them on my neck," cried a voice.

" Yes, yes. He means it as a caress."

" You may have my share of his caresses ! " cried the sitter in a quavering voice.

" Do not repulse him. It might be serious. He is well

202

disposed.. But he has his feelings, no doubt, like the rest of us."

The creature had resumed its stealthy progress. Now it turned the end of the table and stood behind the three friends. Its breath came in quick puffs at the back of their necks. Suddenly Lord Roxton gave a loud exclamation of disgust.

" Quiet ! Quiet ! " said Maupuis.

" It's licking my hand !" cried Roxton.

An instant later Malone was aware of a shaggy head extended between Lord Roxton and himself. With his left hand he could feel long, coarse hair. It turned towards him, and it needed all his self-control to hold his hand still when a long soft tongue caressed it. Then it was gone.

" In heaven's name, what is it ?" he asked.

" We have been asked not to photograph it. Possibly the light would infuriate it. The command through the medium was definite. We can only say that it is either an ape-like man or a man-like ape. We have seen it more clearly than to-night. The face is Simian, but the brow is straight; the arms long, the hands huge, the body covered with hair."

" Tom Linden gave us something better than that," whispered Mailey. He spoke low but Richet caught the words.

" All Nature is the field of our study, Mr. Mailey. It is not for us to choose. Shall we classify the flowers but neglect the fungi ?"

" But you admit it is dangerous."

" The X-rays were dangerous. How many martyrs lost their arms, joint by joint, before those dangers were realized ? And yet it was necessary. So it is with us. We do not know yet what it is that we are doing. But if we can indeed show the world that this Pithecanthropus can come to us from the Invisible, and depart again as it came, then the knowledge is so tremendous that even if he tore us to pieces with those formidable claws it would none the less be our duty to go forward with our experiments."

" Science can be heroic," said Mailey. " Who can deny it ? And yet I have heard these very scientific men tell us that we imperil our reason when we try to get in touch with spiritual forces. Gladly would we sacrifice our reason, or our lives, if we could help mankind. Should we not do as much for spiritual advance as they for material ?"

The lights had been turned up and there was a pause for relaxation before the great experiment of the evening was attempted. The men broke into little groups, chatting in hushed tones over their recent experience. Looking round at the comfortable room with its up-to-date appliances, the strange bird and the stealthy monster seemed like dreams. And yet they had been very real, as was shown presently by the photographer, who had been allowed to leave and now rushed excitedly from the adjacent dark room waving the plate which he had just developed and fixed. He held it up against the light, and there, sure enough, was the bald head of the medium sunk between his hands, and crouching closely over his shoulders the outline of that ominous figure. Dr. Maupuis rubbed his little fat hands with glee. Like all pioneers he had endured much persecution from the Parisian Press, and every fresh phenomenon was another weapon for his own defence.

" *Nous marchons ! Hein ! Nous marchons !*" he kept on repeating, while Richet, lost in thought, answered mechanically:

" *Oui, mon ami, vous marchez !*"

The little Galician was sitting nibbling a biscuit with a glass of red wine before him. Malone went round to him and found that he had been in America and could talk a little English.

" Are you tired ? Does it exhaust you ?"

" In moderation, no. Two sittings a week. Behold my allowance. The doctor will allow no more."

" Do you remember anything ?"

" It comes to me like dreams. A little here—a little there."

204

" Has the power always been with you ?"

" Yes, yes, ever since a child. And my father, and my uncle. Their talk was of visions. For me, I would go and sit in the woods and strange animals would come round me. It did me such a surprise when I found that the other children could not see them."

" *Est ce que vous êtes prêtes ?*" asked Dr. Maupuis.

" *Parfaitement,*" answered the medium, brushing away the crumbs. The doctor lit a spirit-lamp under one of the zinc buckets.

" We are about to co-operate in an experiment, gentlemen, which should, once and for all, convince the world as to the existence of these ectoplasmic forms. Their nature may be disputed, but their objectivity will be beyond doubt from now onwards unless my plans miscarry. I would first explain these two buckets to you. This one, which I am warming, contains paraffin, which is now in process of liquefaction. This other contains water. Those who have not been present before must understand that Panbek's phenomena occur usually in the same order, and that at this stage of the evening we may expect the apparition of the old man. To-night we lie in wait for the old man, and we shall, I hope, immortalize him in the history of psychic research. I resume my seat, and I switch on the red light, Number Three, which allows of greater visibility."

The circle was now quite visible. The medium's head had fallen forward and his deep snoring showed that he was already in trance. Every face was turned towards him, for the wonderful process of materialization was going on before their very eyes. At first it was a swirl of light, steam-like vapour which circled round his head. Then there was a waving, as of white diaphanous drapery, behind him. It thickened. It coalesced. It hardened in outline and took definite shape. There was a head. There were shoulders. Arms grew out from them. Yes, there could not be a doubt of it—there was a man, an old man, standing behind the chair. He moved his head slowly from side to side. He seemed to be peering in indecision towards the company.

One could imagine that he was asking himself, " Where am I, and what am I here for ?"

" He does not speak, but he hears and has intelligence," said Dr. Maupuis, glancing over his shoulder at the apparition. " We are here, sir, in the hope that you will aid us in a very important experiment. May we count upon your co-operation ?"

The figure bowed his head in assent.

" We thank you. When you have attained your full power you will, no doubt, move away from the medium."

The figure again bowed, but remained motionless. It seemed to Malone that it was growing denser every moment. He caught glimpses of the face. It was certainly an old man, heavy-faced, long-nosed, with a curiously projecting lower lip. Suddenly with a brusque movement it stood clear from Panbeck and stepped out into the room.

" Now, sir," said Maupuis in his precise fashion. " You will perceive the zinc bucket upon the left. I would beg you to have the kindness to approach it and to plunge your right hand into it."

The figure moved across. He seemed interested in the buckets, for he examined them with some attention. Then he dipped one of his hands into that which the doctor had indicated.

" Excellent !" cried Maupuis, his voice shrill with excitement. " Now, sir, might I ask you to have the kindness to dip the same hand into the cold water of the other bucket."

The form did so.

" Now, sir, you would bring our experiment to complete success if you would lay your hand upon the table, and while it is resting there you would yourself dematerialize and return into the medium."

The figure bowed its comprehension and assent. Then it slowly advanced towards the table, stooped over it, extended its hand—and vanished. The heavy breathing of the medium ceased and he moved uneasily as if about to wake. Maupuis turned on the white light, and threw up his hands with a loud cry of wonder and joy which was echoed by the company.

On the shining wooden surface of the table there lay a delicate yellow-pink glove of paraffin, broad at the knuckles, thin at the wrist, two of the fingers bent down to the palm. Maupuis was beside himself with delight. He broke off a small bit of the wax from the wrist and handed it to an assistant, who hurried from the room.

" It is final !" he cried. " What can they say now ? Gentlemen, I appeal to you. You have seen what occurred. Can any of you give any rational explanation of that paraffin mould, save that it was the result of dematerialization of the hand within it ?"

" I can see no other solution," Richet answered. " But you have to do with very obstinate and very prejudiced people. If they cannot deny it, they will probably ignore it."

" The Press is here and the Press represents the public," said Maupuis. " For the Press Engleesh, Monsieur Malone," he went on in his broken way. " Is it that you can see any answer ?"

" I can see none," Malone answered.

" And you, monsieur ?" addressing the representative of the *Matin*."

The Frenchman shrugged his shoulders.

" For us who had the privilege of being present it was indeed convincing," said he, " and yet you will certainly be met with objections. They will not realize how fragile this thing is. They will say that the medium brought it on his person and laid it upon the table."

Maupuis clapped his hands triumphantly. His assistant had just brought him a slip of paper from the next room.

" Your objection is already answered," he cried, waving the paper in the air. " I had foreseen it and I had put some cholesterine among the paraffin in the zinc pail. You may have observed that I broke off a corner of the mould. It was for purpose of chemical analysis. This has now been done. It is here and cholesterine has been detected."

"Excellent !" said the French journalist. "You have closed the last hole. But what next ?"

"What we have done once we can do again," Maupuis answered. "I will prepare a number of these moulds. In some cases I will have fists and hands. Then I will have plaster casts made from them. I will run the plaster inside the mould. It is delicate, but it can be done. I will have dozens of them so treated, and I will send them broadcast to every capital in the world that people may see with their own eyes. Will that not at last convince them of the reality of our conclusions ?"

"Do not hope for too much, my poor friend," said Richet, with his hand upon the shoulder of the enthusiast. "You have not yet realized the enormous *vis inertiæ* of the world. But as you have said, ' *Vous marchez—vous marchez toujours*'."

"And our march is regulated," said Mailey. "There is a gradual release to accommodate it to the receptivity of mankind."

Richet smiled and shook his head.

"Always transcendental, Monsieur Mailey ! Always seeing more than meets the eye and changing science into philosophy ! I fear you are incorrigible. Is your position reasonable ?"

"Professor Richet," said Mailey, very earnestly, "I would beg you to answer the same question. I have a deep respect for your talents and complete sympathy with your caution, but have you not come to the dividing of the ways ? You are now in the position that you admit—you must admit—that an intelligent apparition in human form, built up from the substance which you have yourself named ectoplasm, can walk the room and carry out instructions while the medium lay senseless under our eyes, and yet you hesitate to assert that spirit has an independent existence. Is *that* reasonable ?"

Richet smiled and shook his head. Without answering he turned and bid farewell to Dr. Maupuis, and to offer him his congratulations. A few minutes later the company had broken up and our friends were in a taxi speeding towards their hotel.

Malone was deeply impressed with what he had seen, and he sat up half the night drawing up a full account of it for the Central News, with the names of those who had endorsed the result—honourable names which no one in the world could associate with folly or deception.

" Surely, surely, this will be a turning point and an epoch." So ran his dream. Two days later he opened the great London dailies one after the other. Columns about football. Columns about golf. A full page as to the value of shares. A long and earnest correspondence in *The Times* about the habits of the lapwing. Not one word in any of them as to the wonders which he had seen and reported. Mailey laughed at his dejected face.

" A mad world, my masters," said he. " A crazy world ! But the end is not yet !"

13. *In Which Professor Challenger Goes Forth to Battle*

PROFESSOR CHALLENGER was in a bad humour, and when that was so his household were made aware of it. Neither were the effects of his wrath confined to those around him, for most of those terrible letters which appeared from time to time in the Press, flaying and scarifying some unhappy opponent, were thunderbolt flashes from an offended Jove who sat in sombre majesty in his study-throne on the heights of a Victoria flat. Servants would hardly dare to enter the room where, glooming and glowering, the maned and bearded head looked up from his papers as a lion from a bone. Only Enid could dare him at such a time, and even she felt occasionally that sinking of the heart which the bravest of tamers may experience as he unbars the gate of the cage. She was not safe from the acridity of his tongue but at least she need not fear physical violence, which was well within the possibilities for others.

209

Sometimes these berserk fits of the famous Professor arose from material causes. " Hepatic, sir, hepatic !" he would explain in extenuation after some aggravated assault. But on this particular occasion he had a very definite cause for discontent. It was Spiritualism !

He never seemed to get away from the accursed superstition—a thing which ran counter to the whole work and philosophy of his lifetime. He attempted to pooh-pooh it, to laugh at it, to ignore it with contempt, but the confounded thing would insist upon obtruding itself once more. On Monday he would write it finally off his books, and before Saturday he would be up to his neck in it again. And the thing was so absurd ! It seemed to him that his mind was being drawn from the great pressing material problems of the Universe in order to waste itself upon Grimm's fairy tales or the ghosts of a sensational novelist.

Then things grew worse. First Malone, who had in his simple fashion been an index figure representing the normal clear-headed human being, had in some way been bedevilled by these people and had committed himself to their pernicious views. Then Enid, his wee-lamb, his one real link with humanity, had also been corrupted. She had agreed with Malone's conclusions. She had even hunted up a good deal of evidence of her own. In vain he had himself investigated a case and proved beyond a shadow of a doubt that the medium was a designing villain who brought messages from a widow's dead husband in order to get the woman into his power. It was a clear case and Enid admitted it. But neither she nor Malone would allow any general application. " There are rogues in every line of life," they would say. " We must judge every movement by the best and not by the worst."

All this was bad enough, but worse still was in store. He had been publicly humiliated by the Spiritualists— and that by a man who admitted that he had had no education and would in any other subject in the world have been seated like a child at the Professor's feet. And yet in public debate . . . but the story must be told.

210

Be it known, then, that Challenger, greatly despising all opposition and with no knowledge of the real strength of the case to be answered, had, in a fatal moment, actually asserted that he would descend from Olympus and would meet in debate any representative whom the other party should select. " I am well aware," he wrote, " that by such condescension I, like any other man of science of equal standing, run the risk of giving a dignity to these absurd and grotesque aberrations of the human brain which they could otherwise not pretend to claim, but we must do our duty to the public, and we must occasionally turn from our serious work and spare a moment in order to sweep away those ephemeral cobwebs which might collect and become offensive if they were not dispersed by the broom of Science." Thus, in a most self-confident fashion, did Goliath go forth to meet his tiny antagonist, an ex-printer's assistant and now the editor of what Challenger would describe as an obscure print devoted to matters of the spirit.

The particulars of the debate are public property, and it is not necessary to tell in any great detail that painful event. It will be remembered that the great man of Science went down to the Queen's Hall accompanied by many rationalist sympathizers who desired to see the final destruction of the visionaries. A large number of these poor deluded creatures also attended, hoping against hope that their champion might not be entirely immolated upon the altar of outraged Science. Between them the two factions filled the hall, and glared at each other with as much enmity as did the Blues and the Greens a thousand years before in the Hippodrome of Constantinople. There on the left of the platform were the solid ranks of those hard and unbending rationalists who look upon the Victorian agnostics as credulous, and refresh their faith by the periodical perusal of the *Literary Gazette* and the *Freethinker*.

There, too, was Dr. Joseph Baumer, the famous lecturer upon the absurdities of religion, together with Mr. Edward Mould, who has insisted so eloquently upon man's claim to ultimate putridity of the body and extinction of the soul. On the other side Mailey's yellow beard flamed like an oriflamme. His wife sat on one side of him and Mervin, the journalist, on the other, while dense ranks of earnest men and women from the Queen Square Spiritual Alliance, from the Psychic College, from the Stead Bureau, and from the outlying churches, assembled in order to encourage their champion in his hopeless task. The genial faces of Bolsover, the grocer, with his Hammersmith friends, Terbane, the railway medium, the Reverend Charles Mason, with his ascetic features, Tom Linden, now happily released from bondage, Mrs. Linden, the Crewe circle, Dr. Atkinson, Lord Roxton, Malone, and many other familiar faces were to be picked out amid that dense wall of humanity. Between the two parties, solemn and stolid and fat, sat Judge Gaverson of the King's Bench, who had consented to preside. It was an interesting and suggestive fact that in this critical debate at which the very core or vital centre of real religion was the issue, the organized churches were entirely aloof and neutral. Drowsy and semi-conscious, they could not discern that the live intellect of the nation was really holding an inquisition upon their bodies to determine whether they were doomed to the extinction towards which they were rapidly drifting, or whether a resuscitation in other forms was among the possibilities of the future.

In front, on one side, with his broad-browed disciples behind him, sat Professor Challenger, portentous and threatening, his Assyrian beard projected in his most aggressive fashion, a half-smile upon his lips, and his eyelids drooping insolently over his intolerant grey eyes. On the corresponding position on the other side was perched a drab and unpretentious person over whose humble head Challenger's hat would have descended to the shoulders. He was pale and apprehensive, glancing across occasionally in apologetic and deprecating fashion at his leonine opponent. Yet those who knew James Smith best were the least alarmed, for they were aware that behind his commonplace and democratic appearance there lay a knowledge of his subject, practical and theoretical, such as few living men possessed. The wise men of the Psychical Research Society are but children in psychic knowledge when compared with such practising Spiritualists as James Smith—men whose whole lives are spent in various forms of communion with the unseen. Such men often lose touch with the world in which they dwell and are useless for its everyday purposes, but the editorship of a live paper and the administration of a wide-spread, scattered community had kept Smith's feet solid upon earth, while his excellent natural faculties, uncorrupted by useless education, had enabled him to concentrate upon the one field of knowledge which offers in itself a sufficient scope for the greatest human intellect. Little as Challenger could appreciate it, the contest was really one between a brilliant discursive amateur and a concentrated highly-specialized professional.

It was admitted on all sides that Challenger's opening half-hour was a magnificent display of oratory and argument. His deep organ voice—such a voice as only a man with a fifty-inch chest can produce—rose and fell in a perfect cadence which enchanted his audience. He was born to sway an assembly—an obvious leader of mankind. In turn he was descriptive, humorous and convincing. He pictured the natural growth of animism among savages cowering under the naked sky, unable to account for the beat of the rain or the roar of the thunder, and seeing a benevolent or malicious intelligence behind those operations of Nature which Science had now classified and explained.

Hence on false premises was built up that belief in spirits or invisible beings outside ourselves, which by some curious atavism was re-emerging in modern days among the less educated strata of mankind. It was the duty of Science to resist retrogressive tendencies of the sort, and it was a sense of that duty which had reluctantly drawn him from the privacy of his study to the publicity of this platform. He rapidly sketched the movement as depicted by its maligners. It was a most unsavoury story as he told it, a story of cracking toe joints, of phosphorescent paint, of muslin ghosts, of a nauseous sordid commission trade betwixt dead

213

men's bones on one side, and widow's tears upon the other. These people were the hyenas of the human race who battened upon the graves. (Cheers from the Rationalists and ironical laughter from the Spiritualists.) They were not all rogues. (" Thank you, Professor !" from a stentorian opponent). But the others were fools (laughter). Was it exaggeration to call man a fool who believed that his grandmother could rap out absurd messages with the leg of a dining-room table ? Had any savages descended to so grotesque a superstition ? These people had taken dignity from death and had brought their own vulgarity into the serene oblivion of the tomb. It was a hateful business. He was sorry to have to speak so strongly, but only the knife or the cautery could deal with so cancerous a growth. Surely man need not trouble himself with grotesque speculations as to the nature of life beyond the grave. We had enough to do in this world. Life was a beautiful thing. The man who appreciated its real duties and beauties would have sufficient to employ him without dabbling in pseudo sciences which had their roots in frauds, exposed already a hundred times and yet finding fresh crowds of foolish devotees whose insane credulity and irrational prejudice made them impervious to all argument.

Such is a most bald and crude summary of this powerful opening argument. The materialists roared their applause; the Spiritualists looked angry and uneasy, while their spokesman rose, pale but resolute, to answer the ponderous onslaught.

His voice and appearance had none of those qualities which made Challenger magnetic, but he was clearly audible and made his points in a precise fashion like a workman who is familiar with his tools. He was so polite and so apologetic at first that he gave the impression of having been cowed. He felt that it was almost presumptuous upon one who had so little advantage of education to measure mental swords for an instant with so renowned an antagonist, one whom he had long revered. It seemed to him, however, that in the long list of the Professor's accomplishments—

accomplishments which had made him a household word throughout the world—there was one missing, and unhappily it was just this one upon which he had been tempted to speak. He had listened to that speech with admiration so far as its eloquence was concerned, but with surprise, and he might almost say with contempt, when he analysed the assertions which were contained in it. It was clear that the Professor had prepared his case by reading all the anti-Spiritualist literature which he could lay his hands upon—a most tainted source of information—while neglecting the works of those who spoke from experience and conviction.

All this talk of cracking joints and other fraudulent tricks was mid-Victorian in its ignorance, and as to the grandmother talking through the leg of a table he, the speaker, could not recognize it as a fair description of Spiritualistic phenomena. Such comparisons reminded one of the jokes about the dancing frogs which impeded the recognition of Volta's early electrical experiments. They were unworthy of Professor Challenger. He must surely be aware that the fraudulent medium was the worst enemy of Spiritualism, that he was denounced by name in the psychic journals whenever he was discovered, and that such exposures were usually made by the Spiritualists themselves who had spoken of " human hyenas " as indignantly as his opponent had done. One did not condemn banks because forgers occasionally used them for nefarious purposes. It was wasting the time of so chosen an audience to descend to such a level of argument. Had Professor Challenger denied the religious implications of Spiritualism while admitting the phenomena, it might have been harder to answer him, but in denying everything he had placed himself in an absolutely impossible position. No doubt Professor Challenger had read the recent work of Professor Richet, the famous physiologist. That work had extended over thirty years. Richet had verified all the phenomena.

Perhaps Professor Challenger would inform the audience what personal experience he had himself had which gave

215

him the right to talk of Richet, or Lombroso, or Crookes, as if they were superstitious savages. Possibly his opponent had conducted experiments in private of which the world knew nothing. In that case he should give them to the world. Until he did so it was unscientific and really indecent to deride men, hardly inferior in scientific reputation to himself, who actually had done such experiments and laid them before the public.

As to the self-sufficiency of this world, a successful Professor with a eupeptic body might take such a view, but if one found oneself with cancer of the stomach in a London garret, one might question the doctrine that there was no need to yearn for any state of being save that in which we found ourselves.

It was a workmanlike effort illustrated with facts, dates and figures. Though it rose to no height of eloquence it contained much which needed an answer. And the sad fact emerged that Challenger was not in a position to answer. He had read up his own case but had neglected that of his adversary, accepting too easily the facile and specious presumptions of incompetent writers who handled a matter which they had not themselves investigated. Instead of answering, Challenger lost his temper. The lion began to roar. He tossed his dark mane and his eyes glowed, while his deep voice reverberated through the hall. Who were these people who took refuge behind a few honoured but misguided names? What right had they to expect serious men of science to suspend their labours in order to waste time in examining their wild surmises? Some things were self-evident and did not require proof. The onus of proof lay with those who made the assertions. If this gentleman, whose name is unfamiliar, claims that he can raise spirits, let him call one up now before a sane and unprejudiced audience. If he says that he receives messages, let him give us the news in advance of the general agencies. (" It has often been done !" from the Spiritualists.) So you say, but I deny it. I am too accustomed to your wild assertions to take them seriously. (Uproar, and Judge

216

Gaverson upon his feet.) If he claims that he has higher inspiration, let him solve the Peckham Rye murder. If he is in touch with angelic beings, let him give us a philosophy which is higher than mortal mind can evolve. This false show of science, this camouflage of ignorance, this babble about ectoplasm and other mythical products of the psychic imagination was mere obscurantism, the bastard offspring of superstition and darkness. Wherever the matter was probed one came upon corruption and mental putrescence. Every medium was a deliberate impostor. (" You are a liar !" in a woman's voice from the neighbourhood of the Lindens.) The voices of the dead had uttered nothing but childish twaddle. The asylums were full of the supporters of the cult and would be fuller still if everyone had his due.

It was a violent but not an effective speech. Evidently the great man was rattled. He realized that there was a case to be met and that he had not provided himself with the material wherewith to meet it. Therefore he had taken refuge in angry words and sweeping assertions which can only be safely made when there is no antagonist present to take advantage of them. The Spiritualists seemed more amused than angry. The materialists fidgeted uneasily in their seats. Then James Smith rose for his last innings. He wore a mischievous smile. There was quiet menace in his whole bearing.

He must ask, he said, for a more scientific attitude from his illustrious opponent. It was an extraordinary fact that many scientific men, when their passions and prejudices were excited, showed a ludicrous disregard for all their own tenets. Of these tenets there was none more rigid than that a subject should be examined before it was condemned. We have seen of late years, in such matters as wireless or heavier-than-air machines, that the most unlikely things may come to pass. It is most dangerous to say á priori that a thing is impossible. Yet this was the error into which Professor Challenger had fallen. He had used the fame which he had rightly won in subjects which he had mastered in order to cast discredit upon a subject which he had not mastered. The fact that a man was a great physiologist and physicist did not in itself make him an authority upon psychic science.

It was perfectly clear that Professor Challenger had not read the standard works upon the subject on which he posed as an authority. Could he tell the audience what the name of Schrenck Notzing's medium was ? He paused for a reply. Could he then tell the name of Dr. Crawford's medium ? Not ? Could he tell them who had been the subject of Professor Zollner's experiments at Leipzig ? What, still silent ? But these were the essential points of the discussion. He had hesitated to be personal, but the Professor's robust language called for corresponding frankness upon his part. Was the Professor aware that this ectoplasm which he derided had been examined lately by twenty German professors—the names were here for reference—and that all had testified to its existence ? How could Professor Challenger deny that which these gentlemen asserted ? Would he contend that they also were criminals or fools ? The fact was that the Professor had come to this hall entirely ignorant of the facts and was now learning them for the first time. He clearly had no perception that Psychic Science had any laws whatever, or he would not have formulated such childish requests as that an ectoplasmic figure should manifest in full light upon this platform when every student was aware that ectoplasm was soluble in light. As to the Peckham Rye murder it had never been claimed that the angel world was an annexe to Scotland Yard. It was mere throwing of dust in the eyes of the public for a man like Professor Challenger——

It was at this moment that the explosion occurred. Challenger had wriggled in his chair. Challenger had tugged at his beard. Challenger had glared at the speaker. Now he suddenly sprang to the side of the chairman's table with the bound of a wounded lion. That gentleman had been lying back half asleep with his fat hands clutched across his ample paunch, but at this sudden apparition he gave a convulsive start which nearly carried him into the orchestra.

" Sit down, sir ! Sit down !" he cried.

" I refuse to sit down," roared Challenger. " Sir, I appeal to you as chairman ! Am I here to be insulted ? These proceedings are intolerable. I will stand it no longer. If my private honour is touched I am justified in taking the matter into my own hands."

Like many men who override the opinions of others, Challenger was exceedingly sensitive when anyone took a liberty with his own. Each successive incisive sentence of his opponent had been like a barbed bandarillo in the flanks of a foaming bull. Now, in speechless fury, he was shaking his huge hairy fist over the chairman's head in the direction of his adversary, whose derisive smile stimulated him to more furious plunges with which he butted the fat president along the platform. The assembly had in an instant become a pandemonium. Half the rationalists were scandalized, while the other half shouted " Shame ! Shame !" as a sign of sympathy with their champion. The Spiritualists had broken into derisive shouts, while some rushed forward to protect their champion from physical assault.

" We must get the old dear out," said Lord Roxton to Malone. " He'll be had for manslaughter if we don't. What I mean, he's not responsible—he'll sock someone and be lagged for it."

The platform had become a seething mob, while the auditorium was little better. Through the crush Malone and Roxton elbowed their way until they reached Challenger's side, and partly by judicious propulsion, partly by artful persuasion, they got him, still bellowing his grievances, out of the building. There was a perfunctory vote to the chairman, and the meeting broke up in riot and confusion.

" The whole episode," remarked *The Times* next morning, " was a deplorable one, and forcibly illustrates the danger of public debates where the subjects are such as to inflame the prejudices of either speakers or audience. Such terms as ' Microcephalous idiot !' or ' Simian survival !' when applied by a world-renowned Professor to an opponent, illustrate the lengths to which such disputants may pèrmit themselves to go."

Thus by a long interpolation we have got back to the fact that Professor Challenger was in the worst of humours as he sat with the above-mentioned copy of *The Times* in his hand and a heavy scowl upon his brow. And yet it was that very moment that the injudicious Malone had chosen in order to ask him the most intimate question which one man can address to another.

Yet perhaps it is hardly fair to our friend's diplomacy to say that he had " chosen " the moment. He had really called in order to see for himself that the man for whom, in spite of his eccentricities, he had a deep reverence and affection, had not suffered from the events of the night before. On that point he was speedily reassured.

" Intolerable !" roared the Professor, in a tone so unchanged that he might have been at it all night. " You were there yourself, Malone. In spite of your inexplicable and misguided sympathy for the fatuous views of these people, you must admit that the whole conduct of the proceedings was intolerable, and that my righteous protest was more than justified. It is possible that when I threw the chairman's table at the President of the Psychic College I passed the bounds of decorum, but the provocation had been excessive. You will remember that this Smith or Brown person—his name is most immaterial—dared to accuse me of ignorance and of throwing dust in the eyes of the audience."

" Quite so," said Malone, soothingly. " Never mind, Professor. You got in one or two pretty hard knocks yourself."

Challenger's grim features unbent and he rubbed his hands with glee.

" Yes, yes, I fancy that some of my thrusts went home. I imagine that they will not be forgotten. When I said that the asylums would be full if every man of them had his due I could see them wince. They all yelped, I remember, like a kennelful of puppies. It was their preposterous claim that I should read their hare-brained literature which caused me to display some little heat. But I hope, my boy, that you have called round this morning in order to tell me that what I said last night has had some effect upon your own mind, and that you have reconsidered these views which are, I confess, a considerable tax upon our friendship."

Malone took his plunge like a man.

"I had something else in my mind when I came here," said he. "You must be aware that your daughter Enid and I have been thrown together a good deal of late. To me, sir, she has become the one woman in the world, and I shall never be happy until she is my wife. I am not rich, but a good sub-editorship has been offered to me and I could well afford to marry. You have known me for some time and I hope you have nothing against me. I trust, therefore, that I may count upon your approval in what I am about to do."

Challenger stroked his beard and his eyelids drooped dangerously over his eyes.

"My perceptions," said he, "are not so dull that I should have failed to observe the relations which have been established between my daughter and yourself. This question however, has become entangled with the other which we were discussing. You have both, I fear, imbibed this poisonous fallacy which I am more and more inclined to devote my life to extirpating. If only on the ground of eugenics, I could not give my sanction to a union which was built up on such a foundation, I must ask you, therefore, for a definite assurance that your views have become more sane. I shall ask the same from her."

And so Malone suddenly found himself also enrolled among the noble army of martyrs. It was a hard dilemma, but he faced it like the man that he was.

"I am sure, sir, that you would not think the better of me if I allowed my views as to truth, whether they be right

221

or wrong, to be swayed by material considerations. I cannot change my opinions even to win Enid. I am sure that she would take the same view."

" Did you not think I had the better last night ?"

" I thought your address was very eloquent."

" Did I not convince you ?"

" Not in the face of the evidence of my own senses."

" Any conjuror could deceive your senses."

" I fear, sir, that my mind is made up on this point."

" Then my mind is made up also," roared Challenger, with a sudden glare. " You will leave this house, sir, and you will return when you have regained your sanity."

" One moment !" said Malone. " I beg, sir, that you will not be precipitate. I value your friendship too much to risk the loss of it if it can, in any way, be avoided. Possibly if I had your guidance I would better understand these things that puzzle me. If I should be able to arrange it would you mind being present personally at one of these demonstrations so that your own trained powers of observation may throw a light upon the things that have puzzled me."

Challenger was enormously open to flattery. He plumed and preened himself now like some great bird.

" If, my dear Malone, I can help you to get this taint— what shall we call it ?—*microbus spiritualensis*—out of your system, I am at your service. I shall be happy to devote a little of my spare time to exposing those specious fallacies to which you have fallen so easy a victim. I would not say that you are entirely devoid of brains, but that your good nature is liable to be imposed upon. I warn you that I shall be an exacting inquirer and bring to the investigation those laboratory methods of which it is generally admitted that I am a master."

" That is what I desire."

" Then you will prepare the occasion and I shall be there. But meanwhile you will clearly understand that I insist upon a promise that this connection with my daughter shall go no further."

Malone hesitated.

" I give my promise for six months," he said at last.

" And what will you do at the end of that time ?"

" I will decide when the time comes," Malone answered diplomatically, and so escaped from a dangerous situation with more credit than at one time seemed probable.

It chanced that, as he emerged upon the landing, Enid who had been engaged in her morning's shopping, appeàred in the lift. Malone's easy Irish conscience allowed him to think that the six months need not start on the instant, so he persuaded Enid to descend in the lift with him. It was one of those lifts which are handled by whoever uses them, and on this occasion it so happened that, in some way best known to Malone, it stuck between the landing stages, and in spite of several impatient rings it remained stuck for a good quarter of an hour. When the machinery resumed its functions, and when Enid was able at last to reach her home and Malone the street, the lovers had prepared themselves to wait for six months with every hope of a successful end to their experiment.

14.   *In Which Challenger Meets a Strange Colleague*

PROFESSOR CHALLENGER was not a man who made friends easily. In order to be his friend you had also to be his dependant. He did not admit of equals. But as a patron he was superb. With his Jovian air, his colossal condescension, his amused smile, his general suggestion of the god descending to the mortal, he could be quite overpowering in his amiability. But he needed certain qualities in return. Stupidity disgusted him. Physical ugliness alienated him. Independence repulsed him. He coveted the man whom all the world would admire, but who in turn would admire the superman above him. Such a man was Dr. Ross Scotton, and for this reason he had been Challenger's favourite pupil.

And now he was sick unto death. Dr. Atkinson of St.

Mary's who had already played some minor part in this record, was attending him, and his reports were increasingly depressing. The illness was that dread disease disseminated sclerosis, and Challenger was aware that Atkinson was no alarmist when he said that a cure was a most remote and unlikely possibility. It seemed a terrible instance of the unreasonable nature of things that a young man of science, capable before he reached his prime of two such works as *The Embryology of the Sympathetic Nervous System* or *The Fallacy of the Obsonic Index*, should be dissolved into his chemical elements with no personal or spiritual residue whatever. And yet the Professor shrugged his huge shoulders, shook his massive head, and accepted the inevitable. Every fresh message was worse than the last, and, finally, there was an ominous silence. Challenger went down once to his young friend's lodging in Gower Street. It was a racking experience, and he did not repeat it. The muscular cramps which are characteristic of the complaint were tying the sufferer into knots, and he was biting his lips to shut down the screams which might have relieved his agony at the expense of his manhood. He seized his mentor by the hand as a drowning man seizes a plank.

" Is it really as you have said ? Is there no hope beyond the six months of torture which I see lying before me ? Can you with all your wisdom and knowledge see no spark of light or life in the dark shadow of eternal dissolution ?"

" Face it, my boy, face it !" said Challenger. " Better to look fact in the face than to console oneself with fancies."

Then the lips parted and the long-pent scream burst forth. Challenger rose and rushed from the room.

But now an amazing development occurred. It began by the appearance of Miss Delicia Freeman.

One morning there came a knock at the door of the Victoria flat. The austere and taciturn Austin looking out at the level of his eyes perceived nothing at all. On glancing downwards, however, he was aware of a small lady, whose delicate face and bright bird-like eyes were turned upwards to his own.

"I want to see the Professor," said she, diving into her handbag for a card.

"Can't see you," said Austin.

"Oh, yes, he can," the small lady answered serenely. There was not a newspaper office, a statesman's sanctum, or a political chancellory which had ever presented a barrier strong enough to hold her back where she believed that there was good work to be done.

"Can't see you," repeated Austin.

"Oh, but really I must, you know," said Miss Freeman, and made a sudden dive past the butler. With unerring instinct she made for the door of the sacred study, knocked, and forthwith entered.

The lion head looked up from behind a desk littered with papers. The lion eyes glared.

"What is the meaning of this intrusion?" the lion roared. The small lady was, however, entirely unabashed. She smiled sweetly at the glowering face.

"I am so glad to make your acquaintance," she said. "My name is Delicia Freeman."

"Austin!" shouted the Professor. The butler's impassive face appeared round the angle of the door. "What is this, Austin. How did this person get here?"

"I couldn't keep her out," wailed Austin. "Come, miss, we've had enough of it."

"No, no! You must not be angry—you really must not," said the lady sweetly. "I was told that you were a perfectly terrible person, but really you are rather a dear."

"Who are you? What do you want? Are you aware that I am one of the most busy men in London?"

Miss Freeman fished about in her bag once more. She was always fishing in that bag, extracting sometimes a leaflet on Armenia, sometimes a pamphlet on Greece, sometimes a note on Zenana Missions, and sometimes a psychic manifesto. On this occasion it was a folded bit of writing-paper which emerged.

"From Dr. Ross Scotton," she said.

It was hastily folded and roughly scribbled—so roughly

as to be hardly legible. Challenger bent his heavy brows over it.

Please, dear friend and guide, listen to what this lady says. I know it is against all your views. And yet I had to do it. You said yourself that I had no hope. I have tested it and it works. I know it seems wild and crazy. But any hope is better than no hope. If you were in my place you would have done the same. Will you not cast out prejudice and see for yourself? Dr. Felkin comes at three.

J. Ross Scotton.

Challenger read it twice over and sighed. The brain was clearly involved in the lesion: " He says I am to listen to you. What is it ? Cut it as short as you can."

" It's a spirit doctor," said the lady.

Challenger bounded in his chair.

" Good God, am I never to get away from this nonsense !" he cried. " Can they not let this poor devil lie quiet on his deathbed but they must play their tricks upon him ?"

Miss Delicia clapped her hands and her quick little eyes twinkled with joy.

" It's *not* his deathbed. He is going to get well."

" Who said so ?"

" Dr. Felkin. He never is wrong."

Challenger snorted.

" Have you seen him lately ?" she asked.

" Not for some weeks."

" But you wouldn't recognise him. He is nearly cured."

" Cured ! Cured of diffused sclerosis in a few weeks !"

" Come and see."

" You want me to aid and abet in some infernal quackery. The next thing, I should see my name on this rascal's testimonials. I know the breed. If I did come I should probably take him by the collar and throw him down the stair."

The lady laughed heartily.

" He would say with Aristides: ' Strike, but hear me '. You will hear him first, however, I am sure. Your pupil is a real chip of yourself. He seems quite ashamed of getting well in such an unorthodox way. It was I who called Dr. Felkin in against his wish."

"Oh, you did, did you? You took a great deal upon yourself."

"I am prepared to take any responsibility, so long as I *know* I am right. I spoke to Dr. Atkinson. He knows a little of psychic matters. He is far less prejudiced than most of you scientific gentlemen. He took the view that when a man was dying, in any case it could matter little what you did. So Dr. Felkin came."

"And pray how did this quack doctor proceed to treat the case?"

"That is what Dr. Ross Scotton wants you to see." She looked at a watch which she dragged from the depths of the bag. "In an hour he will be there. I'll tell your friend you are coming. I am sure you would not disappoint him. Oh!" She dived into the bag again. "Here is a recent note upon the Bessarabian question. It is much more serious than people think. You will just have time to read it before you come. So good-bye, dear Professor, and *au revoir!*"

She beamed at the scowling lion and departed.

But she had succeeded in her mission, which was a way she had. There was something compelling in the absolutely unselfish enthusiasm of this small person who would, at a moment's notice, take on anyone from a Mormon Elder to an Albanian brigand, loving the culprit and mourning the sin. Challenger came under the spell, and shortly after three he stumped his way up the narrow stair and blocked the door of the humble bedroom where his favourite pupil lay stricken. Ross Scotton lay stretched upon the bed in a red dressing-gown, and his teacher saw, with a start of surprised joy, that his face had filled out and that the light of life and hope had come back into his eyes.

"Yes, I'm beating it!" he cried. "Ever since Felkin held his first consultation with Atkinson I have felt the life-force stealing back into me. Oh, chief, it is a fearful thing

227

to lie awake at night and feel these cursed microbes nibbling away at the very roots of your life ! I could almost hear them at it. And the cramps when my body—like a badly articulated skeleton—would all get twisted into one rigid tangle ! But now, except some dyspepsia and urticaria of the palms, I am free from pain. And all on account of this dear fellow here who has helped me."

He motioned with his hand as if alluding to someone present. Challenger looked round with a glare, expecting to find some smug charlatan behind him. But no doctor was there. A frail young woman, who seemed to be a nurse, quiet, unobtrusive, and with a wealth of brown hair, was dozing in a corner. Miss Delicia, smiling demurely, stood in the window.

" I am glad you are better, my dear boy," said Challenger. " But do not tamper with your reason. Such a complaint has its natural systole and diastole."

" Talk to him, Dr. Felkin. Clear his mind for him," said the invalid.

Challenger looked up at the cornice and round at the skirting. His pupil was clearly addressing some doctor in the room and yet none was visible. Surely his aberration had not reached the point when he thought that actual floating apparitions were directing his cure.

" Indeed, it needs some clearing," said a deep and virile voice at his elbow. He bounded round. It was the frail young woman who was talking.

" Let me introduce you to Dr. Felkin," said Miss Delicia, with a mischievous laugh.

" What tomfoolery is this ?" cried Challenger.

The young woman rose and fumbled at the side of her dress. Then she made an impatient gesture with her hand.

" Time was, my dear colleague, when a snuff-box was as much part of my equipment as my phlebotomy case. I lived before the days of Laennec, and we carried no stethoscope, but we had our little chirurgical battery, none the less. But the snuff-box was a peace-offering, and I was about to offer it to you, but, alas ! it has had its day."

Challenger stood with staring eyes and dilated nostrils while this speech was delivered. Then he turned to the bed.

" Do you mean to say that this is your doctor—that you take the advice of this person ?"

The young girl drew herself up very stiffly.

" Sir, I will not bandy words with you. I perceive very clearly that you are one of those who have been so immersed in material knowledge that you have had no time to devote to the possibilities of the spirit."

" I certainly have no time for nonsense," said Challenger.

" My dear chief !" cried a voice from the bed. " I beg you to bear in mind how much Dr. Felkin has already done for me. You saw how I was a month ago, and you see how I am now. You would not offend my best friend."

" I certainly think, Professor, that you owe dear Dr. Felkin an apology," said Miss Delicia.

" A private lunatic asylum !" snorted Challenger. Then, playing up to his part, he assumed the ponderous elephantine irony which was one of his most effective weapons in dealing with recalcitrant students.

" Perhaps, young lady—or shall I say elderly and most venerable Professor ?—you will permit a mere raw earthly student, who has no more knowledge than this world can give, to sit humbly in a corner and possibly to learn a little from your methods and your teaching." This speech was delivered with his shoulders up to his ears, his eyelids over his eyes, and his palms extended in front—an alarming statue of sarcasm. Dr. Felkin, however, was striding with heavy and impatient steps about the room, and took little notice.

" Quite so ! Quite so !" she said carelessly. " Get into the corner and stay there. Above all, stop talking, as this case calls for all my faculties." He turned with a masterful air towards the patient. Well, well, you are coming along. In two months you will be in the class-room."

" Oh, it is impossible !" cried Ross Scotton, with a half sob.

"Not so. I guarantee it. I do not make false promises."

"I'll answer for that," said Miss Delicia. "I say, dear Doctor, do tell us who you were when you were alive."

"Tut! tut! The unchanging woman. They gossiped in my time and they gossip still. No! no! We will have a look at our young friend here. Pulse! The intermittent beat has gone. That is something gained. Temperature —obviously normal. Blood pressure—still higher than I like. Digestion—much to be desired. What you moderns call a hunger-strike would not be amiss. Well, the general conditions are tolerable. Let us see the local centre of the mischief. Pull your shirt down, sir! Lie on your face. Excellent!" She passed her fingers with great force and precision down the upper part of the spine, and then dug in her knuckles with a sudden force which made the sufferer yelp. That is better! There is—as I have explained—a slight want of alignment in the cervical vertibræ which has, as I perceive it, the effect of lessening the foramina through which the nerve roots emerge. This has caused compression, and as these nerves are really the conductors of vital force, it has upset the whole equilibrium of the parts supplied. My eyes are the same as your clumsy X-rays, and I clearly perceive that the position is almost restored, and the fatal constriction removed. I hope, sir," to Challenger, "that I make the pathology of this interesting case intelligible to you."

Challenger grunted his general hostility and disagreement.

"I will clear up any little difficulties which may linger in your mind. But, meantime, my dear lad, you are a credit to me, and I rejoice in your progress. You will present my compliments to my colleague of earth, Dr. Atkinson, and tell him that I can suggest nothing more. The medium is a little weary, poor girl, so I will not remain longer to-day."

"But you said you would tell us who you were."

"Indeed, there is little to say. I was a very undistinguished practitioner. I sat under the great Abernethy in my youth, and perhaps imbibed something of his methods. When I passed over in early middle age I continued my studies, and was permitted, if I could find some suitable means of expression, to do something to help humanity. You understand, of course, that it is only by serving and self-abnegation that we advance in the higher world. This is my service, and I can only thank kind Fate that I was able to find in this girl a being whose vibrations so correspond with my own that I can easily assume control of her body."

"And where is she ?" asked the patient.

" She is waiting beside me and will presently re-enter her own frame. As to you, sir," turning to Challenger, " you are a man of character and learning, but you are clearly embedded in that materialism which is the special curse of your age. Let me assure you that the medical profession, which is supreme upon earth for the disinterested work of its members, has yielded too much to the dogmatism of such men as you, and has unduly neglected that spiritual element in man which is far more important than your herbs and your minerals. There is a life-force, sir, and it is in the control of this life force that the medicine of the future lies. If you shut your mind to it, it can only mean that the confidence of the public will turn to those who are ready to adopt every means of cure, whether they have the approval of your authorities or not."

Never could young Ross Scotton forget that scene. The Professor, the master, the supreme chief, he who had to be addressed with bated breath sat with half-opened mouth and staring eyes, leaning forward in his chair, while in front of him the slight young woman shaking her mop of brown hair and wagging an admonitory forefinger, spoke to him as a father speaks to a refractory child. So intense was her power that Challenger, for the instant, was constrained to accept the situation. He gasped and grunted, but no retort came to his lips. The girl turned away and sat down on a chair.

" He is going," said Miss Delicia.

"But not yet gone," replied the girl with a smile. "Yes, I must go, for I have much to do. This is not my only medium of expression, and I am due in Edinburgh in a few minutes. But be of good heart, young man. I will set my assistant with two extra batteries to increase your vitality so far as your system will permit. As to you, sir," to Challenger, "I would implore you to beware of the egotism of brain and the self-concentration of intellect. Store what is old, but be ever receptive to what is new, and judge it not as you may wish it, but as God has designed it."

She gave a deep sigh and sank back in her chair. There was a minute of dead silence while she lay with her head upon her breast. Then, with another sigh and a shiver, she opened a pair of very bewildered blue eyes.

"Well, has he been?" she asked in a gentle feminine voice.

"Indeed, yes!" cried the patient. "He was great. He says I shall be in the class-room in two months."

"Splendid! Any directions for me?"

"Just the special massage as before. But he is going to put on two new spirit batteries if I can stand it."

"My word, he won't be long now!" Suddenly the girl's eyes lit on Challenger and she stopped in confusion.

"This is Nurse Ursula," said Miss Delicia. "Nurse, let me present you to the famous Professor Challenger."

Challenger was great in his manner towards women, especially if the particular woman happened to be a young and pretty girl. He advanced now as Solomon may have advanced to the Queen of Sheba, took her hand, and patted her hair with patriarchal assurance.

"My dear, you are far too young and charming for such deceit. Have done with it for ever. Be content to be a bewitching nurse and resign all claim to the higher functions of doctor. Where, may I ask, did you pick up all this jargon about cervical vertebræ and posterior foramina?"

Nurse Ursula looked helplessly round as one who finds herself suddenly in the clutches of a gorilla.

"She does not understand a word you say!" cried the

man on the bed. " Oh, chief, you must make an effort to face ·the real situation ! I know what a readjustment it means. In my small way I have had to undergo it myself. But, believe me, you see everything through a prism instead of through plate-glass until you understand the spiritual factor."

Challenger continued his paternal attentions, though the frightened lady had begun to shrink from him.

" Come now," said he, " who was the clever doctor with whom you acted as nurse—the man who taught you all these fine words ? You must feel that it is hopeless to deceive me. You will be much happier, dear child, when you have made a clean breast of it all, and when we can laugh together over the lecture which you inflicted upon me."

An unexpected interruption came to check Challenger's exploration of the young woman's conscience or motives. The invalid was sitting up, a vivid red patch against his white pillows, and he was speaking with an energy which was in itself an indication of his coming cure.

" Professor Challenger !" he cried, " you are insulting my best friend. Under this roof at least she shall be safe from the sneers of scientific prejudice. I beg you to leave the room if you cannot address Nurse Ursula in a more respectful manner."

Challenger glared, but the peacemaking Delicia was at work in a moment.

" You are far too hasty, dear Dr. Ross Scotton !" she cried. " Professor Challenger has had no time to understand this. You were just as sceptical yourself at first. How can you blame him ?"

" Yes, yes, that is true," said the young doctor. " It seemed to me to open the door to all the quackery in the Universe—indeed it does, but the fact remains."

" ' One thing I know that whereas I was blind now I see'," quoted Miss Delicia. " Ah, Professor, you may raise your eyebrows and shrug your shoulders, but we've dropped something into your big mind this afternoon which will grow and grow until no man can see the end of it." She dived into the bag. "There is a little slip here ' Brain *versus* Soul '. I do hope, dear Professor, that you will read it and then pass it on."

15. *In Which Traps are Laid for a Great Quarry*

MALONE was bound in honour not to speak of love to Enid Challenger, but looks can speak, and so their communications had not broken down completely. In all other ways he adhered closely to the agreement, though the situation was a difficult one. It was the more difficult since he was a constant visitor to the Professor, and now that the irritation of the debate was over, a very welcome one. The one object of Malone's life was to get the great man's sympathetic consideration of those psychic subjects which had gained such a hold upon himself. This he pursued with assiduity, but also with great caution, for he knew that the lava was thin, and that a fiery explosion was always possible. Once or twice it came and caused Malone to drop the subject for a week or two, until the ground seemed a little more firm.

Malone developed a remarkable cunning in his approaches. One favourite device was to consult Challenger upon some scientific point—on the zoological importance of the Straits of Banda, for example, or the Insects of the Malay Archipelago, and lead him on until Challenger in due course would explain that our knowledge on the point was due to Alfred Russel Wallace. " Oh, really ! To Wallace the Spiritualist !" Malone would say in an innocent voice, on which Challenger would glare and change the topic.

Sometimes it was Lodge that Malone would use as a trap. " I suppose you think highly of him."

" The first brain in Europe," said Challenger.

" He is the greatest authority on ether, is he not ?"

" Undoubtedly."

" Of course, I only know him by his psychic works."

Challenger would shut up like a clam. Then Malone would wait a few days and remark casually: " Have you ever met Lombroso !"

" Yes, at the Congress at Milan."

" I have been reading a book of his."

" Criminology, I presume ?"

" No, it was called *After Death—What* ?"

" I have not heard of it."

" It discusses the psychic question."

" Ah, a man of Lombroso's penetrating brain would make short work of the fallacies of these charlatans."

" No, it is written to support them."

" Well, even the greatest mind has its inexplicable weakness." Thus, with infinite patience and cunning did Malone drop his little drops of reason in the hope of slowly wearing away the casing of prejudice, but no very visible effects could be seen. Some stronger measure must be adopted, and Malone determined upon direct demonstration. But how, whem, and where? Those were the all-important points upon which he determined to consult Algernon Mailey. One spring afternoon found him back in that drawing-room where he had once rolled upon the carpet in the embrace of Silas Linden. He found the Reverend Charles Mason, and Smith, the hero of the Queen's Hall debate, in deep consultation with Mailey upon a subject which may seem much more important to our descendants than those topics which now bulk large in the eyes of the public. It was no less than whether the psychic movement in Britain was destined to take a Unitarian or a Trinitarian course. Smith had always been in favour of the former, as had the old leaders of the movement and the present organized Spiritualist Churches. On the other hand, Charles Mason was a loyal son of the Anglican Church, and was the spokesman of a host of others, including such weighty names as Lodge and Barrett among the laymen, or Wilberforce, Haweis and Chambers among the clergy, who clung fast to the old teachings while admitting the fact of spirit communication. Mailey stood between the two parties, and, like the zealous referee in a boxing-match who separates the two combatants, he always took a chance of getting a knock from each. Malone was only too glad to listen, for now that he realized that the future of the world might be bound up in this movement, every phase of it was of intense interest to him. Mason was holding forth in his earnest but good-humoured way as he entered.

"The people are not ready for a great change. It is not necessary. We have only to add our living knowledge and direct communion of the saints to the splendid liturgy and traditions of the Church, and you will have a driving force which will revitalize all religion. You can't pull a thing up from the roots like that. Even the early Christians found that they could not, and so they made all sorts of concessions to the religions around them."

"Which was exactly what ruined them," said Smith. "That was the real end of the Church in its original strength and purity."

"It lasted, anyhow."

"But it was never the same from the time that villain Constantine laid his hands on it."

"Oh, come!" said Mailey. "You must not write down the first Christian emperor as a villain."

But Smith was a forthright, uncompromising, bull-doggy antagonist. "What other name will you give to a man who murdered half his own family?"

"Well, his personal character is not the question. We were talking of the organization of the Christian Church."

"You don't mind my frankness, Mr. Mason?"

Mason smiled his jolly smile. "So long as you grant me the existence of the New Testament I don't care what you do. If you were to prove that our Lord was a myth, as that German Drews tried to do, it would not in the least affect me so long as I could point to that body of sublime teaching. It must have come from somewhere, and I adopt it and say, ' That is my creed '."

"Oh, well, there is not so much between us on that point," said Smith. "If there is any better teaching I have not

236

seen it. It is good enough to go on with, anyhow. But we want to cut out the frills and superfluities. Where did they all come from? They were compromises with many religions, so that our friend C. could get uniformity in his world-wide Empire. He made a patchwork quilt of it. He took an Egyptian ritual—vestments, mitre, crozier, tonsure, marriage ring—all Egyptian. The Easter ceremonies are pagan and refer to the vernal equinox. Confirmation is mithraism. So is baptism, only it was blood instead of water. As to the sacrificial meal . . ."

Mason put his fingers in his ears. " This is some old lecture of yours," he laughed. " Hire a hall, but don't obtrude it in a private house. But, seriously, Smith, all this is beside the question. If it is true it will not affect my position at all, which is that we have a great body of doctrine which is working well, and which is regarded with veneration by many people, your humble servant included, and that it would be wrong and foolish to scrap it. Surely you must agree."

" No, I don't," Smith answered, setting his obstinate jaw. " You are thinking too much of the feelings of your blessed church-goers. But you have also to think of the nine people out of ten who never enter into a church. They have been choked off by what they, including your humble servant, consider to be unreasonable and fantastic. How will you gain them while you continue to offer them the same things, even though you mix spirit-teaching with it? If, however, you approach these agnostic or atheistic ones, and say to them: ' I quite agree that all this is unreal and is tainted by a long history of violence and reaction. But here we have something pure and new. Come and examine it !' In that way I could coax them back into a belief in God and in all the fundamentals of religion without their having to do violence to their reason by accepting your theology."

Mailey had been tugging at his tawny beard while he listened to these conflicting counsels. Knowing the two men he was aware that there was not really much between

237

them, when one got past mere words, for Smith revered the Christ as a God-like man, and Mason as a man-like God, and the upshot was much the same. At the same time he knew that their more extreme followers on either side were in very truth widely separated, so that compromise became impossible.

"What I can't understand," said Malone, "is why you don't ask your spirit friends these questions and abide by their decisions."

"It is not so simple as you think," Mailey answered. "We all carry on our earthly prejudices after death, and we all find ourselves in an atmosphere which more or less represents them. Thus each would echo his old views at first. Then in time the spirit broadens out and it ends in a universal creed which includes only the brotherhood of man and the fatherhood of God. But that takes time. I have heard most furious bigots talking through the veil."

"So have I, for that matter," said Malone, "and in this very room. But what about the materialists? They at least cannot remain unchanged."

"I believe their mind influences their state and that they lie inert for ages sometimes, under their own obsession that nothing can occur. Then at last they wake, realize their own loss of time, and finally, in many cases, get to the head of the procession, since they are often men of fine character and influenced by lofty motives however mistaken in their views."

"Yes, they are often among the salt of the earth," said the clergyman heartily.

"And they offer the very best recruits for our movement," said Smith. "There comes such a reaction when they find by the evidence of their own senses that there really is intelligent force outside themselves, that it gives them an enthusiasm that makes them ideal missionaries. You fellows who have a religion and then add to it cannot even imagine what it means to the man who has a complete vacuum and suddenly finds something to fill it. When I meet some poor earnest chap feeling out into the darkness I just yearn to put it into his hand."

At this stage, tea and Mrs. Mailey appeared together. But the conversation did not flag. It is one of the characteristics of those who explore psychic possibilities that the subject is so many-sided and the interest so intense that when they meet together they plunge into the most fascinating exchange of views and experiences. It was with some difficulty that Malone got the conversation round to that which had been the particular object of his visit. He could have found no group of men more fit to advise him, and all were equally keen that so great a man as Challenger should have the best available.

Where should it be? On that they were unanimous. The large séance room of the Psychic College was the most select, the most comfortable, in every way the best appointed in London. When should it be? The sooner the better. Every spiritualist and every medium would surely put any engagement aside in order to help on such an occasion.

"Who should the medium be? Ah! There was the rub. Of course, the Bolsover circle would be ideal. It was private and unpaid, but Bolsover was a man of quick temper and Challenger was sure to be very insulting and annoying. The meeting might end in riot and fiasco. Such a chance should not be taken. Was it worth while to take him over to Paris? But who would take the responsibility of letting loose such a bull in Dr. Maupuis' china-shop?

"He would probably seize pithecanthropus by the throat and risk every life in the room," said Mailey. "No, no, it would never do."

"There is no doubt that Banderby is the strongest physical medium in England," said Smith. "But we all know what his personal character is. You could not rely upon him."

"Why not?" asked Malone. "What's the matter with him?"

Smith raised his hand to his lips.

"He has gone the way that many a medium has gone before him."

"But surely," said Malone, "that is a strong argument

against our cause. How can a thing be good if it leads to such a result ?"

" Do you consider poetry to be good ?"

" Why, of course I do !"

" Yet Poe was a drunkard, and Coleridge an addict, and Byron a rake, and Verlaine a degenerate. You have to separate the man from the thing. The genius has to pay a ransom for his genius in the instability of his temperament. A great medium is even more sensitive than a genius. Many are beautiful in their lives. Some are not. The excuse for them is great. They practise a most exhausting profession and stimulants are needed. Then they lose control. But their physical mediumship carries on all the same."

" Which reminds me of a story about Banderby," said Mailey. " Perhaps you have not seen him, Malone. He is a funny figure at any time—a little, round, bouncing man who has not seen his own toes for years. When drunk he is funnier still. A few weeks ago I got an urgent message that he was in the bar of a certain hotel, and too far gone to get home unassisted. A friend and I set forth to rescue him. We got him home after some unsavoury adventures, and what would the man do but insist upon holding a séance. We tried to restrain him, but the trumpet was on a side-table, and he suddenly switched off the light. In an instant the phenomena began. Never were they more powerful. But they were interrupted by Princeps, his control, who seized the trumpet and began belabouring him with it. ' You rascal ! You drunken rascal ! How dare you !' The trumpet was all dinted with the blows. Banderby ran bellowing out of the room, and we took our departure."

" Well, it wasn't the medium that time, at any rate," said Mason. " But about Professor Challenger—it would never do to risk the chance."

" What about Tom Linden ?" asked Mrs. Mailey.

Mailey shook his head.

" Tom has never been quite the same since his imprisonment. These fools not only persecute our precious mediums, but they ruin their powers. It is like putting a razor into a damp place and then expecting it to have a fine edge."

" What ! Has he lost his powers ?"

" Well, I would not go so far as that. But they are not so good as they were. He sees a disguised policeman in every sitter and it distracts him. Still, he is dependable so far as he goes. Yes, on the whole we had better have Tom."

" And the sitters ?"

" I expect Professor Challenger may wish to bring a friend or two of his own."

" They will form a horrible block of vibrations. We must have some of our own sympathetic people to counteract it. There is Delicia Freeman. She would come. I would come myself. You would come, Mason ?"

" Of course I would."

" And you, Smith ?"

" No, no ! I have my paper to look after, three services, two burials, one marriage, and five meetings all next week."

" Well, we can easily get one or two more. Eight is Linden's favourite number. So now, Malone, you have only to get the great man's consent and the date."

" And the spirit of confirmation," said Mason, seriously. " We must take our partners into consultation."

" Of course we must, padre. That is the right note to strike. Well, that's settled, Malone, and we can only await the event."

As it chanced, a very different event was awaiting Malone that evening, and he came upon one of those chasms which unexpectedly open across the path of life. When, in his ordinary routine, he reached the office of the *Gazette*, he was informed by the commissionaire that Mr. Beaumont desired to see him. Malone's immediate superior was the old Scotch sub-editor, Mr. McArdle, and it was rare indeed for the supreme editor to cast a glimpse down from that peak whence he surveyed the kingdoms of the world, or to show any cognizance of his humble fellow-workers upon the slopes beneath him. The great man, clean-shaven, prosperous and capable, sat in his palatial sanctum amid a rich assortment of old oak furniture and sealing-wax-red leather. He continued his letter when Malone entered, and only raised his shrewd, grey eyes after some minutes' interval.

"Ah, Mr. Malone, good evening! I have wanted to see you for some little time. Won't you sit down? It is in reference to these articles on psychic matters which you have been writing. You opened them in a tone of healthy scepticism, tempered by humour, which was very acceptable both to me and to our public. I regret, however, to observe that your view changed as you proceeded, and that you have now assumed a position in which you really seem to condone some of these practices. That, I need not say, is not the policy of the *Gazette*, and we should have discontinued the articles had it not been that we had announced a series by an impartial investigator. We have to continue but the tone must change."

"What do you wish me to do, sir?"

"You must get the funny side of it again. That is what our public loves. Poke fun at it all. Call up the maiden aunt and make her talk in an amusing fashion. You grasp my meaning?"

"I am afraid, sir, it has ceased to seem funny in my eyes. On the contrary, I take it more and more seriously."

Beaumont shook his solemn head.

"So, unfortunately, do our subscribers." He had a small pile of letters upon the desk beside him and he took one up.

"Look at this: 'I had always regarded your paper as a God-fearing publication, and I would remind you that such practices as your correspondent seems to condone are expressly forbidden both in Leviticus and Deuteronomy. I should share your sin if I continued to be a subscriber'."

"Bigoted ass!" muttered Malone.

"So he may be, but the penny of a bigoted ass is as good as any other penny. Here is another letter: 'Surely in this age of free-thought and enlightenment you are not helping a movement which tries to lead us back to the exploded idea of angelic and diabolic intelligences outside ourselves. If so, I must ask you to cancel my subscription'."

" It would be amusing, sir, to shut these various objectors up in a room and let them settle it among themselves."

" That may be, Mr. Malone, but what I have to consider is the circulation of the *Gazette*."

" Don't you think, sir, that possibly you underrate the intelligence of the public, and that behind these extremists of various sorts there is a vast body of people who have been impressed by the utterances of so many great and honourable witnesses ? Is it not our duty to keep these people abreast of the real facts without making fun of them ?"

Mr. Beaumont shrugged his shoulders.

" The Spiritualists must fight their own battle. This is not a propaganda newspaper, and we make no pretence to lead the public on religious beliefs."

" No, no, I only meant as to the actual facts. Look how systematically they are kept in the dark. When, for example, did one ever read an intelligent article upon ectoplasm in any London paper ? Who would imagine that this all-important substance has been examined and described and endorsed by men of science with innumerable photographs to prove their words ?"

" Well, well," said Beaumont, impatiently. " I am afraid I am too busy to argue the question. The point of this interview is that I have had a letter from Mr. Cornelius to say that we must at once take another line."

Mr. Cornelius was the owner of the *Gazette*, having become so, not from any personal merit, but because his father left him some millions, part of which he expended upon this purchase. He seldom was seen in the office himself, but occasionally a paragraph in the paper recorded that his yacht had touched at Mentone and that he had been seen at the Monte Carlo tables, or that he was expected in Leicestershire for the season. He was a man of no force of brain or character, though occasionally he swayed public affairs by a manifesto printed in larger type upon his own front page. Without being dissolute, he was a free liver, living in a constant luxury which placed him always on the edge of vice and occasionally over the border. Malone's hot blood flushed to his head as he thought of this trifler, this insect, coming between mankind and a message of instruction and consolation descending from above. And yet those clumsy, childish fingers could actually turn the tap and cut off the divine stream, however much it might break through in other quarters.

"So that is final, Mr. Malone," said Beaumont, with the manner of one who ends an argument.

"Quite final!" said Malone. "So final that it marks the end of my connection with your paper. I have a six months' contract. When it ends, I go!"

"Please yourself, Mr. Malone." Mr. Beaumont went on with his writing.

Malone, with the flush of battle still upon him, went into McArdle's room and told him what had happened. The old Scotch sub-editor was very perturbed.

"Eh, man, it's that Irish blood of yours. A drop o' Scotch is a good thing, either in your veins or at the bottom o' a glass. Go back, man, and say you have reconseedered!"

"Not I! The idea of this man Cornelius, with his pot-belly and red face, and—well, you know all about his private life—the idea of such a man dictating what folk are to believe, and asking me to make fun of the holiest thing on this earth!"

"Man, you'll be ruined!"

"Well, better men than I have been ruined over this cause. But I'll get another job."

"Not if Cornelius can stop you. If you get the name of an insubordinate dog there is no place for you in Fleet Street."

"It's a damned shame!" cried Malone. "The way this thing has been treated is a disgrace to journalism. It's not Britain alone. America is worse. We seem to have the lowest, most soulless folk that ever lived on the Press— good-hearted fellows too, but material to a man. And these are the leaders of the people! It's awful!"

McArdle put a fatherly hand upon the young man' shoulder.

" Weel, weel, lad, we take the world as we find it. We didn't make it and we're no reesponsible. Give it time ! Give it time ! We're a' in such a hurry. Gang hame, now, think it over, remember your career, that young leddy of yours, and then come back and eat the old pie that all of us have to eat if we are to keep our places in the world."

16. In Which Challenger has the Experience of his Lifetime

SO now the nets were set and the pit was dug and the hunters were all ready for the great quarry, but the question was whether the creature would allow himself to be driven in the right direction. Had Challenger been told that the meeting was really held in the hope of putting convincing evidence before him as to the truth of spirit intercourse with the aim of his eventual conversion, it would have roused mingled anger and derision in his breast. But the clever Malone, aided and abetted by Enid, still put forward the idea that his presence would be a protection against fraud, and that he would be able to point out to them how and why they had been deceived. With this thought in his mind, Challenger gave a contemptuous and condescending consent to the proposal that he should grace with his presence a proceeding which was, in his opinion, more fitted to the stone cabin of a neolithic savage than to the serious attention of one who represented the accumulated culture and wisdom of the human race.

Enid accompanied her father, and he also brought with him a curious companion who was strange both to Malone and to the rest of the company. This was a large, raw-boned Scottish youth, with a freckled face, a huge figure, and a taciturnity which nothing could penetrate. No question could discover where his interests in psychic research might lie, and the only positive thing obtained from him was that his name was Nicholl. Malone and Mailey went together to the rendezvous at Holland Park, where they found awaiting them Delicia Freeman, the Rev. Charles Mason, Mr. and Mrs. Ogilvy of the College, Mr. Bolsover of Hammersmith, and Lord Roxton, who had become assiduous in his psychic studies, and was rapidly progressing in knowledge. There were nine in all, a mixed, inharmonious assembly, from which no experienced investigator could expect great results. On entering the séance room Linden was found seated in the armchair, his wife beside him, and was introduced collectively to the company, most of whom were already his friends. Challenger took up the matter at once with the air of a man who will stand no nonsense.

"Is this the medium?" he asked, eyeing Linden with much disfavour.

"Yes."

"Has he been searched?"

"Not yet."

"Who will search him?"

"Two men of the company have been selected."

Challenger sniffed his suspicions.

"Which men?" he asked.

"It is suggested that you and your friend, Mr. Nicholl, shall do so. There is a bedroom next door."

Poor Linden was marched off between them in a manner which reminded him unpleasantly of his prison experiences. He had been nervous before, but this ordeal and the overpowering presence of Challenger made him still more. He shook his head mournfully at Mailey when he reappeared.

"I doubt we will get nothing to-day. Maybe it would be wise to postpone the sitting," said he.

Mailey came round and patted him on the shoulder, while Mrs. Linden took his hand.

"It's all right, Tom," said Mailey. "Remember that you have a bodyguard of friends round you who won't see you ill-used." Then Mailey spoke to Challenger in a sterner way than was his wont. "I beg you to remember, sir, that a medium is as delicate an instrument as any to be found in your laboratories. Do not abuse it. I presume that you found nothing compromising upon his person?"

"No, sir, I did not. And as a result he assures us that we will get nothing to-day."

"He says so because your manner has disturbed him. You must treat him more gently."

Challenger's expression did not promise any amendment. His eyes fell upon Mrs. Linden.

"I understand that this person is the medium's wife. She should also be searched."

"That is a matter of course," said the Scotsman Ogilvy. "My wife and your daughter will take her out. But I beg you, Professor Challenger, to be as harmonious as you can, and to remember that we are all as interested in the results as you are, so that the whole company will suffer if you should disturb the conditions."

Mr. Bolsover, the grocer, rose with as much dignity as if he were presiding at his favourite temple.

"I move," said he, "that Professor Challenger be searched."

Challenger's beard bristled with anger.

"Search me! What do you mean, sir?"

Bolsover was not to be intimidated.

"You are here not as our friend but as our enemy. If you was to prove fraud it would be a personal triumph for you—see? Therefore I, for one, says as you should be searched."

"Do you mean to insinuate, sir, that I am capable of cheating?" trumpeted Challenger.

"Well, Professor, we are all accused of it in turn," said Mailey smiling. "We all feel as indignant as you are at first, but after a time you get used to it. I've been called a liar, a lunatic—goodness knows what. What does it matter?"

"It is a monstrous proposition," said Challenger, glaring all round him.

"Well, sir," said Ogilvy, who was a particularly pertinacious Scot. "Of course, it is open to you to walk out of the room and leave us. But if you sit, you must sit under what we consider to be scientific conditions. It is not scientific that a man who is known to be bitterly hostile to the movement should sit with us in the dark with no check as to what he may have in his pockets."

"Come, come!" cried Malone. "Surely we can trust to the honour of Professor Challenger."

"That's all very well," said Bolsover. "I did not observe that Professor Challenger trusted so very much to the honour of Mr. and Mrs. Linden."

"We have cause to be careful," said Ogilvy. "I can assure you that there are frauds practised on mediums just as there are frauds practised by mediums. I could give you plenty of examples. No, sir, you will have to be searched."

"It won't take a minute," said Lord Roxton. "What I mean, young Malone here and I could give you a once over in no time."

"Quite so, come on!" said Malone.

And so Challenger, like a red-eyed bull with dilating nostrils, was led from the room. A few minutes later, all preliminaries being completed, they were seated in the circle and the séance had begun.

But already the conditions had been destroyed. Those meticulous researchers who insist upon tying up a medium until the poor creature resembles a fowl trussed for roasting, or who glare their suspicions at him before the lights are lowered, do not realize that they are like people who add moisture to gunpowder and then expect to explode it. They ruin their own results, and then when those results do not occur imagine that their own astuteness, rather than their own lack of understanding, has been the cause.

Hence it is that at humble gatherings all over the land, in an atmosphere of sympathy and of reverence, there are such happenings as the cold man of "Science" is never privileged to see.

All the sitters felt churned up by the preliminary altercation, but how much more did it mean to the sensitive centre of it all! To him the room was filled with conflicting rushes and eddies of psychic power, whirling this way or that, and as difficult for him to navigate as the rapids below Niagara. He groaned in his despair. Everything was mixed and confused. He was beginning as usual with his clairvoyance, but names buzzed in his etheric ears without sequence or order. The word " John " seemed to predominate, so he said. Did " John " mean anything to anyone ? A cavernous laugh from Challenger was the only reply. Then he had the surname of Chapman. Yes, Mailey had lost a friend named Chapman. But, it was years ago and there seemed no reason for his presence, nor could he furnish his Christian name. " Budworth "—no; no one would own to a friend named Budworth. Definite messages came across, but they seemed to have no reference to the present company. Everything was going amiss, and Malone's spirits sank to zero. Challenger sniffed so loudly that Ogilvy remonstrated.

" You make matters worse, sir, when you show your feelings," said he. " I can assure you that in ten years of constant experience I have never known the medium so far out, and I attribute it entirely to your own conduct."

" Quite so," said Challenger with satisfaction.

" I am afraid it is no use, Tom," said Mrs. Linden. " How are you feeling now, dear? Would you wish to stop?"

But Linden under all his gentle exterior, was a fighter. He had in another form those same qualities which had brought his brother within an ace of the Lonsdale Belt.

" No, I think, maybe, it is only the mental part that is confused. If I am in trance I'll get past that. The physicals may be better. Anyhow I'll try."

The lights were turned lower until they were a mere crimson glimmer. The curtain of the cabinet was drawn. Outside it on the one side, dimly outlined to his audience, Tom Linden, breathing stertorously in his trance, lay back in a wooden armchair. His wife kept watch and ward at the other side of the cabinet.

But nothing happened.

Quarter of an hour passed. Then another quarter of an

hour. The company was patient, but Challenger had begun to fidget in his seat. Everything seemed to have gone cold and dead. Not only was nothing happening, but somehow all expectation of anything happening seemed to have passed away.

" It's no use !" cried Mailey at last.

" I fear not," said Malone.

The medium stirred and groaned; he was waking up. Challenger gave an ostentatious yawn.

" Is not this a waste of time ?" he asked.

Mrs. Linden was passing her hand over the medium's head and brow. His eyes had opened.

" Any results ?" he asked.

" It's no use, Tom. We shall have to postpone."

" I think so, too, " said Mailey.

" It is a great strain upon him under these adverse conditions," remarked Ogilvy, looking angrily at Challenger.

" I should think so," said the latter with a complacent smile.

But Linden was not to be beaten

" The conditions are bad," said he. " The vibrations are all wrong. But I'll try inside the cabinet. It concentrates the force."

" Well, it's the last chance," said Mailey. " We may as well try it."

The armchair was lifted inside the cloth tent and the medium followed, drawing the curtain behind him.

" It condenses the ectoplasmic emanations," Ogilvy explained.

" No doubt," said Challenger. " At the same time in the interests of truth, I must point out that the disappearance of the medium is most regrettable."

" For goodness sake, don't start wrangling again," cried Mailey with impatience. " Let us get some results, and then it will be time enough to discuss their value."

Again there was a weary wait. Then came some hollow groanings from inside the cabinet. The Spiritualists sat up expectantly.

" That's ectoplasm," said Ogilvy. " It always causes pain on emission."

The words were hardly out of his mouth when the curtains were torn open with sudden violence and a rattling of all the rings. In the dark aperture there was outlined a vague white figure. It advanced slowly and with hesitation into the centre of the room. In the red-tinted gloom all definite outline was lost, and it appeared simply as a moving white patch in the darkness. With the deliberation which suggested fear it came, step by step, until it was opposite the professor.

" Now !" he bellowed in his stentorian voice.

There was a shout, a scream, a crash. " I've got him !" roared someone. " Turn up the lights !" yelled another. " Be careful ! You may kill the medium !" cried a third. The circle was broken. Challenger rushed to the switch and put on all the lights. The place was so flooded with radiance that it was some seconds before the bewildered and half-blinded spectators could see the details.

When they had recovered their sight and their balance, the spectacle was a deplorable one for the majority of the company. Tom Linden, looking white, dazed, and ill, was seated upon the ground. Over him stood the huge young Scotsman who had borne him to earth; while Mrs. Linden, kneeling beside her husband, was glaring up at his assailant. There was a silence as the company surveyed the scene. It was broken by Professor Challenger.

" Well, gentlemen, I presume that there is no more to be said. Your medium has been exposed as he deserved to be. You can see now the nature of your ghosts. I must thank Mr. Nicholl, who, I may remark, is the famous football player of that name, for the prompt way in which he has carried out his instructions."

" I collared him low," said the tall youth. " He was easy."

" You did it very effectively. You have done public service by helping to expose a heartless cheat. I need not say that a prosecution will follow."

251

But Mailey now intervened and with such authority that Challenger was forced to listen.

"Your mistake is not unnatural, sir, though the course which you adopted in your ignorance is one which might well have been fatal to the medium."

"My ignorance indeed! If you speak like that I warn you that I will look upon you not as dupes, but as accomplices."

"One moment, Professor Challenger. I would ask you one direct question, and I ask for an equally direct reply. Was not the figure which we all saw before this painful episode a white figure?"

"Yes, it was."

"You see now that the medium is entirely dressed in black. Where is the white garment?"

"It is immaterial to me where it is. No doubt his wife and himself are prepared for all eventualities. They have their own means of secreting the sheet, or whatever it may have been. These details can be explained in the police court."

"Examine now. Search the room for anything white."

"I know nothing of the room. I can only use my common sense. The man is exposed masquerading as a spirit. Into what corner or crevice he has thrust his disguise is a matter of small importance."

"On the contrary, it is a vital matter. What you have seen has not been an imposture, but has been a very real phenomenon."

Challenger laughed.

"Yes, sir, a very real phenomenon. You have seen a transfiguration which is the half-way state of materialization. You will kindly realize that spirit guides, who conduct such affairs, care nothing for your doubts and suspicions. They set themselves to get certain results, and if they are prevented by the infirmities of the circle from getting them one way they get them in another, without consulting your prejudice or convenience. In this case being unable, owing to the evil conditions which you have yourself created, to build up an ectoplasmic form they wrapped the unconscious medium in an ectoplasmic covering, and sent him forth from the cabinet. He is as innocent of imposture as you are."

"I swear to God," said Linden, "that from the time I entered the cabinet until I found myself upon the floor I knew nothing." He had staggered to his feet and was shaking all over in his agitation, so that he could not hold the glass of water which his wife had brought him.

Challenger shrugged his shoulders.

"Your excuses," he said, "only open up fresh abysses of credulity. My own duty is obvious, and it will be done to the uttermost. Whatever you have to say will, no doubt, receive such consideration as it deserves from the magistrate." Then Professor Challenger turned to go as one who has triumphantly accomplished that for which he came. "Come, Enid!" said he.

And now occurred a development so sudden, so unexpected, so dramatic, that no one present will ever cease to have it in vivid memory.

No answer was returned to Challenger's call.

Everyone else had risen to their feet. Only Enid remained in her chair. She sat with her head on one shoulder, her eyes closed, her hair partly loosened—a model for a sculptor.

"She is asleep," said Challenger. "Wake up, Enid. I am going."

There was no response from the girl. Mailey was bending over her.

"Hush! Don't disturb her! She is in trance."

Challenger rushed forward. "What have you done? Your infernal hankey-pankey has frightened her. She has fainted."

Mailey had raised her eyelid.

"No, no, her eyes are turned up. She is in trance. Your daughter, sir, is a powerful medium."

"A medium! You are raving. Wake up girl,! Wake up !"

" For God's sake leave her ! You may regret it all your
life if you don't. It is not safe to break abruptly into the
mediumistic trance."

Challenger stood in bewilderment. For once his presence
of mind had deserted him. Was it possible that his child
stood on the edge of some mysterious precipice and that
he might push her over ?

" What shall I do ?" he asked helplessly.

" Have no fear. All will be well. Sit down ! Sit down,
all of you. Ah ! she is about to speak."

The girl had stirred. She had sat straight in her chair.
Her lips trembled. One hand was outstretched:

" For him !" she cried, pointing to Challenger. " He
must not hurt my Medi. It is a message. For him."

There was breathless silence among the persons who had
gathered round the girl.

" Who speaks ?" asked Mailey.

" Victor speaks. Victor. He shall not hurt my Medi.
I have a message. For him !"

" Yes, yes. What is the message ?"

" His wife is here."

" Yes !"

" She says that she has been once before. That she came
through this girl. It was after she was cremated. She knock
and he hear her knocking, but not understand."

" Does this mean anything to you, Professor Challenger ?"

His great eyebrows were bunched over his suspicious,
questioning eyes, and he glared like a beast at bay from one
to the other of the faces round him. There was a trick—
a vile trick. They had suborned his own daughter. It was
damnable. He would expose them, every one. No, he
had no questions to ask. He could see through it all. She
had been won over. He could not have believed it of her,
and yet it must be so. She was doing it for Malone's sake.
A woman would do anything for a man she loved. Yes, it
was damnable. Far from being softened he was more
vindictive than ever. His furious face, his broken words,
expressed his convictions.

Again the girl's arm shot out, pointing in front of her.
" Another message !"
" To whom ?"
" To him. The man who wanted to hurt my Medi. He must not hurt my Medi. A man here—two men—wish to give him a message."
" Yes, Victor, let us have it."
" First man's name is . . ." The girl's head slanted and her ear was upturned, as if listening. " Yes, yes, I have it ! It is Al-Al-Aldridge."
" Does that mean anything to you ?"
Challenger staggered. A look of absolute wonder had come upon his face.
" What is the second man ?" he asked.
" Ware. Yes that is it. Ware."
Challenger sat down suddenly. He passed his hand over his brow. He was deadly pale. His face was clammy with sweat.
" Do you know them ?"
" I knew two men of those names."
" They have message for you," said the girl.
Challenger seemed to brace himself for a blow.
" Well, what is it ?"
" Too private. Not speak, all these people here."
" We shall wait outside," said Mailey. " Come, friends, let the Professor have his message."
They moved towards the door leaving the man seated in front of his daughter. An unwonted nervousness seemed suddenly to seize him. " Malone, stay with me !"
The door closed and the three were left together.
" What is the message ?"
" It is about a powder."
" Yes, yes."
" A grey powder ?"
" Yes."
" The message that men want me to say is: ' You did not kill us '."
" Ask them then—ask them—how did they die ?" His

255

voice was broken and his great frame was quivering with his emotion.

" They die disease."

" What disease ?"

" New—new . . . What that ? . . . Pneumonia."

Challenger sank back in his chair with an immense sigh of relief. " My God !" he cried, wiping his brow. Then: " Call in the others, Malone."

They had waited on the landing and now streamed into the room. Challenger had risen to meet them. His first words were to Tom Linden. He spoke like a shaken man whose pride for the instant was broken.

" As to you, sir, I do not presume to judge you. A thing has occurred to me which is so strange, and also so certain, since my own trained senses have attested it, that I am not prepared to deny any explanation which has been offered of your previous conduct. I beg to withdraw any injurious expressions I may have used."

Tom Linden was a true Christian in his character. His forgiveness was instant and sincere.

" I cannot doubt that my daughter has some strange power which bears out much which you, Mr. Mailey, have told me. I was justified in my scientific scepticism, but you have to-day offered me some incontrovertible evidence."

" We all go through the same experience, Professor. We doubt, and then in turn we are doubted."

" I can hardly conceive that my word will be doubted upon such a point," said Challenger, with dignity. " I can truly say that I have had information to-night which no living person upon this earth was in a position to give. So much is beyond all question."

" The young lady is better," said Mrs. Linden.

Enid was sitting up and staring round her with bewildered eyes.

" What has happened, Father ? I seem to have been asleep."

" All right, dear. We will talk of that later. Come home with me now. I have much to think over. Perhaps you will come back with us, Malone. I feel that I owe you some explanation."

When Professor Challenger reached his flat, he gave Austin orders that he was on no account to be disturbed, and he led the way into his library, where he sat in his big armchair with Malone upon his left and his daughter upon his right. He had stretched out his great paw and enclosed Enid's small hand.

" My dear," he said, after a long silence, " I cannot doubt that you are possessed of a strange power, for it has been shown to me to-night with a fullness and a clearness which is final. Since you have it I cannot deny that others may have it also, and the general idea of mediumship has entered within my conceptions of what is possible. I will not discuss the question, for my thoughts are still confused upon the subject, and I will need to thrash the thing out with you, young Malone, and with your friends, before I can get a more definite idea. I will only say that my mind has received a shock, and that a new avenue of knowledge seems to have opened up before me."

" We shall be proud indeed," said Malone, " if we can help you."

Challenger gave a wry smile.

" Yes, I have no doubt that a headline in your paper, ' Conversion of Professor Challenger ' would be a triumph. I warn you that I have not got so far."

" We certainly would do nothing premature and your opinions may remain entirely private."

" I have never lacked the moral courage to proclaim my opinions when they are formed, but the time has not yet come. However, I have received two messages to-night, and I can only ascribe to them an extra-corporeal origin. I take it for granted, Enid, that you were indeed insensible."

" I assure you, Father, that I knew nothing."

" Quite so. You have always been incapable of deceit. First there came a message from your mother. She assured me that she had indeed produced those sounds which I heard and of which I have told you. It is clear now that you were the medium and that you were not in sleep but in trance. It is incredible, inconceivable, grotesquely wonderful—but it would seem to be true."

" Crookes used almost those very words," said Malone. He wrote that it was all ' perfectly impossible and absolutely true '."

" I owe him an apology. Perhaps I owe a good many people an apology."

" None will ever be asked for," said Malone. " These people are not made that way."

" It is the second case which I would explain." The Professor fidgeted uneasily in his chair. " It is a matter of great privacy—one to which I have never alluded, and which no one on earth could have known. Since you heard so much you may as well hear all.

" It happened when I was a young physician, and it is not too much to say that it cast a cloud over my life—a cloud which has only been raised to-night. Others may try to explain what has occurred by telepathy, by subconscious mind action, by what they will, but I cannot doubt—it is impossible to doubt—that a message has come to me from the dead.

" There was a new drug under discussion at that time. It is useless to enter into details which you would be incapable of appreciating. Suffice it that it was of the datura family which supplies deadly poisons as well as powerful medicines. I had received one of the earliest specimens, and I desired my name to be associated with the first exploration of its properties. I gave it to two men, Ware and Aldridge. I gave it in what I thought was a safe dose. They were patients, you understand, in my ward in a public hospital. Both were found dead in the morning.

" I had given it secretly. None knew of it. There was no scandal for they were both very ill, and their death seemed natural. But in my own heart I had fears. I believed that I had killed them. It has always been a dark background to my life. You heard yourselves to-night that it was from the disease, and not from the drug that they died."

" Poor Dad !" whispered Enid patting the great hirsute hand. " Poor Dad ! What you must have suffered !"

Challenger was too proud a man to stand pity, even from his own daughter. He pulled away his hand.

" I worked for science," he said. " Science must take risks. I do not know that I am to blame. And yet—and yet—my heart is very light to-night."

17. Where the Mists Clear Away

MALONE had lost his billet and had found his way in Fleet Street blocked by the rumour of his independence. His place upon the staff had been taken by a young and drunken Jew, who had at once won his spurs by a series of highly humorous articles upon psychic matters, peppered with assurances that he approached the subject with a perfectly open and impartial mind. His final device of offering five thousand pounds if the spirits of the dead would place the three first horses in the coming Derby, and his demonstration that ectoplasm was in truth the froth of bottle porter artfully concealed by the medium, are newspaper stunts, which are within the recollection of the reader.

But the path which closed on one side had opened on the other. Challenger, lost in his daring dreams and ingenious experiments, had long needed an active, clear-headed man to manage his business interests, and to control his world-wide patents. There were many devices, the fruits of his life's work, which brought in income, but had to be carefully watched and guarded. His automatic alarm for ships in shallow waters, his device for deflecting a torpedo, his new and economical method of separating nitrogen from the air, his radical improvements in wireless transmission and his novel treatment of pitch blend, were all money-makers. Enraged by the attitude of Cornelius, the Professor placed the management of all these in the hands of his prospective son-in-law, who diligently guarded his interests.

Challenger had himself altered. His colleagues, and those about him, observed the change without clearly perceiving the cause. He was gentler, humbler, and more spiritual man. Deep in his soul was the conviction that he, the champion of scientific method and of truth, had, in fact, for many years been unscientific in his methods, and a formidable obstruction to the advance of the human soul through the jungle of the unknown. It was this self-condemnation which had wrought the change in his character. Also, with characteristic energy, he had plunged into the wonderful literature of the subject, and as, without the prejudice which had formerly darkened his brain, he read the illuminating testimony of Hare, de Morgan, Crookes, Lombroso, Barrett, Lodge, and so many other great men, he marvelled that he could ever for one instant have imagined that such a consensus of opinion could be founded upon error. His violent and whole-hearted nature made him take up the psychic cause with the same vehemence, and even occasionally the same intolerance with which he had once denounced it, and the old lion bared his teeth and roared back at those who had once been his associates.

His remarkable article in the *Spectator* began, " The obtuse incredulity and stubborn unreason of the prelates who refused to look through the telescope of Galileo and to observe the moons of Jupiter, has been far transcended in our own days by those noisy controversialists, who rashly express extreme opinions upon those psychic matters which they have never had either the time, or the inclination to examine "; while in a final sentence he expressed his conviction that his opponents " did not in truth represent the thought of the twentieth century, but might rather be regarded as mental fossils dug from some early Pliocene horizon ". Critics raised their hands in horror, as is their wont, against the robust language of the article, though violence of attack has for so many years been condoned in the case of those who are in opposition. So we may leave Challenger, his black mane slowly turning to grey, but his great brain growing ever stronger and more virile as it faces such problems as the future had in store—a future which had ceased to be bounded by the narrow horizon of death, and which now stretches away into the infinite possibilities and developments of continued survival of personality, character and work.

The marriage had taken place. It was a quiet function, but no prophet could ever have foretold the guests whom Enid's father had assembled in the Whitehall Rooms. They were a happy crowd, all welded together by the opposition of the world, and united in one common knowledge. There was the Rev. Charles Mason, who had officiated at the ceremony, and if ever a saint's blessing consecrated a union, so it had been that morning. Now in his black garb with his cheery toothsome smile, he was moving about among the crowd carrying peace and kindliness with him. The yellow-bearded Mailey, the old warrior, scarred with many combats and eager for more, stood beside his wife, the gentle squire who bore his weapons and nerved his arm. There was Dr. Maupuis from Paris, trying to make the waiter understand that he wanted coffee, and being presented with tooth-picks, while the gaunt Lord Roxton viewed his efforts with cynical amusement. There, too, was the good Bolsover with several of the Hammersmith circle, and Tom Linden with his wife, and Smith, the fighting bull-dog from the north, and Dr. Atkinson, and Marvin the psychic editor with his kind wife, and the two Ogilvies, and little Miss Delicia with her bag and her tracts, and Dr. Ross Scotton, now successfully cured, and Dr. Felkin who had cured him so far as his earthly representative, Nurse Ursula, could fill his place. All these and many more were visible to our two-inch spectrum of colour, and audible to our four octaves of sound. How many others, outside those narrow limitations, may have added their presence and their blessing—who shall say?

One last scene before we close the record. It was in a sitting-room of the Imperial Hotel at Folkestone. At the

261

window sat Mr. and Mrs. Edward Malone gazing westwards down Channel at an angry evening sky. Great purple tentacles, threatening forerunners from what lay unseen and unknown beyond the horizon, were writhing up towards the zenith. Below, the little Dieppe boat was panting eagerly homewards. Far out the great ships were keeping mid-channel as scenting danger to come. The vague threat of that menacing sky acted subconsciously upon the minds of both of them.

"Tell me, Enid," said Malone, " of all our wonderful psychic experiences, which is now most vivid in your mind?"

" It is curious that you should ask, Ned, for I was thinking of it at that moment. I suppose it was the association of ideas with that terrible sky. It was of Miromar I was thinking, the strange mystery man with his words of doom."

" And so was I."

" Have you heard of him since?"

" Once and once only. It was on a Sunday morning in Hyde Park. He was speaking to a little group of men. I mixed with the crowd and listened. It was the same warning."

" How did they take it? Did they laugh?"

" Well, you have seen and heard him. You could not laugh, could you?"

" No, indeed. But you don't take it seriously, Ned, do you? Look at the solid old earth of England. Look at our great hotel and the people on the Lees, and the stodgy morning papers and all the settled order of a civilized land. Do you really think that anything could come to destroy it all?"

" Who knows? Miromar is not the only one who says so."

" Does he call it the end of the world?"

" No, no, it is the rebirth of the world—of the true world, the world as God meant it to be."

" It is a tremendous message. But what is amiss? Why should so dreadful a Judgment fall?"

" It is the materialism, the wooden formalities of the churches, the alienation of all spiritual impulses, the denial of the Unseen, the ridicule of this new revelation—these are the causes according to him."

" Surely the world has been worse before now ?"

" But never with the same advantages—never with the education and knowledge and so-called civilization, which should have led it to higher things. Look how everything has been turned to evil. We got the knowledge of airships. We bomb cities with them. We learn how to steam under the sea. We murder seamen with our new knowledge. We gain command over chemicals. We turn them into explosives or poison gases. It goes from worse to worse. At the present moment every nation upon earth is plotting secretly how it can best poison the others. Did God create the planet for this end, and is it likely that He will allow it to go on from bad to worse ?"

" Is it you or Miromar who is talking now ?"

" Well, I have myself been brooding over the matter, and all my thoughts seem to justify his conclusions. I read a spirit message which Charles Mason wrote. It was: ' The most dangerous condition for a man or a nation is when his intellectual side is more developed than his spiritual'. Is that not exactly the condition of the world to-day?"

" And how will it come ?"

" Ah, there I can only take Miromar's word for it. He speaks of a breaking of all the phials. There is war, famine, pestilence, earthquake, flood, tidal waves—all ending in peace and glory unutterable."

The great purple streamers were right across the sky. A dull crimson glare, a lurid angry glow, was spreading in the west. Enid shuddered as she watched it.

" One thing we have learned," said he. " It is that two souls, where real love exists, go on and on without a break through all the spheres. Why, then, should you and I fear death, or anything which life or death can bring ?"

She smiled and put her hand in his.

" Why indeed ?" said she.

APPENDICES

NOTE ON CHAPTER 2

CLAIRVOYANCE IN SPIRITUALISTIC CHURCHES

THIS phenomenon, as exhibited in Spiritualistic churches or temples, as the Spiritualists usually call them, varies very much in quality. So uncertain is it that many congregations have given it up entirely, as it has become rather a source of scandal than of edification. On the other hand there are occasions, the conditions being good, the audience sympathetic and the medium in good form, when the results are nothing short of amazing. I was present on one occasion when Mr. Tom Tyrell, of Blackburn, speaking in a sudden call at Doncaster—a town with which he was unfamiliar —got not only the descriptions but even the names of a number of people which were recognized by the different individuals to whom he pointed. I have known Mr. Vout Peters also to give forty descriptions in a foreign city (Liège) where he had never been before, with only one failure, which was afterwards explained. Such results are far above coincidence. What their true *raison d'etre* may be has yet to be determined. It has seemed to me sometimes that the vapour which becomes visible as a solid in ectoplasm, may in its more volatile condition fill the hall, and that a spirit coming within it may show up as an invisible shooting star comes into view when it crosses the atmosphere of the earth. No doubt the illustration is only an analogy but it may suggest a line of thought.

I remember being present on two occasions in Boston, Massachusetts, when clergymen gave clairvoyance from the steps of the altar, and with complete success. It struck me as an admirable reproduction of those apostolic conditions when they taught " not only by words but also by power ". All this has to come back into the Christian religion before it will be revitalized and restored to its prestine power. It cannot, however, be done in a day. We want less faith and more knowledge.

NOTE ON CHAPTER 9

EARTHBOUND SPIRITS

THIS chapter may be regarded as sensational, but as a fact there is no incident in it for which chapter and verse may not be given. The incident of Nell Gwynne, mentioned by Lord Roxton, was told me by Colonel Cornwallis West as having occurred in a country house of his own. Visitors had met the wraith in the passages and had afterwards, when they saw the portrait of Nell Gwynne which hung in a sitting-room, exclaimed, " Why, there is the woman I met ".

The adventure of the terrible occupant of the deserted house is taken with very little change from the experience of Lord St. Audries in a haunted house near Torquay. This gallant soldier told the story himself in *The Weekly Dispatch* (Dec., 1921), and it is admirably retold in Mrs. Violet Tweedale's *Phantoms of the Dawn*. As to the conversation carried on between the clergyman and the earthbound spirit, the same authoress has described a similar one when recording the adventures of Lord and Lady Wynford in Glamis Castle (*Ghosts I Have Seen*, p. 175).

Whence such a spirit draws its stock of material energy is an unsolved problem. It is probably from some mediumistic individual in the neighbourhood. In the extremely interesting case quoted by the Rev. Chas. Mason in the narrative and very carefully observed by the Psychic Research Society of Reykjavik in Iceland, the formidable earthbound creature proclaimed how it got its vitality. The man was in life a fisherman of rough and violent character who had committed suicide. He attached himself to the medium, followed him to the séances of the Society, and caused indescribable confusion and alarm, until he was exorcised by some such means as described in the story. A long account appeared in the *Proceedings of the American Society of Psychic Research* and also in the organ of the Psychic College, *Psychic Research* for January, 1925. Iceland, it may be remarked, is very advanced in psychic science, and in proportion to its population or opportunities is probably ahead of any other country. The Bishop of Reykjavik is President of the Psychic Society, which is surely a lesson to our own prelates whose disassociation from the study of such matters is little less than a scandal. The matter relates to the nature of the soul and to its fate in the Beyond, yet there are, I believe, fewer students of the matter among our spiritual guides than among any other profession.

NOTE ON CHAPTER 10

RESCUE CIRCLES

THE scenes in this chapter are drawn very closely either from personal experience or from the reports of careful and trustworthy experimenters. Among the latter are Mr. Tozer of Melbourne, and Mr. McFarlane of Southsea, both of whom have run methodical circles for the purpose of giving help to earthbound spirits. Detailed accounts of experiences which I have personally had in the former circles are to be found in Chapters IV and VI of my

Wanderings of a Spiritualist. I may add that in my own domestic circle, under my wife's mediumship, we have been privileged to bring hope and knowledge to some of these unhappy beings.

Full reports of a number of these dramatic conversations are to be found in the last hundred pages of the late Admiral Usborne Moore's *Glimpses of the Next State*. It should be said that the Admiral was not personally present at these sittings, but that they were carried out by people in whom he had every confidence, and that they were confirmed by sworn affidavits of the sitters. " The high character of Mr. Leander Fisher ", says the Admiral, " is sufficient voucher for their authenticity ". The same may be said of Mr. E. G. Randall, who has published many such cases. He is one of the leading lawyers of Buffalo, while Mr. Fisher is a Professor of Music in that city.

The natural objection is that, granting the honesty of the investigators, the whole experience may be in some way subjective and have no relation to real facts. Dealing with this the Admiral says: " I made inquiries as to whether any of the spirits, thus brought to understand that they had entered a new state of consciousness, had been satisfactorily identified. The reply was that many had been discovered, but after several had been verified it was considered useless to go on searching for the relatives and places of abode in earth life of the remainder. Such inquiries involved much time and labour, and always ended with the same result ". In one of the cases cited (*op. cit.*, p. 524) there is the prototype of the fashionable woman who died in her sleep, as depicted in the text. In all these instances the returning spirit did not realize that its earth life was over.

The case of the clergyman and of the sailor from the *Monmouth* both occurred in my presence at the circle of Mr. Tozer.

The dramatic case where the spirit of a man (it was the case of several men in the original) manifested at the very time of the accident which caused their death, and where the names were afterwards verified in the newspaper report, is given by Mr. E. G. Randall. Another example given by that gentleman may be added for the consideration of those who have not realized how cogent is the evidence, and how necessary for us to reconsider our views of death. It is in *The Dead Have Never Died* (p. 104).

" I recall an incident that will appeal to the purely materialistic. I was one of my father's executors, and after his dissolution and the settlement of his estate, speaking to me from the next plane, he told me one night that I had overlooked an item that he wanted to mention to me.

" I replied: ' Your mind was ever centred on the accumulation of money. Why take up the time that is so limited with the discussion of your estate ? It has already been divided '.

267

" ' Yes ', he answered, ' I know that, but I worked too hard for my money to have it lost, and there is an asset remaining that you have not discovered '.

" ' Well ', I said ' if that be true, tell me about it '.

" He answered: ' Some years before I left I loaned a small sum of money to Susan Stone, who resided in Pennsylvania, and I took from her a promissory note upon which, under the laws of that State, I was entitled to enter a judgment at once without suit. I was somewhat anxious about the loan, so, before its maturity, I took the note and filed it with the prothonotary at Erie, Pennsylvania, and he entered judgment, which became a lien on her property. In my books of account there was no reference to that note or judgment. If you will go to the prothonotary's office in Erie, you will find the judgment on record, and I want you to collect it. There are many things that you don't know about and this is one of them '.

" I was much surprised at the information thus received, and naturally sent for a transcript of that judgment. I found it entered Oct. 21, 1896, and with that evidence of the indebtedness I collected from the judgment debtor 70 dollars with interest. I question if anyone knew of that transaction besides the makers of the note and the prothonotary at Erie. Certainly I did not know about it. I had no reason to suspect it. The psychic present at that interview could not have known about the matter, and I certainly collected the money. My father's voice was clearly recognizable on that occasion, as it has been on hundreds of others, and I cite this instance for the benefit of those who measure everything from a monetary standpoint."

The most striking, however, of all these posthumous communications are to be found in *Thirty Years Among the Dead*, by Dr. Wickland of Los Angeles. This, like many other valuable books of the sort, can only be obtained in Great Britain at the Psychic Bookshop in Victoria Street, S.W.

Dr. Wickland and his heroic wife have done work which deserves the very closest attention from the alienists of the world. If he makes his point, and the case is a strong one, he not only revolutionizes all our ideas about insanity, but he cuts deep also into our views of criminology, and may well show that we have been punishing as criminals people who were more deserving of commiseration than of censure.

Having framed the view that many cases of mania were due to obsession from undeveloped entities, and having found out by some line of inquiry, which is not clear to me, that such entities are exceedingly sensitive to static electricity when it is passed through the body which they have invaded, he founded his treatment with remarkable results upon this hypothesis. The third factor in his system was the discovery that such entities were more easily, dislodged if a vacant body was provided for their temporary reception. Therein lies the heroism of Mrs. Wickland, a very charming and cultivated lady, who sits in hypnotic trance beside the subject ready to receive the invader when he is driven forth. It is through the lips of this lady that the identity and character of the undeveloped spirit are determined.

The subject having been strapped to the electric chair—the strapping is very necessary as many are violent maniacs—the power is turned on. It does not affect the patient, since it is static in its nature, but it causes acute discomfort to the parasitical spirit, who rapidly takes refuge in the unconscious form of Mrs. Wickland. Then follow the amazing conversations which are chronicled in this volume. The spirit is cross-questioned by the doctor, is admonished, instructed, and finally dismissed either in the care of some ministering spirit who superintends the proceedings, or relegated to the charge of some sterner attendant who will hold him in check should he be unrepentant.

To the scientist who is unfamiliar with psychic work such a bald statement sounds wild, and I do not myself claim that Dr. Wickland has finally made out his case, but I do say that our experiences at rescue circles bear out the general idea, and that he has admittedly cured many cases which others have found intractable. Occasionally there is very cogent confirmation. Thus in the case of one female spirit who bitterly bewailed that she had not taken enough carbolic acid the week before, the name and address being correctly given (*op. cit.*, p. 39).

It is not apparently everyone who is open to this invasion, but only those who are in some peculiar way psychic sensitives. The discovery, when fully made out, will be one of the root facts of the psychology and jurisprudence of the future.

NOTE ON CHAPTER 12

DR. MAUPUIS'S EXPERIMENTS

THE Dr. Maupuis of the narrative is, as every student of psychic research will realize, the late Dr. Geley, whose splendid work on this subject will ensure his permanent fame. His was a brain of the first order, coupled with a moral courage which enabled him to face with equanimity the cynicism and levity of his critics. With rare judgment he never went further than the facts carried him, and yet never flinched from the furthest point which his reason and the evidence would justify. By the munificence of Mr. Jean Meyer he had been placed at the head of the Institut Métapsychique, admirably equipped for scientific work, and he got the full value out of that equipment. When a British Jean Meyer makes his appearance he will get no return for his money if he does not choose a progressive brain to drive his machine. The great endowment left to the Stanford University of California has been practically wasted, because those in charge of it were not Geleys or Richets.

The account of Pithecanthropus is taken from the *Bulletin de l'Institut Métapsychique*. A well-known lady has described to me how the creature pressed between her and her neighbour, and how she placed her hand upon his shaggy skin. An account of this séance is to be found in Geley's *L'Ectoplasmie et la Clairvoyance* (Felix Alcau), p. 345. On page 296 is a photograph of the strange bird of prey upon the medium's head. It would take the credulity of a MacCabe to imagine that all this is imposture.

These various animal types may assume very bizarre forms. In an unpublished manuscript by Colonel Ochorowitz, which I have been privileged to see, some new developments are described which are not only formidable but also unlike any creature with which we are acquainted.

Since animal forms of this nature have materialized under the mediumship both of Kluski and of Guzik, their formation would seem to depend rather upon one of the sitters than upon either of the mediums unless we can disconnect them entirely from the circle. It is usually an axiom among Spiritualists that the spirit visitors to a circle represent in some way the mental and spiritual tendency of the circle. Thus, in nearly forty years of experience, I have never heard an obscene or blasphemous word at a séance because such séances have been run in a reverent and religious fashion. The question therefore may arise whether sittings which are held for purely scientific and experimental purposes, without the least recognition of their extreme religious significance, may not evoke less desirable manifestations of psychic force. The high character, however, of men like Richet and Geley ensure that the general tendency shall be good.

It might be argued that a subject with such possibilities had better be left alone. The answer seems to be that these manifestations are, fortunately, very rare, whereas the daily comfort of spirit intercourse illumines thousands of lives. We do not abandon exploration because the land explored contains some noxious creatures. To abandon the subject would be to hand it over to such forces of evil as chose to explore it while depriving ourselves of that knowledge which would aid us in understanding and counteracting their results.

Also published by Impala

The Maracot Deep
Sir Arthur Conan Doyle
Paperback ISBN 0 9549943 4 5

When The World Screamed *with*
The Lost World
Sir Arthur Conan Doyle
Paperback ISBN 0 9549943 6 1

Sportsman, doctor, historian and writer, Sir Arthur Conan Doyle (1859-1930) created one of the most enduring - indeed, legendary - characters in English literature: Sherlock Holmes, the brilliantly observational denizen of 221B Baker Street. Conan Doyle was born of Irish parents in Edinburgh and educated partly in Great Britain and partly in Germany. He qualified as a medical doctor in Southsea, but the absence of both patients and revenue persuaded him, as he himself has related, to turn his daydreams into imaginative writings. The result was a true stroke of genius, the creation of the great detective and his honest, down-to-earth colleague and 'chronicler', Dr Watson. In addition to his works of fiction, Conan Doyle was also a superb physical specimen and an avid boxer. In 1894 at Davos, Switzerland, he invented and subsequently popularized the concept of skiing as a sport. He also served as an army doctor in the war between England and the Boers of South Africa at the beginning of the 20th century, wrote a history of that war and was appointed official War Historian of the 1914-18 World War. His keen sense of justice involved him in two notorious cases of mistaken identity, those of Edaljee in 1903 and Oscar Slater in 1909. Conan Doyle personally, at his own expense, fought the courts on behalf of these two men, both total strangers to him, because he felt that they had been wrongfully convicted. Conan Doyle was an idealist who believed in his country and 'fair play'. In his writings, women tend to be modest, charming, faithful, beautiful and in need of defence. Gentlemen are honest, altruistic, gallant and brilliant. But Conan Doyle's fertile brain also conjured up an opposing criminal class of extraordinary depravity and ingenuity, led by the diabolical and brilliant Professor Moriarty, Holmes's arch enemy.

From Buzan's Book of Genius, by Tony Buzan and Raymond Keene.